Corporate Innovation Strategies

Smart Innovation Set

coordinated by
Dimitri Uzunidis

Volume 33

Corporate Innovation Strategies

Corporate Social Responsibility and Shared Value Creation

Nacer Gasmi

iSTE

WILEY

First published 2020 in Great Britain and the United States by ISTE Ltd and John Wiley & Sons, Inc.

ISTE Ltd
27-37 St George's Road
London SW19 4EU
UK

www.iste.co.uk

John Wiley & Sons, Inc.
111 River Street
Hoboken, NJ 07030
USA

www.wiley.com

Library of Congress Control Number: 2020944437

British Library Cataloguing-in-Publication Data
A CIP record for this book is available from the British Library
ISBN 978-1-78630-654-8

FSC
www.fsc.org
MIX
Paper from responsible sources
FSC® C013604

Contents

Introduction

Human behavior has always been evaluated, both in terms of its effectiveness and acceptability. Companies are not immune to this type of behavior (Pasquero 2007). The effective component of corporate behavior, which is associated with financial performance, has always been at the heart of corporate discourse. This performance has led companies to only focus on innovation strategies that are likely to further enhance their competitiveness and therefore their profitability. Yet, increasingly, the acceptable dimension of their activities for external and internal stakeholders is also becoming a decisive strategic issue for companies. In recent years, there has been an expectation from consumers that a company's brands should not only offer them functional advantages, but that companies should also invest in corporate social responsibility (CSR) initiatives, that is, community initiatives. Since World War II, through their activities to create value (profit), multinationals have generated significant growth that has made it possible to significantly reduce the rate of global poverty and to create positive externalities, such as new jobs, new services and state budgetary contributions through various taxes (Kaplan *et al.* 2018).

Unfortunately, this growth has not benefited all populations. In developed economies, the most recent gains have benefitted a small proportion of the population, while many members of the working, rural and urban classes have suffered as a result of socio-economic decline. In addition, these enterprises often induce negative social and/or environmental externalities, such as lay-offs, psychosocial risks, occupational accidents and pollution due to climate deregulation. The trajectory of production models is always shaped by the economic, social and political climate of a given period. Until the 1980s, responses to problems of social responsibility were part of a reactive approach to gradually adapt to environmental and social regulations (Berry and Rondinelli 1998).

While the idea of CSR is sometimes presented as a novelty (d'Humières and Chauveau 2001), concerns about the consequences of economic activities have always been prevalent. The idea of CSR, which involves discourse and practice between businesses and society, dates back at least to the beginning of the 20th Century in North America (Acquier and Gond 2007). In the industrial era, paternalism was an early modern form of CSR. Today, social practices must be sustainable because, as Lars Rebien Sorensen, CEO of the Novo Nordisk Group, pointed out, "corporate social responsibility is nothing more than maximizing the value of the company over time, because in the long run, social and environmental problems become financial problems" (Ignatius 2015). The justification for CSR is associated with the representation of the nature and role of the enterprise and its *raison d'être*.

The more a company is concerned about the impact its activities may have on the rest of society, the more it is considered a socially responsible company (Pasquero 2007). CSR thus becomes an exemplary positive theoretical approach, as it challenges the contractual-legal vision of the company. This contractual vision of CSR, which advocates a more partnership-based approach to corporate governance, is part of the process of creating shared value (CSV). The correlation between societal progress and commercial success is becoming increasingly apparent. To this end, "if all companies could stimulate societal progress in all regions of the world, the result would be a decrease in poverty, pollution, disease, and an increase in corporate profits" (Kramer and Pfitzer 2017). According to these authors, there are two reasons why CSR practice has become imperative for companies. The first concerns the questioning of the legitimacy of businesses, which have come to be perceived as thriving at the expense of the community as a whole. The second relates to the numerous global problems, ranging from inequality to global warming, which are of such magnitude that solutions require the expertise and inspirational models of the private sector. Much of the work on CSR focuses on its contributions to business and society. This type of strategy involves devising responses to social and environmental problems generated by a company's internal activities, or to problems that are external to it. Until the 2000s, strategies for integrating these issues were mainly the prerogative of large companies. Environmental and societal issues, which threaten people and companies in all countries, require companies to redefine their societal strategies and business philosophy, in order to create new value and prosper, by sharply reducing negative societal externalities generated by their activities, or by creating positive externalities (Winston 2017). Thus, all companies, whatever their activity and size, must take into account both financial and non-financial issues in their daily management, that is, to move towards global performance, because, as Lash and Wellington (2007) point out, societal issues present risks that may be irreversible for them and for society. Companies' interest in societal issues and their solutions is part of a strategic logic that requires all organizations to formalize their ideology. This ideology includes all of their values (social, environmental, organizational ethics) and shared beliefs about their mission (Desreumaux 2005), and goes beyond profit creation and compliance with regulations. The integration of societal issues into a company's strategy therefore forms part of new trends that are raising awareness of two major strategic issues, united by a common goal.

The first issue corresponds to a strategy of legitimization anchored in the company's institutional communication (Dimaggio and Powell 1983; Suchman 1995; Philips *et al.* 2004), and in the congruence of the company's values with those deemed appropriate by society (Philippe 2006). The second issue, described as Porter's hypothesis, subordinates societal investment to a vision based on the reduction of negative social and/or environmental externalities produced by the firm's activities (societal performance) while improving its competitive advantage (financial performance). The concept of externalities generates external effects (positive or negative) that generally refer to relations between agents that do not pass through the price mechanism (i.e. non-market effects) and therefore do not receive monetary compensation. Positive societal externalities correspond to environmental and/or social practices that are perceived as generating private costs and collective environmental and social benefits. Their production thus contributes to the well-being of agents other than the adopter (Gasmi and Grolleau 2003). In the case of negative externalities, their counterpart is left to the stakeholders. Positive environmental and/or social externalities therefore result from innovations, to enable the company that develops them to "correct" market "failures" and, in particular, the negative external effects on society (Daudigeos and Valiorgue 2010), that result from its economic activity. Kapp (1971) defines these effects as direct or indirect losses incurred by third parties or the general public, as a result of a company's activity. For example, a negative social externality may be associated with the manufacture of products that have a negative impact on customers (e.g. processed food products that lead to obesity), and a positive social externality may be associated with the manufacture of products that improve the health of customers (e.g. organically produced food products). Negative environmental effects can, for example, correspond to practices that generate greenhouse gas (GHG) emissions and therefore pollution, non-recycled waste, etc., while a positive environmental externality corresponds to practices that reduce these negative effects.

With the CSV approach, societal issues are the source of pressures that companies cannot avoid, but must be able to analyze and anticipate. The reinforcement of these pressures is likely to enhance the company's image, as well as considerably reduce its room to maneuver, due to regulatory constraints, public protests, boycott operations organized by activists (environmentalists, etc.) and media campaigns (Boiral and Joly 1992; Gasmi and Grolleau 2005). As a result, many companies only became aware of this after being surprised by public reactions to issues that they had not previously thought of, as being part of their professional responsibilities (Porter and Kramer 2010). While in the past, companies were rarely seen as actors of societal change, in recent years, CSR practices based on CSV have made real opportunities for companies to reduce negative externalities, while improving their competitive advantage and their relationships with key stakeholders. The common principle of all approaches to these practices is that companies cannot limit their activities to the sole objective of profit maximization, without taking into account their responsibility to society as a whole. Governments and businesses must play a key role in reducing negative human-induced societal externalities and corporate activities in a meaningful way, in order to sustainably safeguard our planet and reduce global poverty. Of the world's top 100 economic powers, 63 are corporations and only 37 are States (Strategor 2013, p. 339). Corporate engagement is essential and desirable, as it will have a considerable and positive impact on society. As a benchmark, institutions – especially supranational and national ones – must consider the importance they have afforded to reduce their budget deficit, by developing appropriate strategies in order to reduce the ecological and social deficit.

While environmental and social practices are becoming a major strategic issue for companies of all sizes (Berger-Douce 2007), many companies do not appreciate the opportunities and benefits of integrating social practices (Porter and Kramer 2010). A few companies are working to secure their value chain, processes and infrastructure, but most continue to operate in ignorance of the societal risks they may face. The importance of CSR practices in companies, and in society in general, is becoming increasingly strong (Lépineux *et al.* 2010), and the formalization of this responsibility is crucial for the company (Gasmi 2014). Not all companies have the same attitude towards CSR practices. Referring to the models proposed by Godet (1991) and Louppe and Rocaboy (1994), four types of strategies can be identified by characterizing social and environmental practices in the firm: 1) a strategy of inactivity or lack of interest in societal issues; 2) a strategy of reactivity to momentarily integrate this issue, in order to preserve the firm's institutional image and propose ad hoc solutions; 3) a pre-emptive strategy to anticipate changes and prepare to react to them (comply with legal obligations, moral demands, etc.); 4) a proactive strategy with an inclusive attitude towards CSR issues, which are considered structural strategic priorities. While companies that integrate their societal strategy in a proactive and CSV-based approach are organizations that exploit the business opportunities offered by this type of strategy as far as possible, many of them do not really take advantage of these opportunities.

Generally speaking, CSR promoters have used four arguments to defend their cause: moral obligation (asserting their duty to be corporate citizens), sustainability, reputation (image) and "legitimacy to operate" (Porter and Kramer 2010).

This book focuses on social and environmental strategies based on CSV and is divided into three parts. The first part presents the theoretical development, which analyzes the challenges of CSR strategies based on CSV. The second part includes two case studies that analyze the different forms of environmental innovation strategies based successively on the concept of "ethical values" and CSV, developed by the Decathlon Group. The third part analyzes the different social innovation strategies capable of inducing CSV.

PART 1

Analysis of Factors Incentivizing Companies to Develop CSV-based Strategies for Societal Innovations

Introduction to Part 1

This theoretical section deals successively with the analysis of the foundations of societal strategies based on the creation of shared value (CSV), the role that these strategies play in correcting and/or anticipating potential damage to the company, social and environmental innovations, as well as in analyzing ecosystems capable of facilitating the implementation of this type of strategy, the key steps in calculating the value of the impact investment and, finally, the development of innovative business models based on CSV.

The radical liberal conception of business has evolved towards a contractual conception of CSR. It is no longer a question of whether the value created by a company is private income for shareholders alone, but that it is also a partnership value for its other stakeholders. The CSV concept proposed by Porter and Kramer (2006) assumes that the firm must develop a societal strategy, while at the same time, extending its governance to its stakeholders. CSR strategies can enable a company to reduce the negative societal externalities brought about by its activities, and produce positive externalities. Moreover, they can limit the pressures exerted by stakeholders, by taking into account their specific expectations and the power and resources they hold which are necessary for the company. Regulatory or hard power authorities intervene at the regulatory level. Soft power players are a powerful source of influence and persuasion, which encourages the company to behave in a way that is acceptable to society. Societal practices will then reinforce the classic attributes of products with tangible and intangible product differentiation attributes. This differentiation is only effective if the company uses labels as a management tool to allow customers to make inferences when making purchases. But these eco-responsible purchasing acts will only increase if customers have a better understanding of the positive issues of CSR for society. The challenge in implementing CSV-based societal strategies is developing an organization capable of innovation in the company's industry. Managers must give priority to societal, technological and organizational innovations that generate CSV for the company, by supporting its overall business strategy; they must also promote the establishment of fruitful collaborations with various actors in their business ecosystems (BE). To accelerate change, the traditional BE must be transformed into a regional societal business ecosystem (RSBE), without constraints and/or additional costs. If businesses want to be more resilient, they will adopt different approaches based on three levers: vision, societal project and partnership. Their competitive advantage will be linked to finding and selecting effective innovation strategies that other stakeholders can buy into. This implies that impact investment will allocate capital to projects that will generate social and environmental benefits, as well as benefits for companies. Some prospective methodology has been developed to estimate the potential benefits of such projects, by calculating a new indicator called the Impact Multiple of Money (IMM), based on the results of relevant foothold studies. Depending on their history and sector, companies must adopt a business model that refers to their value chain and its impact on the competitive environment, industrial investment choices and product life cycles. They can choose between three types of business models: repair (if they do not practice CSR), innovation (if they develop a new business) or the creation of a business from scratch. In all of the business models, they will have to achieve specific competitive and societal objectives.

1

Foundations of the Societal Strategy Based on Creating Shared Value (CSV)

Existing literature on CSR focuses on two opposing visions that have different consequences.

1.1. The issues at stake in the liberal and contractual conceptions of CSR

The first vision is a radical liberal conception, which is taken up by Levitt (1958) and Friedman (1970) in particular, who consider that the sole social responsibility of a company is to make profit. In this approach, the State is the only political and public actor, while companies, as private, non-political actors, are exempt from exposing their decisions to public scrutiny, or justifying their behavior, if they comply with the regulations in force and the morality of the practice (Friedman 1962, 1970). Companies are rarely seen as agents of societal change, even though, as Kramer and Pfitzer (2017) point out, the correlation between social progress and business success is becoming increasingly evident. The second vision is the instrumental position of CSR, which can be seen in the works of Mitchell *et al.* (1997), Jensen (2002), and Sundaram and Inkpen (2004). CSR CSV can be called "strategic" because it affects the firm's position in relation to its competitors and goes far beyond action, to correct or anticipate potential damage to the firm (boycott, etc.). When this strategy is associated with competitive societal innovation, the company can improve its financial and societal performance. Profit maximization is one of the ultimate objectives of a company, but does not contradict the consideration of the interests of its various stakeholders. With this contractual conception of CSR, the company becomes a major economic and social player. The two visions of CSR differ in terms of the nature of the value created. The radical liberal vision is limited to the creation of shareholder value, but has evolved with the emergence of partnership value creation (Charreaux and Desbrières 1998). According to these authors, in the traditional financial approach, the value created is equal to the income received by shareholders, whereas partnership value is based on an overall measure of income created by the firm in relation to its stakeholders, not just the shareholders. Partnership value creation does not focus entirely on the process of value creation and sharing, but is merely an extension of the creation of shareholder value to other stakeholders, such as employees (Gautier *et al.* 2013). In recent years, companies have become increasingly interested in creating shared value (CSV), thanks to CSR practices as part of the contractual approach, which advocate a partnership-based mode of governance. In this case, taking into account the expectations of the various internal and external stakeholders with regard to acceptable behavior in the company's activities is at the heart of the CSR concept. Jensen (2002) acknowledges that the partnership perspective of stakeholder-based governance can contribute to maximizing the firm's market value. This valuation led him to propose the concept of "enlightened value maximization". Subsequently, the innovative concept of "creating shared value" was mainly proposed by Porter and Kramer (2006, 2011). In their 2006 article, this concept was based on the interrelationships that existed between companies and society, whereas in their 2011 article, they considered that companies were not able to seize the opportunities that CSR represented, in terms of overall performance (financial and societal). For Pfitzer *et al.* (2014), the shared value is "the implication of integrating a social mission into the culture of the company and the allocation of resources towards the development of innovations that can help solve social problems". For Kramer and Pfitzer (2017), CSV is "the creation of profit (business success) for the company while generating benefits for society". These various definitions all converge towards the same principle: the activities of the company can affect society, and society can in turn affect the company.

1.2. CSR as a lever for adapting corporate governance

This interdependence means that companies have an interest in finding solutions to societal challenges. With the CSV approach, CSR must be understood as a set of discourses and practices, which work towards extending corporate governance to its various stakeholders (Dupuis 2008). A stakeholder refers to a group or individual that can affect or is affected by the achievement of the organization's objectives (Freeman 1984). Nowadays, it has become imperative for companies to place their overall strategy within a CSV-based perspective and better identify their CSR, by explicitly taking into account the expectations of their internal and external stakeholders. Therefore, the company is at the heart of a set of relations with stakeholders that are no longer just organizational (shareholders and management), but also involve internal (employees) and external stakeholders, who have an interest in its activities and decisions. The sharing of returns and externalities must then be regulated through quasi-contractual arrangements (Freeman 1984). With CSV, the integration of societal issues must be thought of as a strategy in its own right, by approaching these issues as a business problem (Porter and Reinhardt 2007). To do so, this integration must be seen as an opportunity to create financial and societal performance.

The integration of CSR thus assumes, as Coriat and Weinstein (1995) point out, a theorization of the firm under its dual organizational and institutional dimension, where profit maximization is no longer the sole or obligatory hypothesis. Therefore, there would be a set of organizational competencies built within a particular institution, where rules are partly imposed by stakeholders with divergent interests (Dupuis 2008). Post *et al.* (2002) identify three categories of stakeholders, distinguished by their strategic dimensions, which can play the role of regulatory mechanisms to encourage companies to develop societal strategies based on CSV. The first category is associated with the "basic resources" dimension that includes shareholders, employees and customers. The second category belongs to the "market" sphere that consists of commercial and competitive partners. The third category belongs to the "socio-political" sphere embodied by the regulatory authorities (hard power) and soft power players, also called "institutional stakeholders". By integrating the expectations of these stakeholders, CSR plays a role in a new approach that consists of adapting the company's governance systems to the realities of new organizational forms. This adaptation implies that the company must respond to the interests of all its internal and external stakeholders in order for its strategy to be viable. To this end, the justification for CSR proposed by stakeholder theory (SHT) gives the firm a role of societal regulation that organizes the interactions between various stakeholders. This theory essentially aims to better understand the company's environment, rather than to help the manager to manipulate it (Mercier and Gond 2005). The SHT approach is based on a representation of the company that is totally embedded in society, its laws, values and culture (Capron and Quairel-Lanoizelée 2007).

2

CSR as a Lever Which Corrects and/or Anticipates Potential Damage to the Company

Potential damage may arise from the pressures that socio-political and/or market stakeholders may exert on the company, if its activities produce negative social and/or environmental externalities, or if it is unaware of their existence.

2.1. CSR as a lever to avoid pressures from socio-political stakeholders

Today, companies feel "almost" obliged to reconsider, indirectly, the way they relate to their internal and external stakeholders. They are increasingly exposed to risks in terms of image (as an institution), legislation (environmental and social risks) and competitiveness, if they do not behave in a way that is acceptable to these stakeholders. Some companies have developed CSR strategies based on creating shared value (CSV) without this being an entirely voluntary or a spontaneous act, but many other companies have only "woken up" after being surprised by the reactions of hard and soft power stakeholders, to issues they had not previously considered as part of their job responsibilities (Porter and Kramer 2010). The relationship between the company and its stakeholders should therefore not be analyzed as a relationship of agency, but as a relationship of dependence on the resources they hold (Quairel and Auberger 2005). This dependence subordinates the firm to the stakeholders and asserts that its sustainability depends on its ability to manage their demands and, above all, on those whose resources and support are decisive for its survival (Pfeffer and Salancik 1978). Managers do not have the same attention for all these institutional stakeholders, who depend on legitimacy, power and urgency (Mitchell *et al.* 1997) and on the interest they may have in the acceptable behavior of the firm. The company's actions are deemed "acceptable" according to criteria adopted by these stakeholders, who hold resources that can make the company vulnerable through the various pressures exerted on it, in order to ensure that it reduces the negative caused by its activities. CSR is therefore a means of mitigating and avoiding these pressures. The strategic approach may lead the firm to think of its relationship with society as a form of implicit contract. This contract may sometimes be forcefully recalled by institutional arrangements embodied by the stakeholders of soft power and hard power.

2.2. CSR as a lever for alleviating or anticipating regulatory pressures

Stakeholders under the authority of regulatory authorities, or hard power, are one of the key levers that can encourage companies to develop societal practices. The intervention of a regulatory authority can be explained by "the complexity inherent in any quality standard that involves various types of players[1] in various types of networks and regimes built on trust or reputation, which calls for the involvement of a public authority, to varying degrees, in the form of economic regulation and, above all, social or qualitative regulation that concerns the conditions of being involved in the activity and the physical characteristics of the products or services offered" (Chanteau 2009). Even if there are situations where individual interest is in line with the collective interest, compliance with the standard is not a given, because, as this author indicates, "the personal ethics of a manager or shareholder can at best only be a source of motivation, because his individual dimension cannot alone institute the quality standard, given that his commitment is more often a conviction than a responsibility". Regulatory authorities are supranational (European Union, WTO, etc.), national (Senate, National Assembly, State) and sub-national (local authorities: town halls, regions, departments). Depending on their powers, they "issue the company with an operating permit" (Eccles and Serafeim 2014) for a standard, a label or guidelines for reducing the negative externalities produced by its activities, or for encouraging the production of positive externalities, by producing public goods, etc. If these negative societal externalities continue to be produced, they can be costly to the firm. Lars Rebien Sorensen[2], CEO of Novo Nordisk, considers that "if we continue to pollute, stricter regulations will be imposed and the cost of energy consumption will be higher". According to Ignatius (2015), "from a social perspective, if we do not treat our employees well, if we do not behave as socially

1 Producers, experts, consumer associations, etc.

2 Excerpt from interview: Ignatius, A. (2015). Lars Rebien Sorensen voted best manager of the year 2015. *Harvard Business Review*, December–January, 98.

responsible companies in our local communities, if we do not offer low-cost products to the poorest countries, governments will impose regulations on us that will ultimately prove very costly". Arguments for companies to reduce negative societal externalities can, according to Crifo and Forget (2014), lead to companies avoiding future burdensome regulation, saving on transaction costs associated with regulatory processes, or even providing a private response to regulatory failures. The reduction in regulatory costs may come from firms engaging in societal investments that generate positive societal externalities beyond what the current law proposes, or before its enactment, so the regulator may weaken its requirements in order to limit the costs it would otherwise impose on less virtuous firms. CSR practice then resembles a form of regulatory pre-emption that avoids stronger future regulatory constraints (Crifo and Forget 2014), and is not intended to weaken the regulatory constraint, but to reduce the frequency of company audits, legal risks (lower environmental and/or social risk) and therefore a potential fine (Crifo and Mottis 2011). A mutual reinforcement exists between CSR and regulation, and beyond this, CSV strategies can also, as Bénabou and Tirole (2010) point out, be a lever for regulation when governments fail. This is the case, for example, when US President Donald Trump decided in early June 2017 to withdraw his country from the Paris climate agreement, stating that "as of today, the United States will cease all implementation of the non-binding Paris Accord and the draconian financial and economic burdens the agreement imposes on our country"[3]. In response to this failure by the government to regulate the environment, some CEOs have responded, including those from big American groups such as Tesla's Elon Musk, Disney's Bob Iger, Jeff Immelet of General Electric and so on. They have decided to continue the fight to reduce the negative environmental externalities produced by the activities of their groups[4].

The pro-social behavior of these CSR managers can be explained by different sources of motivation, ranging from pure selfishness to totally altruistic concerns (Grolleau *et al.* 2009). Purely altruistic behavior may promote values that are not shared by regulators. As individuals' preferences are heterogeneous, it is therefore inevitable that the values of some managers do not fully reflect those of public policies. Altruistic motivation is also justified by image concerns, which thus serve as an inexpensive incentive for accountability. In this case, responsible behavior generates an image value that potentially increases the private individual performance of the company and thus reduces the cost of the negative societal externality to be corrected. Motivation can also be explained by considerations of personal and social

3 Excerpt from Donald Trump's speech on the withdrawal of the United States on June 1, 2017.

4 *Le Monde*, June 3, 2017.

esteem (Bénabou and Tirole 2010), in order to buy "free societal prestige" and demonstrate one's generosity to others (Tirole 2009). CSR practices play the role of self-regulation, are motivated by moral concerns (Baron 2001) and can thus be considered a non-monetary managerial advantage (Baron *et al.* 2008) for the company.

2.3. CSR as a lever to avoid or mitigate the pressures exerted by soft power

Firms may also be led to adopt CSV strategies in response to actual or potential pressures from soft power stakeholders, who are considered by Van den Berghe and Louche (2005) as private, non-market and invisible political actors. The concept of soft power is defined by Nye (1990) as an ability to make others "want what you want", developed during the years of Clinton's presidency in the United States. Soft power refers to the power of influence and persuasion as a mode of regulation. These stakeholders, who may or may not have a voluntary or involuntary relationship with the company, under a rather implicit or moral contract, accept being exposed to certain risks. They are mainly embodied in a set of actors from civil society such as non-governmental organizations (NGOs), whistle-blowers, local communities, trade unions, scientists, ordinary citizens, the traditional or social media, public opinion and rating agencies[5] (Gasmi and Grolleau 2005). Van den Berghe and Louche (2005) point out that "stimulated and influenced by this invisible hand, market parties also start to consider CSR and good corporate governance as the prerequisite for sustainable growth and welfare within a globalizing business environment". Soft power actors, such as NGOs, play a key role in identifying and issuing alerts to denounce companies with irresponsible behavior that causes negative social and/or environmental externalities produced by their activities, to encourage them to develop CSR practices that can reduce these externalities or generate positive externalities. This is the case, for example, with Nike, which was the target of attention (Kahle *et al.* 2000) due to its societal practices. The group has been the subject of numerous counter-advertisements, television and radio reports, anti-Nike websites, with particularly devastating effects, and even a film, *The Big One*[6] (1998), which reveals the deplorable working conditions of its sub-contractors (Gasmi and Grolleau 2005). The same is true of the Volkswagen group, which set up

5 These agencies assess and rate responsible business practices on environmental, social and governance (ESG) issues.

6 American documentary film by Michael Moore released in 1998. The film denounces the practices of multinationals that lay off their staff while they make a profit, such as Nike, whose subcontractors use child labor.

a vast system of rigging anti-pollution tests on 11 million vehicles worldwide, a system exposed by the International Council on Clean Transportation (ICCT), an American NGO specializing in clean transport, which decided to test the GHG emissions of certain diesel cars[7]. The group faced a potential fine of up to $18 billion and was also fined 1 billion euros[8] in June 2018, by the public prosecutor's office in Brunswick, Germany. Challenging the monopoly of traditional forms of regulation (market, state, etc.), soft power stakeholders are increasingly calling for alternative societal regulation of economic activities. In the eyes of the public, they also represent a credible source of information[9] and action on companies, particularly on multinationals (Gasmi and Grolleau 2005). The legitimacy (voluntary commitment to the general interest) and the power of pressure that these stakeholders have exerted clearly demonstrate their ability to hold companies accountable for the negative social and/or environmental externalities produced by their activities (Porter and Kramer 2010). These pressures may lead companies to consider reducing these externalities. Soft power actors grant the company a "license to operate", that is, they give "their approval" for the company to operate (Eccles and Serafeim 2014), while companies with questionable behavior may be "deprived" of it (Post *et al.* 2002). NGOs, described as private political actors by Baron (2001), threaten companies that behave irresponsibly, by conducting campaigns based on boycotting, denigration, revelations, etc. (Eccles and Serafeim 2014). The effectiveness of these threats above all concerns the most visible companies that are well known by the public. CSR can therefore play a role in reducing the risk of boycotts or hostile media campaigns initiated by soft power players. The institutional determining factors embodied by the stakeholders in the socio-political sphere, encourage companies to implement strategies based on CSV, which fall into two groups.

The first corresponds to the power or dependence on the resources that these stakeholders hold and that are likely to make the enterprise fragile, hence the *legitimacy to operate* and the urgency to address the environmental and social problems it poses (Mitchell *et al.* 1997). *Legitimacy* thus provides a concrete way for the firm to identify and make decisions about the social and environmental issues that matter to its stakeholders (Porter and Kramer 2010), by developing innovations in products, processes and business models that can provide reliable solutions to these issues. The second area, which leads the company to deploy societal approaches, is related to opportunities to improve relations with these stakeholders

7 *Le Monde*, Économie & Entreprise supplement, Thursday September 24, 2015.

8 *Le Monde*, Économie & Entreprise supplement, Wednesday June 20, 2018.

9 This credibility stems from their independence, their activism in relation to companies and the fact that the actions they defend are not in their own interests.

through CSV-based strategies. The challenge of societal commitment is then part of a strategy of institutional legitimization within the company (Dimaggio and Powell 1983; Suchman 1995). According to classical economic theory, this legitimacy is determined by the market, that is, the firm is considered an entity that is distinct from its environment, whereas with CSR, firms are part of systems that are strongly constrained by the environment in which they operate. Their legitimacy therefore does not only derive from profit-making or strict compliance with the law (Chelli 2011), but is more in line with a socio-political framework, rather than a market framework. The concept of organizational legitimacy is therefore not synonymous with legality, but rather refers to the conformity of a company's objectives, products and procedures, with the societal norms and values that prevail in its field of activity. Legitimacy is also a congruence between the values associated with a company's activities and the norms of acceptable behavior, defined by the social system to which it belongs. It provides the company with the approval of society and the opportunity to obtain the resources it needs to survive. Legitimacy could therefore be the result of a cyclical and dynamic process, involving a number of legitimization strategies (Chelli 2011). The question of legitimacy, which is consubstantial with social order, rests on people's adherence to rationality and legality, that is, on the belief in the force of law and regulations (Capron and Quairel-Lanoizelée 2007). CSR thus offers the possibility of being a decisive lever which can be used to create legitimacy for the business. The aim of CSR strategies based on CSV is to lead the company to internalize the externalities produced by its activities and meet the expectations of all its stakeholders belonging to the socio-political sphere and the market. With CSR, the company's legitimacy is not only limited to that of the market but also depends on the legitimacy granted by society.

2.4. CSR as a lever for securing a competitive advantage, reducing negative societal externalities or producing positive externalities

For Quairel (2013), "questioning the link between the concept of CSR and competition highlights the theoretical and managerial oppositions of CSR, and economic approaches." This work is in line with a CSV vision: therefore, the business has a responsibility to reinforce the "classic"[10] attributes of products with social and/or environmental attributes, producing tangible and intangible differentiation that can further enhance its competitive advantage. Tangible societal attributes are those that improve the intrinsic quality of the product, resulting in a

10 A product is classified as "conventional" if it does not contain tangible or intangible "environmental and/or social" attributes.

private benefit to the customer. Intangible attributes are those that provide a collective benefit to society. These societal attributes play a pivotal role in the process of securing the company's competitive edge, as they help to further enhance the level of differentiating attributes of the "expandable core" of products, not only, as Wessel and Christensen (2014) point out, by facilitating simple price competition but also by strengthening the intrinsic quality of the product brought about by social and environmental innovations (product safety and comfort, increase in its life cycle, etc.) and by societal values (e.g. GHG reduction, water rationalization, improved consumer health, i.e. societal performance). The integration of societal practices thus modifies the "center of gravity" of product differentiation attributes. This center of gravity is at the confluence of the "production" of two attribute polarities: tangible attributes representing the polarity of the deepening of rational motivations (key lever of the act of purchasing) and intangible attributes linked to the reduction of negative environmental and/or social externalities or to the genesis of positive externalities representing the polarity of virtue, therefore of general interest (Gasmi 2014). Societal strategies based on CSV therefore show the ideal facet of a company's activities: innovating to meet a societal need (societal performance) while generating profit (financial performance) (Porter and Kramer 2011; Pfitzer *et al.* 2014; Kramer and Pfitzer 2017; etc.). If this process can lead to a competitive advantage for the company, and profit for society, then there is nothing to prevent a company from engaging in a social and environmental program that will have a positive impact on its corporate image. If this program can also lead to positive societal outcomes, and ultimately to employee and shareholder satisfaction, then it can be judged positively in moral terms (Deslandes 2012). If the demand for "societal" benefits is part of an attempt to take better account of the positive environmental and social impacts of the company's activity, then a shared value is created with its stakeholders in the market and in the socio-political sphere (Porter and Kramer 2011). This shared value enables the company to establish relationships of trust with these stakeholders and to demonstrate the sincerity of its ethical commitment. The company then gains a competitive advantage resulting from the quality of its relationships with these stakeholders, which is the major competitive route in CSR (Quairel 2013). This advantage, which is linked to the voluntary integration of the company's environmental and social issues into its global strategy, is part of a logic of anticipating the changing behavior of consumers, suppliers, investors, etc., and that of its employees, with regard to these issues. In this case, the advantage that the integration of CSV societal practices can bring is not limited to improving the company's relations with its institutional stakeholders (hard power and soft power) and those of the market but also concerns its relations with its internal stakeholders.

<table>
<tr><td colspan="4">No poverty (1)</td><td colspan="4">Zero hunger (2)</td><td colspan="4">Good health and well-being (3)</td></tr>
<tr><td colspan="4">Quality education (4)</td><td colspan="4">Gender equality (5)</td><td colspan="4">Clean water and sanitation (6)</td></tr>
<tr><td colspan="4">Affordable and clean energy (7)</td><td colspan="4">Decent work, economic growth (8)</td><td colspan="4">Industry, innovation and infrastructure (9)</td></tr>
<tr><td colspan="4">Reduced inequalities (10)</td><td colspan="4">Sustainable cities and communities (11)</td><td colspan="4">Responsible consumption and production (12)</td></tr>
<tr><td colspan="4">Climate change (13)</td><td colspan="4">Life below water (14)</td><td colspan="4">Life on land (15)</td></tr>
<tr><td colspan="4">Peace, justice and strong institutions (16)</td><td colspan="8">Partnerships for the goals (17)</td></tr>
<tr><td colspan="12">380 million jobs would be created by 2030
if these 17 global goals were achieved in four areas</td></tr>
<tr><td colspan="3">Food: $2.3 trillion</td><td colspan="3">Cities: $3.7 trillion</td><td colspan="3">Energy, materials: $4.3 trillion</td><td colspan="3">Health and well-being: $1.8 trillion</td></tr>
</table>

Table 2.1. *Summary of opportunities achieved through sustainable development practices (Laurent 2017)*

As a result, companies are increasingly expected to address the CSV issue and have a great deal of scope to improve the quality of life for the world's poor. Despite powerful incentives, a unique capacity to foster large-scale societal change and enormous potential to develop inclusive growth with cost-effective societal strategies to address poverty and inequality (Kaplan *et al.* 2018), many companies are not fully exploiting this potential and should be aware of the various opportunities specific to their sectors. A study was conducted by Laurent (2017)[11] on the state of the sustainable development issue, an opportunity that amounts to billions of dollars. The estimated value of the 60 business opportunities identified is $12.1 trillion per year by 2030. These opportunities would contribute to the achievement of the 17 UN global Sustainable Development Goals (SDGs) in the areas of food and agriculture, cities, energy and materials, and health and well-being (see Table 2.1).

To broaden the scope of possibilities, CSR managers should evaluate all the options offered by three areas to build a competitive societal mission strategy that will lead to a competitive advantage for the company (Bharadwaj and Rodriguez-Vilá 2018). The first is "a brand heritage study to identify the most important benefits the brand offers to help them identify the societal needs that the brand can meet". For example, the Dove brand was not sold as a soap product, but as a beauty product. Putting beauty first is therefore at the heart of the brand's value proposition. It is

11 The author of this study drew on United Nations sources: Business & Sustainable Development Commission (2017). Better Business, Better World. Report, United Nations.

logical that the brand should focus on societal needs relating to the perception of beauty. The second area concerns "consumers and the difficulty of identifying in an exhaustive way the societal issues to which they are attuned". The company needs to focus on the "cultural tensions" that affect consumers and relate to the brand's heritage. These tensions may, for example, be "preserving the core of the brand attributes that have formed its identity to date, while reinforcing it with tangible societal attributes". The brand then becomes relevant to consumers when it provides solutions to these tensions. The third area concerns "product or industry-related externalities". This involves identifying the indirect costs incurred or benefit obtained by a third party (Gasmi and Grolleau 2003), arising from the production or use of the company's branded products. A company can thus build an effective corporate mission strategy by choosing one of these areas. However, taking all three areas into account can offer real opportunities for CSV. There are two conditions for a successful CSV-based societal process. The first condition is to develop social and/or environmental innovations capable of capitalizing on the opportunities they will produce. The second is to turn a societal cause into a competitive advantage, so CSR project managers must fight against two types of obstacles which they may encounter. The first is the difficulty of changing goals after this societal mission has been chosen, because its success depends on the legitimacy of the company. Changing commitment, or delivering an inconsistent message, can be perceived by stakeholders in the socio-political sphere and the market as an incongruous act, because according to Tirole (2009), the company may be seen as an entity that seeks to buy "free" "social prestige" to show its generosity to these stakeholders. The second obstacle is associated with the appeal of the idea of "doing good", which may distract CSR managers from the brand's essential needs. Turning a societal cause into a competitive advantage always attracts criticism, which has both supporters and opponents. CSR managers must therefore assess whether the relevant stakeholders are willing to accept and support societal strategies based on CSV. Thus, depending on their expectations, there may be four potential situations. One is related to stakeholders who react negatively and do not support the company's societal strategy. This attitude may be the source of three factors: a gap between the message communicated by the brand and that practiced by the company (Gasmi 2014), a politicization of the message and a mistrust of the company's motivation. This is the case with companies in the food industry that are often criticized by consumers, parents, NGOs, etc., for their contribution, through some of their products, to the increase in the rate of obesity among children. The other three situations may, for example, concern the Nike group which, in the 1990s, developed a policy of outsourcing its production activities to low-cost countries, especially in Asia (Gasmi and Grolleau 2005). Thus, the first situation corresponds to the stakeholders who benefit from the outsourcing strategy and are relatively unconcerned about the ethical consequences, including consumers, shareholders, workers and outsourcing countries, as well as competitors. These stakeholders value the choice of outsourcing, putting ethical considerations on the back burner for the benefit of the company, allowing it to make private economic profit. The second situation represents the soft power players (NGOs, etc.) who are particularly sensitive to the ethical consequences of Nike's strategic choices. Finally, the third concerns public authorities and workers in the countries where the subcontracting is taking place. These actors remain at a distance from the ethical choices made by the multinational for different reasons, essentially based on considerations of lesser harm for some and of attractiveness and economic development for others. The public authorities of some Asian countries are happy to welcome foreign companies that provide their workers with jobs and salaries. The vulnerability of the workers employed, along with their demographic and cultural profile, makes them more conciliatory and less demanding with regard to the ethical problem; moreover, alternative job offers are very limited and the workers are at great risk of exploitation (Gasmi and Grolleau 2005). Workers and public authorities may even defend the notion of low costs in order not to compromise their competitive advantages, thus encouraging these companies to invest in their country to promote their economic development. All categories of stakeholders show that a societal cause is unlikely to escape criticism, and CSR managers must set themselves a goal so that the defenders of the societal mission outnumber those that oppose it.

Certainly, CSV-based societal strategies can have a positive effect on the legitimacy of a company's activities by reducing negative externalities or generating positive externalities while improving its competitive advantage. But the key factor of "competitive advantage" is only effective if customers perceive and consider both intangible (collective benefit) and tangible (individual private benefit to the customer) social and/or environmental attributes as an element of product differentiation and integrate them into their purchasing act. The appropriation of these attributes is not an intrinsic value for customers, as it depends on the level of their attention to CSR practices and their labels as management tools, in order to make inferences about these tools to differentiate the "societal products" that should correspond to their expectations. Labels, attention and appropriation therefore play a decisive role in the purchasing act.

2.4.1. *Labels, a tool for managing the appropriation of CSR as differentiating attributes*

Societal attributes are based on the notion of trust (trust attributes), and the differentiation strategy that they can play raises questions about the asymmetry of information to which the customer may be exposed when making a purchase. Trust attributes have the peculiarity that they are practically never verified by the buyer before or after the purchase (Nelson 1970; Darby and Karni 1973). From this perspective, the social or environmental label, as a management tool linked to societal innovations, can reduce this asymmetry of information. A management tool corresponds to "any sign, technique or local and elementary know-how aimed at orienting or facilitating collective, individual and microsocial action" (de Vaujany 2006). A label, as a distinctive sign affixed to the product, makes it possible, in principle, to transform trust attributes into search attributes[12] and to solve the problem of information asymmetry between the seller and the consumer (Caswell 1998). The societal label then plays four major roles in optimizing the process of appropriating these societal attributes of product differentiation. First, it communicates to the customer a mass of information on the social and/or environmental practices developed by the company and the nature of the attributes (tangible and/or intangible) of differentiation that they can produce. Second, it provides a guarantee of trust as a credible societal attribute for the customer. This trust, which is a determining factor in the decision to purchase societal products, is the consequence of a belief created on the basis of information communicated by the company through its labels, and not of objective verification by the buyer (Gasmi and Grolleau 2002). Third, it can reinforce the competitive advantage that these attributes can generate (Quairel 2013). Fourth, the label also aims to push customers towards choosing products with societal attributes so that they can make inferences about CSR as a way of differentiating these products in their purchasing act. The concept of "appropriation" is defined as "the process by which the subject reconstructs for himself patterns of use of an artefact in the course of an activity that is meaningful to him" (Rabardel 1995). The label certainly plays a decisive role in the act of purchasing, but appropriation also depends on the attitudes that the customer may have towards CSR practices and the label as a management tool in general. In order to facilitate this appropriation, the company must place it in a *psycho-cognitive appropriation perspective*. This perspective, described as "pragmatic" and "semiotic" by Lorino (2002), fits into theoretical frameworks that are increasingly oriented towards a socio-cognitive prism, by adopting a structuration's stance, in which the label is no longer considered as a lever for the rationality of the actors (clients) (de Vaujany 2006; Aggeri and Labatut 2010; Grimand 2012). The label then takes the form of an artifact for the action of a client in a situation, who will interpret it by giving it a meaning according to an individually and socially constructed pattern of use (Martineau 2012). The psycho-cognitive approach, which conceives appropriation as a process of acquiring new knowledge about management tools (labels), assumes that clients must develop a logic for optimizing the allocation of their attention (Kessous *et al.* 2010), with respect to these tools and the information they convey.

12 Search attributes are properties of products that consumers can check and evaluate before making a purchase (Nelson 1970; Darby and Karni 1973).

2.4.2. *Process of optimizing customer focus on societal attributes*

The process of caring about societal attributes is a prerequisite for customers to take ownership of them when they make a purchase. At the end of the 1990s, the issue of socially responsible consumption (SRC) began to take hold as a necessary change in consumer behavior in the markets (Dubuisson-Quellier 2013). SRC is "the fact that an individual buys goods or services that have a positive (or less negative) impact on his environment and uses his purchasing power to express his social and/or environmental concerns" (François-Lecompte 2005), or that he integrates into his individual choices or consumption practices, considerations linked to collective well-being (Dubuisson-Quellier 2013). Drawing on the work of McInnis *et al.* (1991), three main steps can explain this process of attentiveness.

The first relates to *the opportunity for customers to expose themselves to these labels* and their *ability to process the information they convey*. Interaction between the labels and the customer implies access to the information environment on societal practices and their management tools. This environment operates at two levels (Garabedian 2007). The first is of a *macroeconomic nature*. The potential consumer of products with societal attributes will need to be informed about the state of the planet's environment (level of soil pollution, toxicity of pesticides, etc.) and social issues (famine, unemployment, child exploitation, working conditions, etc.). The second level is of a *microeconomic nature*. In this case, the information should focus on CSR in general, societal products and labels as management tools. Do these products contain the expected "socially responsible" attributes? Do these labels really correspond to the nature of the societal practice communicated? Is accessibility to this informational environment on CSR and management tools (labels) the main additional attribute of product quality? (Roger 2000).

The second stage concerns the *client's cognitive ability to process and understand the information transmitted by the labels*. This understanding must focus on the mechanisms that lead CSR to "produce" societal attributes of differentiation. The ability to identify these attributes and to recognize their contribution (private and/or collective benefit) must not present any ambiguity in the client's interpretation so as to allow inferences to be established. The term inference refers to the ability of a source of information to convey clarifications on these attributes that are not directly related to them (Larceneux 2002). The novelty of labels as management tools and societal attributes may afford the key factors of "opportunity" and "cognitive capacity", a role of "pre-appropriation" of these attributes as a differentiating element in their act of purchasing.

The third step is to *assess the potential of a market for products* that incorporate "societal" attributes as an element of differentiation, as well as the profile of the customers who are capable of consuming them. Consumption has a role of social representation, whose functioning is structured around a central core[13] and peripheral elements (Gonzalez *et al.* 2009). Champniss *et al.* (2015) point out that customers are very social animals, belonging to categories which each have a well-defined identity, so, according to Garabedian (2007), they can be considered as heterogeneous agents in the face of societal problems.

Roughly three categories of consumers can be distinguished. The first corresponds to consumers who are part of a rationality whose core is instrumental (selfish) in consuming "socially responsible" products. They may give priority to CSR practices that "manufacture" attributes that improve the intrinsic quality of the product and provide them with a tangible individual private benefit. These consumers may agree that it is important for companies to develop CSR practices, but they refuse to accept the consequences, that is, higher prices, lower quality products (Carrigan and Attala 2001) and a negative image. This is the case, for example, with luxury clothing, as Achabou and Dekhili (2013) have shown that consumers perceive products made from recycled materials negatively (i.e. have a negative image of them). Selfish consumers are motivated more by their own interests (well-being) than by those of society (d'Astous and Legendre 2009). The second is made up of consumers who adopt a rationality whose core is "hybrid" (instrumental and axiological), that is, they are interested in the societal practices of the company that bring them a tangible individual private benefit (health and well-being, etc.), while generating a collective benefit. They are concerned with societal practices that "produce" attributes that improve the intrinsic quality of products (instrumental rationality) but are also sensitive to the reduction of negative social and environmental externalities or the generation of positive externalities (axiological rationality). Finally, the third category concerns consumers whose behavior is axiologically rational and who are motivated by the extra-economic dimensions of the purchasing act (Desjeux 2003). For them, the purchase is not limited to the need for use, but responds to a broader satisfaction that includes moral satisfaction. It is a question of giving meaning to their act of purchasing, so consuming "socially responsible" products enables them to achieve the ethical values which they aspire to hold. For d'Astous and Legendre (2009), "these consumers are people who take into account the societal consequences of their consumption and use their purchasing power and their purchasing act to influence society". They are interested in the moral rules of the market economy and think that companies should preserve the environment and respect social values (François-Lecompte and Valette-Florence 2006). It is the intangible attribute embodied by the virtue of improving a company's civic image that is valued. These consumers express militant or political positions in

13 The core is the fundamental element of the representation: it determines both the meaning and the organization of the representation.

their commercial choices, especially, according to Tirole (2009), if the visibility of their altruistic consumption is high.

2.4.3. *Factors determining consumer eco-responsibility*

This seems to be a good time to launch sustainable offers, and most consumers seem to appreciate environmentally friendly products and services. However, according to White *et al.* (2020), "a recent survey shows that 65% of consumers of them say they want to buy brands committed to sustainable development, but only 26% actually do so". This gap between intention and action needs to be reduced in order to achieve the sustainable development goals of companies, as well as sustainable development across the world as a whole. Unilever estimates that approximately 70% of its GHGs depend on the types of products sold, their use and the recycling of packaging in an environmentally responsible manner. In recent years, the authors have "conducted their own experiments and used the interventions of legislators, marketing, economic and psychological research to find ways to encourage sustainable consumption, thus matching consumer behavior with the principles they espouse". They identified five actions that companies can use.

The first concerns the *use of social pressure*. White and Simpson advised the City of Calgary in Alberta, Canada, who wanted to improve the recycling of grass clippings from lawns, "to try to change people's attitudes by using "social norms", that is, tacit conventions that define acceptable behavior in a group and that people must respect if they want to fit in." Social pressure is an extension of the theory of engagement. For example, White, Simpson and the city conducted a field study on messages that had been posted on the doors of residents' homes ("Your neighbors recycle grass. You can do it too") and observed that in two weeks, the grass recycling rate of residents was double that of a control group. Moreover, *advocates of sustainable behavior are more convincing when they themselves have adopted such behavior*. According to White *et al.* (2020), a study found that 63% more people invested in solar panels when a supporter of these products explained the reasons that they had installed them in their own home. On the other hand, "social norms may not appeal to some consumers, such as men who associate sustainability with femininity and reject it, unless a brand is already linked to masculinity and virility". For example, Jack Daniel's[14] integrates sustainability into its brand strategy (sale of residual products and unused resources, no landfill) and links sustainability, quality and taste. In general, "social pressure can increase if sustainable behaviors are made more visible (no waste to be recycled or composted in a transparent garbage bag), more public (sticker on a car windshield indicating that the engine should be turned

14 American distillery company of Tennessee whiskey, founded by Jack Daniel.

off while waiting for a child to leave school), or competitive (singling out students who compost to encourage others to do the same)".

The second step is to *promote good habits*. People have routines for moving, buying, eating and recycling products and packaging. "Sustainable consumption behaviors require breaking bad habits, which are often due to signals in familiar contexts." For example, using a disposable coffee cup (a habit repeated 500 billion times a year worldwide) can respond to signals such as a disposable cup offered by a bartender, or a trash can with a picture of a cup on it. "Companies need to improve the design of their products, but above all make sustainable behavior a default choice." In Germany, researchers have found that 94% of people conserve clean electricity when it is supplied by default in residential buildings. This approach shows that this type of strategy can be generalized for other areas of activity. For example, making green alternatives such as reusable hand towels and electronic bank statements the default option can increase the rate of take-up. In California (United States), restaurants offer beverages without plastic straws as part of their dining service in order to limit customer demand for straws. White *et al.* (2020) propose three techniques for developing good habits. *Incentives in the form of simple written messages* can remind people of behaviors that they should develop in certain places, such as encouraging recycling near appropriate bins. *Feedback* can provide indications of repeated behaviors such as on fuel consumption and mileage when driving a vehicle. *Sustainable motivation levers* may be different for different companies. For example, in the UK, Coca-Cola and Merlin Entertainments have installed "reverse vending machines" to recycle plastic bottles and allow consumers to benefit from half-price entrance tickets to amusement parks. "Yet if these levers are removed, the desired behavior may disappear. They can also destroy consumers' intrinsic desire to change behavior." Researchers have found that external incentives ("Save money!") combined with intrinsic motivations ("Protect the environment!") lead to less desire for a sustainable product than intrinsic motivations alone. "An external incentive could therefore have a 'crowding out effect' on an intrinsic motivation. However, major changes in people's lives, such as moving, changing jobs, etc., cause them to change their habits." A study was carried out on 400 households that had recently moved, and another 400 households that had not moved. Half of the households in both groups attended an interview and received samples of environmentally friendly products and information on sustainable development. The adoption of green behaviors was more likely among households that had moved than others.

The third step is to take advantage of the *domino effect*. "If consumers are encouraged to develop environmentally responsible habits, positive effects can logically be brought about. By deciding to behave in an environmentally friendly manner, they are likely to make other changes that are beneficial to society." White *et al.* (2020) report that Ikea launched a sustainability initiative, *Live Lagom* (*lagom* means “the right amount” in Swedish), and then studied the journey of a core group of its customers. The company found that although they started by reducing food waste, they often continued to work on other areas, such as energy conservation. In addition, Ikea observed a *snowball effect,* with customers taking small actions and then moving on to more significant projects. For example, the purchase of LED light bulbs could lead consumers to dress warmer and lower the temperature of their homes, change curtains and blinds to reduce heat loss, buy more energy-efficient appliances, etc. “While these actions help to make consumers more sustainable in their purchasing decisions, the effects can also be negative: a single environmental action can lead to less environmentally friendly behavior. This attitude, referred to as ‘licensing’ by researchers, occurs when a consumer feels that an initial ethical action allows him or her to behave less virtuously later on.” For example, according to these authors, researchers have found that people who made a virtual eco-responsible purchase displayed less socially beneficial behavior than people who made a traditional virtual purchase. “Businesses can address this problem by requiring that the first action for the environment requires a lot of effort, an obligation that leads to a commitment”. “If consumers are only encouraged to make smaller commitments, it is better not to mention these types of actions, as they will likely practice lazy activism or slacktivism.”

The fourth step is to *speak from the head or heart.* According to White *et al.* (2020), corporate communication influences the adoption of responsible behavior by consumers. Launching and/or promoting a product, a service or a campaign requires marketers to choose between *emotional levers* and *rational arguments,* two strategies that are effective if certain conditions are met. The first plays on the fact that “consumers are more likely to be eco-responsible when they derive positive emotions, such as hope and pride”. Bacardi, a spirits company, and the NGO Lonely Whale have collaborated to try and eliminate a billion single-use plastic straws, using the hashtag *#thefuturedoesntsuck* to promote events and call on consumers to take action. The pride felt by participants in a study who were publicly praised each week for their energy efforts led them to step up these efforts. On the other hand, these authors point out that “a negative emotion, such as guilt, is an effective motivator only if it is used carefully”. During one experiment, *responsibility was subtly emphasized* (choosing a product publicly) and 84% of consumers bought Fair Trade products because they were so afraid of feeling guilty if they did not. Conversely, when *their guilt was explicitly solicited* (“How can you enjoy a cup of tea knowing that the people who produce this tea are not being treated fairly?”), they reacted very badly and only 40% of them chose environmentally friendly products. The second strategy “appeals to reason”. In 2010, Unilever took into account results which concluded that “people change their habits if they are sure that their actions will have a real impact, that is, if they have an individual impact”. The company therefore launched a campaign on its ecologically produced palm oil, with a photograph of an unspoiled rainforest and the slogan “What you buy at the supermarket can change the world… Small actions, big difference”. Thus, “the marketing of a sustainable product depends on communication of the potential effects of its use on the environment. The provision of information on sustainable behavior and its consequences is of decisive importance”, especially for products with high prices and deferred profits. A study by Hardisty (2020) has shown that when purchasing household appliances or electronics, consumers think little about their energy efficiency or care less about it than about their price. On the other hand, White *et al.* found that “a message geared towards the potential losses to the community in the event of insufficient household recycling is most effective if there is information on when the bins are taken out, what materials to recycle, etc.”. This method reassures people who are afraid of losing something and therefore have an “aversion to loss”.

The fifth step proposes *favoring experience over materialism*. Some companies have set up business models to make consumers more receptive to ecological alternatives. “In *the experience economy*, they offer experience-based solutions that are an alternative to material goods.” For example, Honeyfund might suggest financing a honeymoon trip rather than the household items on a wedding list. This makes the buyers and the bride and groom seem happier, with more meaningful memories. “*With the sharing economy*, companies specialize in sharing and renting products or services rather than selling them, which reduces their environmental footprint. Others offer recycling after the products have been used.” For example, Eileen Fisher and Patagonia encourage their customers to buy high-quality clothing that they can wear for a long time, and then send it back to the company to be refurbished and resold to perpetuate a sustainable circular economy.

Businesses are increasingly communicating with consumers about the sustainability of their brands to increase their market share and contribute to the development of a sustainable lifestyle. The authors of this study recommend that companies should better understand the wants and needs of their target markets, as well as the obstacles and benefits of behavioral change, and adapt their market strategies. “Applying the fundamentals of marketing to engage consumers with a brand’s *raison d’être* and successfully promoting sustainable consumption are the key challenges for companies in the future. The more companies overcome them, the more the sustainable business will emerge as a ‘smart’ business.”

3

Innovation and Ecosystem as Key to the Success of CSV-based Societal Strategies

The concepts of innovation and innovation mapping, the key role that the ecosystem can play, and the process of implementing societal strategies based on creating shared value (CSV), require clarification.

3.1. Innovation as a fundamental lever for developing CSV-based strategies

The constant challenge in implementing societal strategies based on CSV is to develop an organization capable of innovation in the field of business activities. According to Pisano (2015), "innovation is often associated with a frustrating quest because failure rates are high, and successful firms fail to maintain their performance levels because of their tendency to adopt fashionable good innovation practices and to imitate the innovator of the moment, which can be a trap, etc." In general, innovations from research to entrepreneurship are mainly aimed at securing a company's competitive advantage, but companies are increasingly interested in societal innovations that create shared value. Buisson and Hyungseok (2018) point out that "these innovations are based on two types of research that are often complementary: scientific research and technical research." Scientific research corresponds, for the most part, to the discoveries exposed in academic journals of the hard sciences, generally based on disruptive technological innovations and also considered difficult to exploit commercially in their current state. Technical research takes place further downstream and is frequently the subject of patent applications.

It is *de facto* more likely to facilitate commercial exploitation by entrepreneurs. Can these two types of research lead to the creation of innovative companies or promote the development of innovations capable of resulting in CSV? To answer this question, these two authors consider that the State can play a central role. They have identified five different areas through which the State can influence the interactions between these two types of research and innovative entrepreneurship: the size of government, the legal framework and security of ownership, access to finance, freedom of international trade and labor and business credit regulations. A strong State presence will naturally reduce the share of the economy that is accessible to innovative entrepreneurs. Technical research therefore leads to more innovative entrepreneurship when the role of the State is limited, whereas a strong State helps scientific research become more efficient in order to transform technical research into innovative enterprises (Buisson and Hyungseok 2018). CSR managers, in choosing the innovations to be developed, must give priority to technical societal (technological, organizational) innovations capable of generating CSV for the company by supporting its overall business strategy. When companies implement this innovation strategy, they determine the amount of investment needed to create an innovative business model. Pisano (2015) proposes an innovation matrix or map composed of four types of innovation: routine, disruptive, radical and architectural (see Table 3.1).

	Makes the most of existing technical expertise	**Requires new skills**
Requires a new business model	*Disruptive innovation*: open-source software, video-on-demand, occasional rental services	*Architectural innovation*: personalized medicines, Internet research for the press
Benefits of the existing business model	*Routine innovation*: new car, new animated film	*Radical innovation*: genetic engineering, biotechnology

Table 3.1. *Innovation matrix (Pisano 2015)*

Routine innovation is based on the company's existing technological skills and is in line with the existing business model and therefore its customers. Disruptive innovation requires a new business model but rarely a technological revolution. As a result, it calls into question the business model of other companies or causes a break with it. Radical innovation is the opposite of disruptive innovation, as the challenge is purely technological, for example, technological innovations in genetic engineering (1970) and biotechnology (1980). Architectural innovation combines the technological disruption with that of the business model (digital photography for Kodak and Polaroid), and this association presupposes that companies have the appropriate skills for the sectors in which they operate. The innovation matrix makes it possible to examine whether a potential innovation is adapted to existing technical capabilities and business models and can therefore be useful in the decision to develop an innovation strategy (Pisano 2015).

To consider these four types of innovations as strategic is to know how to balance and pace them. In an innovation strategy, the need for a company to change its dominant patterns is key. This is the case, for example, with firms that integrate societal practices into their overall strategies and transition from innovations that improve their competitive advantage to CSV-based strategies. Firms may then face the challenge of building and sustaining the capacity to innovate in societal strategies. Since CSV-based innovations are relatively new, the problem with efforts to put them into practice may stem mainly from the lack of a clear innovation strategy, in other words "a commitment to a set of coherent and mutually reinforcing policies or behaviors that are designed to achieve a specific competitive and societal goal" (Pisano 2015). According to Martin (2019), an innovation with a successful societal mission must be "capable of bringing to light a process that can lead to two concepts: reduced waste of resources and increased productivity of the firm." These two concepts influence the organization of the company's work. This author underlines that it was Frederick Winslow Taylor who first considered management a science, thus initiating a movement that reached its apogee with William Edwards Deming and his conception of a comprehensive quality management system to eliminate all losses from production processes. Smith, Ricardo, Taylor and Deming made this management a science whose objective became the elimination of waste of time, raw materials or capital. For a company that makes its innovation strategy part of its societal mission, the fight against waste must be par for the course.

According to Pisano (2019), "a culture favorable to innovation improves the bottom line (financial performance) of companies and can be valued by their managers and employees." To put it into practice, this author proposes five recommendations. First, CSR managers must develop *a tolerant attitude to failure, but zero tolerance to incompetence* (an important characteristic of innovative cultures). Second, companies must have *a willingness to experiment, within a very rigorous framework,* meaning that they are *comfortable with uncertainty and ambiguity,* making attempts to learn rather than to design a product or service that is immediately marketable. Third, *psychological security, with brutal candor,* is needed within the company to enable its stakeholders to talk openly and honestly about their problems *without fear of reprisals*. Fourth, *collaborating and upholding individual responsibility* must result in information, input and maximum integration of the contributions of all potential contributors. Fifth, *non-hierarchical but strong leadership* should be developed. Generally speaking, an organization chart is a fairly good reflection of the structural organization of a company, but it reveals little about its culture, that is, about the behaviors of individuals, their interactions according to their functions, etc.

Moreover, to succeed in a societal-mission-type innovation strategy, the strategy must always be linked to the company's culture. "The strategy provides a formal logic for defining the (societal) goals of the company and provides a framework for employees and partners to achieve them" (Groysberg *et al.* 2018). The strategy should also provide clarity and coherence for collective action and decision-making. It should be based on a set of choices that aim to mobilize individuals, and be reinforced, often both by concrete rewards when goals are achieved and by sanctions when they are not.

Culture expresses values based on *organizational ethics and beliefs* while guiding activity through *common assumptions and group rules*. Culture is also the tacit social order of a company: it can shape attitudes and behavior in a varied and sustainable way. "When it is aligned with personal values, motivations and needs, culture can release amounts of energy that can achieve a common purpose and stimulate the company's ability to thrive" (Groysberg *et al.* 2018). According to these authors, based on an amalgamation of the major works by mainly Edgar Schein, Shalom Schwarts and Geert Hofstede, four cultural attributes are generally accepted. First, *culture must be shared, as it is associated with the phenomenon of the group,* that is, it cannot exist in a single individual and cannot represent the simple average of individual characteristics. It is embodied in shared behaviors, values and assumptions that are often linked to unspoken rules. Second, culture is pervasive, in other words, it permeates many levels, can be applied very broadly within the organization and is clearly manifested in collective behaviors through implicit assumptions, also known as "action logic" (mental models for interpreting and responding to the world around us). Third, *culture must be sustainable* because it can influence the thoughts and actions of group members over the long term. It is therefore a self-reinforcing societal model that becomes increasingly resistant to change and external influences. Fourth, *culture is implicit* – this important aspect is often overlooked. Despite its subliminal nature, it acts as a kind of non-verbal language. The reactions of individuals in their relationships, or in the face of change, vary according to the culture of the company (see Figure 3.1).

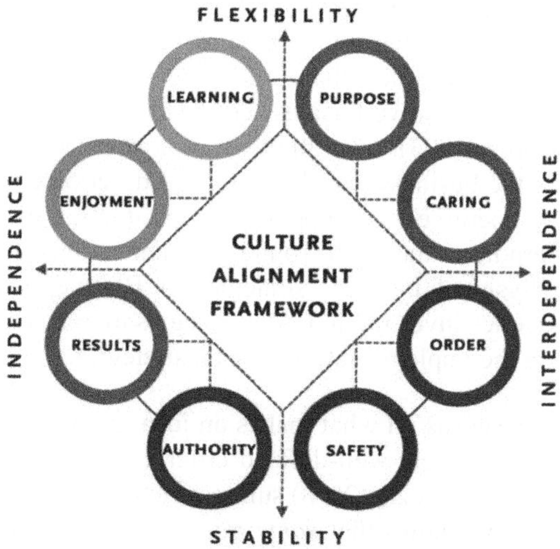

Figure 3.1. *Integrated cultivation framework (Spencer Stuart, cited by Pisano (2015))*

In order to acquire a capacity for innovation, CSR managers, who alone are competent for managing such a complex system, must first define a societal strategy capable of facilitating CSV. In this case, the leadership of these managers and the creation of an innovative organization are intimately linked. The challenge of this leadership is to take responsibility for the processes, structures, talents and behaviors that will transform the company by integrating societal strategies based on CSV, whereas, until now, it has mainly been limited to developing innovations that can secure its competitive advantage. CSR managers must now look for opportunities for innovation that will structure CSV-related ideas into concepts and product models by choosing which actions to take. According to Hill *et al.* (2015), "the leadership role of these managers is primarily to create a community that is willing and able to generate new societal ideas over time." In a study conducted by the same authors on the role of the leader in creating a more innovative organization, the managers who were surveyed had a wide variety of profiles, but they all envisioned leadership in the same way: they all had a conventional viewpoint. For them, leadership was about setting the course to follow and is effective so long as the solution to a problem is simple and known. However, if the problem requires a truly original response, no one can decide in advance what that response will be. By definition, leadership does not mean developing and selling a vision to individuals in order to motivate them to put these innovations into practice. The question is therefore not only "how should they organize themselves to make societal innovation happen?" but also "how do they make it happen?" At the end of the study, the authors concluded that "the notion of visionary leaders is so widespread that many of them have been forced to rethink and redefine their functions before their organizations can truly become and remain innovative in CSV strategies." Companies must therefore develop these strategies not only by making trade-offs but also by building a competitive business ecosystem (BE) that can facilitate their realization. It was Moore (1993), over 20 years ago, who introduced and transposed the notion of a BE to the business world, in order to describe companies that "work cooperatively and competitively to support new products, satisfy customer needs and eventually incorporate the next round of innovations." As an innovative approach to the analysis of business strategies, a BE has enabled the strategic management of companies investing in CSV strategies to evolve and thus becomes a key tool in facilitating the implementation of such strategies.

There is no real consensus on what makes an idea innovative and what makes it valuable, even though relatively well-defined criteria can predict who will generate creative ideas. Chamorro-Premuzic (2018) summarizes a detailed review of more than 100 scientific studies and shows that *some people are significantly more likely to come up with new and useful ideas, regardless of their area of expertise, profession and background*. According to this author, "these individuals tend to have a recurring set of psychological and behavioral characteristics and are better at identifying problems rather than solving them." Above all, "they are passionate, sensitive, with an insatiable spirit, open to new experiences, non-conformist and curious." These aspects of their personality determine the creative potential of each individual rather than their IQ, academic performance or motivation. Creativity alone is not enough to innovate, as it also requires the development, production and implementation of the innovative idea. The essential difference between creativity and innovation is execution, in other words, the ability to transform an idea into a successful business, service or product. Entrepreneurship is therefore a process by which creative ideas become useful innovations, and it involves human action which depends on the decisions and behaviors of certain people. To this end, one logical approach to understanding the essence of innovation is to study the fundamental characteristics of entrepreneurial minds, that is, people who are a force for innovation. The research highlights five key variables in addition to creativity (Chamorro-Premuzic 2018). The first relates to *the opportunism of the individual* whose mind helps identify market gaps and opportunities that are at the heart of the process of entrepreneurial strategies and innovation. Opportunists seem to be programmed for novelty, as they are eager for new and complex experiences and seek variety in all aspects of their lives. The second is associated with *serious education and training*, which are essential for learning how to note promising new opportunities. Without expertise, it is difficult to distinguish between information that is relevant ("signals") and information that is irrelevant ("noise"). The third variable *is a proactive nature and great perseverance*, which enables an individual to better exploit newly identified opportunities. Effective innovators are also very determined, resilient and energetic. The fourth relates to *prudence*. Successful innovators are more organized, cautious and averse to risks than the rest of the population. In the entrepreneurial process, high risk-taking is quite common when starting a business, but success does not really depend on it. Finally, the fifth variable relates to the *social capital on which effective innovators rely* throughout this process, which is always a team effort. These innovators tend to *use their connections and networks* to mobilize resources and skills and build strong alliances inside and outside the firm. In addition, they tend to have a very high emotional quotient (EQ). While these five characteristics play a critical role in the entrepreneurial process, true innovation is unlikely to succeed without a meaningful mission or a clear long-term vision. Vision is where entrepreneurship and leadership meet, so it is the ability to inspire others to be innovators and to succeed in innovation that is crucial for the company.

3.2. Analysis of the ecosystem's role in the process of implementing CSV strategies

Companies seeking new economic opportunities, and aspiring to gain public trust, must understand that in adopting CSV strategies, they will inevitably encounter obstacles, as none of them can act alone and each of them exists within an ecosystem in which societal conditions are likely to hinder their markets and restrict the productivity of their suppliers and distributors, etc. (Kramer and Pfitzer 2017). In addition, public policies introduce their own limits, and cultural norms influence demand. All these situations are beyond the control of any one company. As a result, many global societal problems require expertise and models inspired by the private sector. In order to undertake CSV efforts, therefore, companies must promote and participate in multi-sectoral coalition efforts. To this end, they need a new framework in which governments and members of society all have an essential role to play, not individually, but collectively. Kania and Kramer (2011) have created a movement called "*collective impact*" to foster successful social sector collaborations and to guide companies in their efforts to bring together diverse actors in their ecosystems to incentivize change. Collective impact is based on the premise that *societal problems arise and persist as a result of a complex combination of actions and omissions* by actors from all sectors (Kramer and Pfitzer 2017). These problems can therefore only be solved through coordinated efforts made by various stakeholders such as public institutions (government agencies, States, communities, etc.), soft power actors (NGOs, scientists, communities, etc.), directly or indirectly affected populations, etc. (Kramer and Pfitzer 2017). Companies that place their strategies within a collective impact perspective will commit to societal progress in various fields (education, health, job creation, etc.) and will also be able to easily identify the economic opportunities of their competitors. However, according to Adner and Kapoor (2017), "any initiative, whether established or disruptive, needs a range of complementary elements such as technologies, services, standards, regulations, etc. to realize its shared value proposition." Since a company is only as good as its ecosystem, the strength and maturity of the ecosystem's components play a key role in the success of such strategies. If the ecosystem of the old technology (competitive advantage) is in place and competitive, then innovation has overcome its disruptive challenges (Adner and Kapoor 2017) and uncovered the nuts and bolts of its operation.

The successful implementation of these strategies requires that CSR managers believe in the power of ecosystems. According to Straub (2019), Peter Drucker points out that "his interest in management stems from his interest in the evolution of relations between individuals and societal institutions", which he calls *social ecology*. This new ecology is not biological and concerns the ecosystems formed by companies and institutions. For this author, the objective is to find "a balance between continuity, on the one hand, and change and innovation, on the other hand, and to enable managers to identify emerging trends so that they can act on them." Drawing on the concepts of ecology and ecosystems can provide an opportunity to better anticipate how technology will change companies and industries in terms of CSV. New perspectives are emerging to understand the business world as a dynamic and evolving force in society, as well as to bring managers to reconsider the way they manage their companies. With this approach, *companies* regain a long neglected identity, that *of organizations with a human dimension, capable of evolving, instead of just being a set of machines*. This paradigm shift with regard to management training and R&D implies a retreat from management theory and practice, which is conditioned by a mechanistic vision of the economy with rational individuals and companies maximizing their utility and profits, respectively, that is, with human robots (employees) and organizational machines (companies). *Human beings* have emotions, aspirations, dreams, idiosyncrasies and *do not appreciate being treated as mere cogs in a machine*. This can lead to a form of *disengagement, defiance* and *poor performance*, as well as *stress, discouragement* and *untapped potential*. A second paradigm concerns the power of ecosystems. According to McKinsey, "these complex networks of interconnected businesses that depend on and feed off of each other can deliver value to customers, end-users and key stakeholders." Upon implementing societal innovations based on CSV, companies have to transform the classical BE into a regional societal business ecosystem (RSBE) and should not consider this transformation as a burden and/or a source of additional costs.

Firms have always focused on innovation strategies that can further secure their competitive position, yet in order to adopt societal strategies based on CSV, there may be, as McCaffery and Pearson (2016) point out, "situations where some of these firms may be hampered by functional fixity and other cognitive biases that cause them to neglect alternative solutions for the establishment of an adequate ecosystem." The term "bias" refers to the distortions between how individuals (customers) must reason to best ensure the validity of their conclusions and how they will actually reason

(Gardair 2007). These two authors consider fixity not only as an effective neurological tactic in everyday life but also as a real obstacle to creativity for companies wishing to develop CSV strategies. These biases, which they must fight against, are briefly summarized as five types of obstacles, four of which are organizational factors related to change (Eccles and Serafeim 2014). The first is associated with *short-term incentives* that often hinder investment ability in competitive societal innovations. Many employees, including managers, are rewarded for short-term performance, whereas CSR practices are part of a long-term vision. The second results from a *lack of expertise*. These new strategies for solving internal and external societal problems arising from a company's activities often involve new skills that may not be available. The third is the *budgetary limitations of the company*. Major societal innovations that require long-term investment may be perceived as very costly and therefore unattractive to managers. The fourth organizational barrier is associated with *investor pressure* on maximum short-term profitability, which the company may not be able to meet. Finally, the fifth may be associated with a *risk of conflict between the elements of the ecosystem of technological and/or organizational innovation strategies* that have been designed to secure a competitive advantage *and those of the new ecosystem that the company needs to put in place to develop innovation strategies based on CSV*. However, this conflict can be mitigated by a standard exchange between certain innovations from the two ecosystems. New societal innovations therefore require significant changes in the existing ecosystem and can then be considered a constraint. The key factor is the time it takes for the new ecosystem to develop to the point where users understand its potential (Adner and Kapoor 2017) and how it works. To combat all these factors that induce this functional fixity, the real challenge for companies is to adopt a flexible behavioral approach to the development of innovation strategies that create shared value, and a specific ecosystem that enables the potential of these strategies to be exploited. The successful development of these strategies requires the RSBE to take into account specific elements. The ecosystems of many companies are limited to incremental societal improvements, with easily justified projects that generate quick returns, such as energy efficiency. Companies need to make a profound change in strategy and philosophy that will make them more resilient and help them create sustainable shared value. With this logic of resilience, they adopt radically different approaches based on three levers: vision, societal project and partnership (Winston 2017). According to Martin (2019), resilience is the ability to return to business as usual following a difficulty, that is, being able to recover from a shock. There is a difference between being adapted to one's environment (which is made possible by efficiency) and being able to adapt to changes in one's environment. Resilient systems are distinguished by the characteristics that efficiency seeks to remove (diversity and redundancy, or underuse of resources in other words).

The vision is for the members of the partnership to dare to ask questions that are considered incongruous, in order to develop societal innovations in a radical way, using science to set ambitious goals and fight against short-termism. This is the case, for example, with a manager of the American logistics group, UPS, who wondered: "Can we reduce vehicle fuel costs by avoiding turning left at a crossroads?". This incongruous idea of not turning left, combined with an organizational innovation, has reduced waiting time at junctions and saved the company 30 million liters of petrol per year. Depending on their sector of activity, the second lever concerns companies that need to have a clear understanding of the real trade-offs to be made between financial and societal performance. The societal project therefore consists of prioritizing major societal innovations that enable the company to rethink products, markets or processes and redefine productivity in the value chain or specific social business models that can generate these trade-offs in a sustainable way (Porter and Kramer 2011; Eccles and Serafeim 2014): for example, GHG emissions are an issue for a coal company, but not for a service organization. This lever lies at the heart of the creation of materiality maps, that is, identifying relevant criteria likely to facilitate CSV. These relevant criteria are assessed according to three categories of evidence. The first is associated with *the collective interest produced by the innovations,* and the second establishes *the positive economic impact for the company* (reduction in costs, increase in profit, turnover, etc.). For the collective interest and the positive economic impact to be viable and profitable, companies should favor, where possible, the use of hybrid societal innovations that do not penalize their competitiveness. "Hybrid societal innovation is an innovation that can significantly reduce the negative social and environmental externalities generated by the company's activities at lower costs, while at the same time generating a competitive advantage for the company" (Gasmi 2017). Finally, the third is related to *prospective adjustment to emerging societal issues* (Eccles and Serafeim 2014). This adjustment means that the company identifies a new issue, not yet mentioned in its evidence-based tests, and its importance, that is, whether or not its consideration is likely to generate positive or negative effects that other stakeholders, sectors or generations will have to manage, or if a systemic break is possible (Eccles and Serafeim 2014). For the societal project to be viable, appropriate responses to two questions must be given. Can societal, technological or organizational innovations, based on CSV, satisfy the needs of current or potential customers? What is the degree of substitution between old and new technology? If the answers provided are capable of delivering on their promises, these innovations will of course be able to establish themselves on the market, but only if they are not overly dependent on other innovations. The pace of substitution plays a key role in the process of accelerating the implementation of CSV-based societal innovations. The rate of resilience is determined by the rate at which problems in the ecosystem of the new technology are solved and whether or not the old technology can exploit opportunities to expand its ecosystem. Adner and Kapoor (2017) propose four models on the rate of substitution (Table 3.2).

		Possibility of extending the ecosystem of the old technology	
		Low	**High**
Disruptive difficulties of the new societal technology based on venture capital	**Important**	*Illusion of resilience*: immobility followed by rapid substitution, GPS navigator versus paper maps	*Robust resilience*: slower substitution, electric versus gasoline cars
	Unimportant	*Creative destruction*: faster substitution, 3D printer versus inkjet printer	*Robust coexistence*: gradual substitution, hybrid versus combustion engines

Table 3.2. *Matrix of patterns of technological substitution rates (Adner and Kapoor 2017)*

		Actors	
		Value chain companies	**Business and other non-commercial stakeholders**
Focus	**Results**	Key strategy: develop sector benchmarks and standard systems to measure societal performance in the value chain	Key strategy: introduce "payment" models for ecosystem services that allow companies to invest in funds that pay local communities to improve conservation and achieve environmental outcomes
	Business processes	Key strategy: identify and share business processes that reduce GHG emissions, natural resource consumption and waste, while protecting the environment	Key strategy: establish wide-ranging collaborations that encourage the business community and other stakeholders to pursue operational innovations and best practices that create shared value

Table 3.3. *Matrix of collaborative models (Nidumolu* et al. *2017)*

The third lever concerns the strategy of the partnership policy, which will be organized around the company's key stakeholders. Nidumolu *et al.* (2017) propose four models of collaboration (see Table 3.3). The partnership policy is based on two inseparable courses of action: management and innovation. Autissier *et al.* (2018) define management as a set of capabilities aimed at making people (here, stakeholders of the firm) cooperate with one another to achieve a goal under cost and time constraints, whereas innovation is aimed at creating new ways for people to cooperate in achieving goals effectively and efficiently, while taking into account societal changes. Inherited from Taylorism, management has built practices on the hierarchical "command/control" model by associating participative loops. In today's rapidly changing world, it is useful to question and redefine what business practices are, that is, managerial innovation, in order to envisage that they will be the new forms of management and form their backbone. These new forms increasingly rely on shared leadership, and the organizational issue is also becoming increasingly cooperative.

<table>
<tr><th></th><th colspan="3">Autonomy development</th></tr>
<tr><th rowspan="3">Delivery development</th><td>Design thinking, codesign</td><td>Network learner</td><td>Incubator, spin-off</td></tr>
<tr><td>Hackathon</td><td>Participatory workshops</td><td>Microplatform, self-contained team</td></tr>
<tr><td>Tutoring, monitoring, peer coaching</td><td>Co-development</td><td>Immersion, disruptive experience</td></tr>
</table>

Table 3.4. *Matrix of collaborative managerial innovations (Autissier* et al. *2018, p. 46)*

The cooperative purpose has always been sought, but the difference comes from the use of individual stances and behaviors. Cooperation is no longer achieved not only through the distribution of activities (organization charts) and the formalization of operations (processes) but also through the commitment and participatory stance of individuals. Partnership or collaboration enables the achievement of societal goals and competitive advantages beyond the scope of the company alone. Autissier *et al.* (2016) conducted an interview study to identify the innovations most favored by the 15 groups of companies that are members of the ESSEC Chair of Change. The various managerial innovations cited were structured along two axes: *delivery* on the *y* axis and *autonomy* on the *x* axis. The notion of *delivery* is defined as the ability to produce and respond to client demand and is a key capacity in today's organizations (Autissier *et al.* 2015), whereas the *autonomy* left to individuals is not only a societal demand but also a factor of collective intelligence conducive to innovation and empowerment practices. These authors identified nine forms of managerial innovation based on collaboration or partnership (see Table 3.4).

The first managerial innovation is associated with *design thinking*, which combines observation of uses and prototyping,[1] and arose in the mid-2000s at Stanford University and in design companies. Codesign thinking is an "agile" method, meaning the ideas resulting from observation of the needs of the beneficiaries are very quickly prototyped to be tested iteratively (Autissier *et al.* 2018). *Codesign* is a process based on the association of all the key stakeholders, in particular the final customer for whom a response to a need with a well-defined use must be found (Autissier *et al.* 2016). The second is the *learning network*, which relies on *non-hierarchical* exchanges to ensure free speech and develop collective intelligence by putting people in situations of collective reflection and action, in order to deal with subjects requiring them to share and construct collective solutions (Autissier *et al.* 2014). The third is the *hackathon, the name derived from* the contraction of the terms "hack", which refers to hacker, meaning to modify or tinker, and "marathon", a long and arduous long-distance race. In the computer world, this concept corresponds to "commando operations" that test ideas and then produce application prototypes in a limited amount of time (Autissier *et al.* 2018). The fourth, known as *peer coaching*, differs from traditional coaching (Lenhardt and Buratti 2013) and has complemented it in recent years. Two people with the same job or different skills exchange information on real-life work situations, with cross-examination according to the coaching techniques, that is, with a coach–coach alternation that supposes active listening (Autissier *et al.* 2016, 2018), which may improve their company's performance. The fifth is associated with the *incubator* and the *spin-off* whose concepts have emerged in light of recent developments in digital transformation. A spin-off consists of creating a subsidiary where volunteer employees work in an entrepreneurial and capital-intensive way (Autissier *et al.* 2016). Projects can thus be developed as in a start-up, without the administrative and political inertia of large companies. The incubator is a variation of a spin-off. Employees work in a "lab" (laboratory)-type structure, which provides them with the resources they need, but they are autonomous in carrying out a project. The incubator can be a temporary organization or a preliminary stage prior to the creation of a spin-off (Autissier and Métais 2016). The sixth is a *set of participatory workshops* where the proposed activities are structured by a script in order to alternate individual, group and collective production times. Facilitators supervise these free expression workshops using the metaplan method or organized with matrices and other figures (Autissier and Moutot 2013). According to these authors, the participants thus have moments of exchange that allow them to stop being embarrassed when tackling certain subjects and/or to promote conviviality if they do not know each other. The sessions last from one to three hours, with a sequence of one to four 45-minute workshops. This type of participatory workshop is also called an icebreaker (Autissier and Moutot 2015). The seventh innovation is associated

1 Cited by Autissier *et al.* (2018, p. 30): Brown (2009). *Change by Design: How Design Thinking Transforms Organizations and Inspires Innovation*. Harper Business, New York.

with the notion of *microplateau* which comes from lean experiments in the Japanese automotive industry, especially at Toyota in the 1970s (Womack *et al.* 2009). Small groups of people are completely autonomous in their internal management and production activities, without hierarchy and without control processes, but with an obligation to produce results. The hierarchy of the company is only called upon when there are problems of coordination and adequacy between allocated resources and results. This strategic approach is aimed at small groups for which the cost of coordination is low (Mucchielli 2015). The eighth concerns *co-development* and is considered a standard for management training and professionalization. The Quebec authors Champagne and Payette (2005) developed this technique, which uses a script in which people grouped in workshops reflect on problematic and/or curious situations on a given topic. The principle of this innovation is for a participant to be a client who presents his or her situation and for the others to act as consultants who propose solutions to this situation. Each participant must play this double role of client and consultant. All must therefore learn to understand and solve different situations in their work environment. At the end of the session, the participants ask themselves how they have worked in terms of personal development. Finally, the ninth managerial innovation based on collaboration is associated with *immersion* and *disruptive experience*. One of the best known immersive techniques is the learning expedition (from the French *expédition apprenante* in Quebec). Autissier *et al.* (2018) point out that its principle is based on visits to companies that share their experience, by people from one or more companies. Meetings last from one to three hours, while cross-immersions can last up to several days, allowing participants to discover new ways of working and to challenge their practices. The disruptive experience aims to create a split in the participants. For example, in the United States, Singularity University offers seminars for decision-makers on themes such as "Change or die" and "Thinking the world of tomorrow". Philosopher and computer scientist Ray Kurtzweil created this structure in 2008 at his NASA research center in Silicon Valley. The researcher believes that change is increasingly rapid and violent and that today's ways of thinking must evolve in order to understand and build the world of tomorrow (Autissier *et al.* 2018). *Singularity* is a notion that emerged in the 1950s, with von Neumann's work, to reveal the tipping point at which technology would supplant humans and the day when machines could create other machines themselves.

The nine forms of innovation that have been identified can be grouped according to their purpose in order to provide a more macro view of managerial innovation (see Table 3.5).

Purposes of managerial innovations	Features of managerial innovations	Forms of managerial innovation
Outsourcing	Creating organizational forms outside traditional boundaries to have smaller and more flexible organizations in developing CSV-based strategies	Incubator and spin-off Immersion and disruptive experience
Collaborative mode	Proposing devices to improve relations between people: seeking collective intelligence by involving more people in problem solving	Participatory workshops Learning networks
Collective creativity	Deploying systems that enable the greatest number of people to be players in innovation by having them propose ideas	Design thinking, codesign Hackathon
Co-learning	Defining learning methods: exchange of experiences and knowledge between people based on a principle of reciprocity and resolution with respect to mutual problems	Tutoring, monitoring and peer coaching, focus group Co-development
Empowerment	Inventing new forms of organization, control and coordination between people, with the possibility of leaving more power to people for their autonomy and accountability	Microplatform, self-contained team

Table 3.5. *Purposes of managerial innovations (Autissier* et al. *2018, p. 53)*

These innovations make it possible to propose an initial model of managerial innovation based on collaborative strategies (Table 3.6).

Modes of collaboration	
Operation	**Stance**
Agility	Commitment
Adaptation	Accountability

Table 3.6. *Structuring of managerial innovations (Autissier* et al. *2018, p. 52)*

All the managerial innovations show that the "collaboration" lever plays a decisive role, because the preservation of resources and the use of their long-term value requires new collaborations that take into account the regional societal business ecosystems (RSBE) as a whole. The partnership is part of a reasoning based on co-creation or co-innovation, in an open approach to the production of an innovative societal strategy and is described as open innovation, the basis of which is theorized by Chesbrough (2003). This concept consists of encouraging the business not to close in on itself, but to open up to other innovative ideas which are capable of bringing about CSV and have been raised by its various stakeholders (customers, employees, suppliers, NGOs, etc.). These stakeholders intervene according to their skills in all stages of product design, such as the definition of essential characteristics, the choice of environmentally friendly materials and processes that reduce the consumption of water, electricity, waste, the drudgery of employee work, the evaluation of the fairest prices and the creation of positive social externalities.

For the three levers (vision, societal project and partnership) to achieve their objectives, CSR managers must integrate six elements (Kramer and Pfitzer 2017) in their RSBEs. The first is the *development of a common action plan* so that participants adopt a common vision and a concerted approach, specific to the societal innovations to be developed that are likely to produce CSV. This plan helps to harmonize their efforts, define the commitment of each partner and determine the sharing and flow of information internally and externally. The second concerns the establishment of *a common system of evaluation* resulting from the choice of a short list of indicators which explain how to measure the success and limitations of these innovations. The third is the *development of mutually supportive actions*, in other words, each partner concentrates on what they can and know how to do, by forming working groups, each of which is dedicated to a different aspect of the problem to be solved. The fourth is to *develop permanent channels of communication* to enable all the RSBE actors to maintain regular and structured exchanges *in order to build trust and coordinate common objectives*. The fifth element concerns the *creation of a structure dedicated to the societal project*, that is, a separate, independently funded team. This structure, which is the backbone of this project, is intended to guide the vision and strategy, support activities, establish common evaluation practices, make policy proposals and mobilize resources, and ensure harmonious communication between all the working groups. Finally, the sixth element stipulates that *a partner company provides the necessary funds* to start the project to transform the ecosystem in order to realize societal projects that create shared value, that is, reconciling financial and societal performance. In addition to these six elements proposed by Kramer and Pfitzer (2017), another key element is to *identify the likely tensions that may exist between stakeholders*: these tensions represent the crux of the problem of innovation in an ecosystem with multiple stakeholders.

Certainly, partnership plays a key role in developing competitive societal innovations based on CSV. But all innovation strategies are fallible, since solving a problem, such as CSV for business, is at the heart of innovation (Satell 2018). No "right" method exists, so innovation must be understood like other business disciplines, in other words, as a set of tools created for specific objectives. This author proposes four types of innovations and examples of problems they can solve (Table 3.7).

<table>
<tr><th></th><th></th><th colspan="2">How well are the areas of competence defined?</th></tr>
<tr><th></th><th></th><th>Not well defined</th><th>Well defined</th></tr>
<tr><td rowspan="2">How well is the problem defined?</td><td>Well defined</td><td>Revolutionary innovation: mavericks, autonomous teams; open innovation/competition</td><td>Continuous innovation: action plans, R&D laboratory, design thinking, acquisitions</td></tr>
<tr><td>Not well defined</td><td>Basic research: research department of university partnerships, specialized journals and conferences</td><td>Disruptive innovation: venture capital model, innovation lab, 15%/20% rule</td></tr>
</table>

Table 3.7. *Types of innovations and the problems they solve (Satell 2018)*

Continuous innovation is part of a logic of constant growth and potential improvement in existing markets, with a clear idea of the problems to be solved and the areas of expertise needed. Companies developing this type of innovation must establish clear action plans, have R&D research laboratories and practice design thinking. Design thinking makes it possible to build prototypes very quickly with the aid of aesthetic and educational designers and test them on users. Teams of developers and users therefore work together for a fixed period of time (usually 2 days) to produce a prototype from a given project.

Revolutionary innovation is associated with a company that faces a problem that is perfectly circumscribed but extremely difficult to solve. Unusual areas of competence must therefore be explored, and in this case, open innovation strategies can be effective. The concept of disruptive innovation described by Clayton Christensen in *The Innovator's Dilemma* was a revelation. By studying the reasons why successful companies lose efficiency, he discovered that in some situations, so-called good practices can be fatal. For example, when the fundamentals of competition change, companies can find themselves performing better and better in areas that customers are less and less interested in. Improving the attributes of the company's product no longer then corresponds to market expectations, and instead innovation is required in terms of a business model capable of producing products that meet these expectations. The fourth innovation corresponds to fundamental research and always starts with the discovery of a new phenomenon. No one could have predicted that Einstein's discoveries would profoundly transform modern science, nor that the universal computer of Alan Turing[2] would become a reality. Some large companies, such as IBM or Procter & Gamble, can afford to invest in basic research laboratories. Others encourage researchers and engineers to participate in in-house conferences to present what they have discovered. A company that has the capacity to work with very high-level scientists thus receives support in terms of skills that enable it to project itself into the future. Companies without such resources can use open innovation or crowdsourcing in terms of business models, such as design thinking, to make very rapid progress. However, there is no single solution to all of a company's problems.

According to a study by Cross *et al.* (2018), collaboration is invading the workspace, silos are breaking down, connectivity is increasing and teamwork is seen as an element of business success. The distribution of this collaborative work is often extremely unbalanced, with 20–35% of value-added collaborations relying on 3–5% of employees. Managers can only manage these collaborations effectively if they distinguish between three types of resources. The first is associated with information resources: knowledge, skills and expertise that can be recorded and transmitted. The second concerns social resources: a person's sensitivity, accessibility and position in the network, which can help colleagues work better together. These two resources can be shared, generally through a simple exchange, without undermining the reservations of the collaborators, and by making it so that a person can certainly offer their knowledge or knowledge of a network, but that they must be able to keep the use of it for their own needs. Finally, the third is made up of personal resources: a person's time and energy. All resources are often, by default, the object of requests for collaboration, such as direct assistance, which may not be necessary and which may put the dynamics of the person's work at a disadvantage.

CSR managers are therefore required to streamline, allocate collaborative responsibilities and reward effective contributions. When it comes to problem solving, innovative managers have always known that a better question leads to a better answer, which can challenge deep-rooted assumptions. For example, we must first evaluate the different strategies for societal missions, brand attributes and innovations that can generate CSV for the company, and then succeed in collaborative work. CSR managers must therefore set up an effective brainstorming

2 Alan Turing, a logic mathematician, worked on the Enigma and Colossus machines to decipher German messages for the British Army during World War II.

strategy with the principle of seeking questions rather than answers. This approach can establish a climate of trust that will then allow problems to be analyzed in greater depth and then resolved effectively, but the appointment of a responsible person and a matrix of sessions is required for this research phase. In addition, partnership stakeholders avoid destructive group dynamics and biases that may thwart their opinions. The philosophy of brainstorming helps to overcome cognitive biases and venture into uncharted territory. For Gregersen (2018), lingering in an interrogative mode does not come naturally to most people who are conditioned, from an early age, to constantly produce only answers. A process needs to be developed to reformulate problems in a new and fruitful way. Since not all questions are of equal interest, it is difficult to predict what kind of questions they should be, and to ensure that they are useful.

To make these sessions more successful, this author proposes three steps. The first is the preparation of the collective work with the choice of a challenge that quickly interests the stakeholders. If this challenge is the societal project, it is ready to be submitted for questions that will move it forward. In traditional brainstorming sessions, which are more concerned with generating answers, individuals outperform groups on average. Indeed, powerful group dynamics such as "social laziness" (relying on the contributions of others) and social anxiety (fear of being judged for one's ideas) can hinder original opinions and inhibit introverted members. On the other hand, the rapid enunciation of a set of questions essentially reverses many of these destructive dynamics by encouraging people to break their habits of social interaction. This approach creates a safe space for all participants (including a more reserved person) to offer a different perspective, as the set of questions does not require everyone to instinctively put forward their point of view. In practice, when the partners are brought together, the brainstorming facilitator should share with them the challenge of the project by quickly presenting the societal problem for a few minutes, in a precise manner without constraining or directing the question(s).

The second step is then to limit the collective production of questions about the challenge to a few minutes (or to about 15 questions), without leaving out any, especially those that are surprising and provocative. However, before giving the floor to the stakeholders in the collaboration, two crucial rules must be clearly stated. First, they can only ask questions and will be reframed by the facilitator if they try to suggest solutions or answer questions from others. Second, no preambles or rationales framing the questions will be allowed so that they do not view the problem in a biased way. Each of them must also check their emotions as the "owner" of the challenge: Are my feelings positive? Neutral? Or negative? It is advisable for them to write down, in a few words, their basic mood at the beginning and end of the sessions, as emotions affect creative energy.

The third step is to identify a goal among the questions that suggests new avenues. Some may be intriguing, appear different from the way problems have been handled so far and may even embarrass the participants. Typically, in 80% of cases, this exercise generates at least one question that usefully reframes the problem and provides a new angle for solving it. Collaboration managers must therefore already identify the key questions that need to be answered in order to make the societal project a success.

To understand the difficulties of implementing societal innovations based on CSV, Kaplan *et al.* (2018) conducted a study by interviewing 30 managers of CSR strategies. The results show that most of these managers believe that the difficulties stem from the implementation of societal projects, their lack of integration into the main activities of the company, problems collaborating with local communities, and lack of relevant indicators to stimulate and evaluate the benefits for the company, and for the targeted populations. These authors have identified another problem that is not related to the implementation of the project but to the limited ambition of these managers who do not place their societal projects in an outlook capable of strengthening their market or moving towards a related market, in order to generate economic value for the business, etc. To solve this problem, they identified eight main questions: do CSV strategies reinforce the brand's product attributes? What new and strategic attributes can they bring out that respond to the cultural environment of the country where the brand is present? Are they difficult for competitors to copy? Can they add value to such strategies by giving the brand access to related markets? The related market can be defined as a market for products that have things in common with existing products. It has the advantage of being based on the sharing of certain resources and therefore a source of cost reduction for the company. By positioning themselves in related markets, can these strategies generally stimulate the company's commercial performance, while reducing the negative societal externalities produced by its activities or by creating positive externalities? Can these markets always generate new products or services for existing and/or potential consumers in other economic sectors? In order to gain a foothold in these related markets, which can be a breeding ground for opportunities, does the company need to categorize the characteristics of the offer with societal connotations, in order to create appropriate offer profiles? What type of ecosystem must be put in place to succeed in these societal missions?

Moreover, according to these authors, clarifying that a societal innovation strategy is capable of creating shared value requires clear answers to five questions. First, how can innovation create value for potential customers? It must make the product more competitive, therefore less expensive, more efficient, easier to use and more luxurious. Second, how will the company capture some of the value generated by societal innovation? Innovations that create shared value can attract imitators faster than customers. Intellectual property is rarely sufficient to protect against competition.

For example, with the advent of organic products, a specific market has developed, which imitators have penetrated by focusing mainly on price reduction and effective mass communication. Companies had to sell their products in conventional markets, popularize the information conveyed by labels so that they could be identified more easily, etc., while the imitators were forced to sell their products on conventional markets. Third, what innovations will enable the company to create value, and what resources should each of them benefit from? In the majority of economic sectors, technological innovation is an essential source of CSV (economic and societal value). But there are other important innovations in some economic areas that are unrelated to new technologies. Indeed, since the early 1990s, many companies have had the imagination and capacity to create innovative business models that facilitate CSV by developing organizational innovations. For example, these innovations allow the reorganization of the architecture of the company's value chain activities, with some of them being regrouped (production, marketing, distribution, logistics, etc.). Fourth, can these strategies reduce negative societal externalities or produce positive social and environmental externalities, while securing the company's competitive advantage? Fifth, how can trade-offs be successfully managed? Each profession seeks out its own interests; only CSR managers can make the best choices for the company, and a clear innovation strategy helps them to better understand societal issues before making these trade-offs.

3.3. Assessing the impact of an innovation on each stakeholder in the ecosystem

According to Ihrig and Macmillan (2018), companies may find it difficult to gain acceptance and success for their innovations in ecosystems composed of many powerful and highly interconnected partners. In some sectors, such as aerospace, electronics, chemicals and construction, it can be difficult for companies to achieve acceptance and success in an ecosystem composed of many powerful and highly interconnected partners. In some sectors, such as in those listed above, simple product or service innovations can therefore be complex. For example, in the mobile phone sector, if Samsung or Huawei launches a new mobile phone, it must be attractive to users, phone operators, major application providers such as Google, etc. This complexity creates benefits companies that know how to manage it, in other words, there is a significant competitive advantage in finding and selecting effective innovation strategies that other stakeholders can buy into.

The same is true in a large company where each activity in the value chain operates in its own ecosystem, with internal and external partners that are often specialized units from very different companies. This is the case for pharmaceutical companies that have long been responsive to the needs of patients, physicians, healthcare providers, insurers, distributors and government agencies. Modifying a drug to improve its effectiveness may be approved by patients and physicians, but it can lead to increased side effects, increased medical insurance costs and increased regulatory costs. To find opportunities for growth, these companies have long focused on developing new drugs and working with partners who still have the same role, without changing the consumer cycle. Yet growth and profitability have become difficult, and many are therefore moving towards service innovations that change consumption patterns and ecosystem functioning, often requiring the buy-in of other stakeholders. A study was conducted by Ihrig and Macmillan (2018) on a large pharmaceutical company – which they dubbed PharmaCo – that wanted to transform its service offering using ideation based on a tool they created that is suitable for sectors where innovations need to be adopted by a multi-stakeholder ecosystem. These authors worked with units based in the United States, the United Kingdom, Brazil and South Korea, but only report a simplified case of a unit that wanted to offer treatment for a chronic disease.

Through a series of workshops, the six stages of the process involve some 20 people from various levels of the company, representing the main functions of its value chain.

The first stage is to identify the main stakeholders and their expectations and needs. For example, for PharmaCo, these are healthcare providers, insurers, commercial channels (pharmacies, etc.) but, above all, patients.

The second stage focuses on mapping their consumption chains in order to identify the key parts of the process that should satisfy their priority need for a product or service. For patients, this chain corresponds to disease awareness, diagnosis, treatment and adherence to treatment. Companies may need to modify their chain, thus creating disruptive innovations that will lead to new relationships in the ecosystem, such as the integration of new stakeholders and a diminished role for others.

The third stage concerns the classification of the key characteristics of the product or service for each stakeholder into three categories: non-negotiable (offer the minimum), differentiators (differentiate positively from competitors) and sources of dissatisfaction (accept unpleasant characteristics).

The fourth stage proposes growth opportunity profiles that result from the search for differentiators capable of improving the characteristics of the offer, or removing sources of dissatisfaction, for each stakeholder.

In order to limit the complications associated with their chronic disease, PharmaCo has established a growth opportunity profile for patients (Table 3.8).

Stages in the consumption chain	**Non-negotiable**	**Differentiators**	**Sources of dissatisfaction**
Awareness	Blood tests at annual check-ups	**Free blood tests in pharmacies**	Diagnostic anxiety
Evaluation, diagnosis	Early and reliable diagnosis by the doctor		Franchise
Treatment	No worsening of the disease	No side effects, simple and infrequent dosages **Discounted or free gym memberships**	**Treatment costs**
Support	Guaranteed availability in pharmacies	**SMS reminders to patients to take their medication**	

Table 3.8. *Patient growth opportunity profile: the existing offer is shown in plain text, while the proposed differentiators are shown in bold (Ihrig and Macmillan 2018)*

The fifth stage is associated with tensions that may exist between stakeholders. These tensions may arise if the most important non-negotiable characteristic of each stakeholder conflicts with the dominant differentiating characteristics of the other stakeholders (Table 3.9).

The sixth and final stage is the identification of tensions that can be overcome and potential innovations that will create the most value in the ecosystem. PharmaCo chose automatic prescription refills, which improved the non-negotiability element for three stakeholders. A communication strategy convinced insurers that this choice would reduce more expensive reimbursements for potential emergency or complication treatments.

To ensure that ecosystem innovation strategies remain sustainably competitive, companies need to be proactive in their approach.

Chronic disease	Suggested differentiators			
Non-negotiable	**Patients: discounted or free gym memberships**	**Providers: automatic prescription renewals**	**Insurers: penalties for non-performance**	**Pharmacies: option to send direct emails to patients**
Patients: at least minimal improvements to health status	**Benefits of healthy living**	**Fewer concerns about renewals**	**Enhanced accountability**	**No trips to pharmacies**
Providers: a respected and profitable activity	**Patients in better shape**	**Fewer side effects to treat**	**More comprehensive examinations**	
Insurers: no net cost increases	Additional initial expenses in sports halls	Increase in the number of applications	**Lower costs**	
Pharmaceuticals: higher margins		**Increase in sales**		**Reduction in pharmacy staff**

Table 3.9. *Impact of differentiators on non-negotiable characteristics: negative impacts are shown in plain text, while positive impacts are shown in bold (Ihrig and Macmillan 2018)*

4

Value of Impact Investment for Societal Innovations

Having identified the difficulties of implementing societal innovations based on creating shared value (CSV), the value of the impact of these innovations for the company and society is crucial. Addy *et al.* (2019) point out that "problems of scarcity and inequality are becoming increasingly pressing, but many investors want to earn economic and societal returns for 'doing good by doing good'". Impact investment can provide capital for projects that will generate social and environmental benefits as well as corporate benefits (CSV). However, opportunities cannot be properly measured from a company's past social and environmental impact data. In addition, estimating the financial returns on a potential investment and the internal rate of return are known valuation tools, but none of them relate to social and environmental benefits in monetary terms, as predicting societal gains is largely a matter of conjecture. This analytical problem has been taken into account by major economic players, including Root Capital, the MacArthur Foundation, Omidyar Network, Skopos Impact Fund, Bridges Impact+, the World Economic Forum and the Rockefeller Foundation, among others. Their collaborative work has produced interesting indicators for impact assessment and management, including social return on investment (SROI). Subsequently, the Impact Management Project (IMP), a collaboration initiated in 2016 by foundations and major investment managers, aimed to structure these indicators in a coherent language and develop several concrete tools to facilitate the implementation of best practices in impact management. The authors of this research worked with Rise Fund, a $2 billion impact investment fund dedicated to growth in companies and managed by TPG Growth and Bridgespan Group, a global social impact consulting firm. They attempted to assess societal impacts and financial performance with the same degree of rigor. Working with experts in the field, Rise Fund and Bridgespan Group were able to develop *a forward-looking methodology* to estimate the financial value of the social and environmental assets that could result from each dollar invested before incurring any costs.

Companies or institutions that are investors in societal impacts can assess the expected return on an opportunity with a new indicator called the Impact Multiple of Money (IMM). If a company wishes to use the IMM, it must already determine the products, services or projects that might justify the effort required to calculate it. Rise Fund qualitatively screens its potential investments to reject those that may not be financially promising, and identify those whose societal impact is likely to be measured positively with IMM. For example, Rise Fund requires a potential societal return on investment of at least $2.50 for every dollar invested, before allocating capital to a company.

4.1. Key steps in calculating the value of the impact investment

Addy *et al.* (2019) propose six steps for calculating an IMM in an investment selection process. The first step is to *assess the relevance and scope of a product, service or project* specific to a company's industry. For example, at the relevance level, an appliance company may wish to invest in innovation strategies that can reduce GHG emissions from its product lines, or a health center provider may wish to assess the social benefits of investing in low-income neighborhoods, to propose that lower-cost care can be provided to the community. As for scope, it concerns the number of people who may be interested in a company's product or service and therefore the assumed significance of the impact of that product or service. For example, Rise Fund calculated the reach of three products from the educational technology company EverFi, which proved significant, before making its first impact investments. The three programs are AlcoholEdu, an online course designed to prevent alcohol abuse among students at more than 400 universities; Haven, an awareness of violence and sexual harassment issues for students at about 650 universities; and a financial education program for students at over 6,100 high schools. The scale of these projects is significant, as it was estimated that nearly 6.1 million people would benefit from them over five years, starting in 2017.

The second step is to *identify the desired social and/or environmental outcomes* and confirm through existing research that they are achievable and measurable. The impact of a social and/or environmental program is about the number of people affected and the improvement achieved, but a small number of people are better than a large number, with very few positive effects. Based on statistics from social science reports in 2010, 2007 and 2016, respectively, AlcoholEdu saved 36 lives out of 2.2 million students enrolled in the program, Haven reduced sexual assaults by 37,898 cases among 2.6 million students, and the third project reached out to 1.3 million students.

The third step is to *estimate the economic value* of societal innovations based on shared value (CSV). Once the desired outcomes are identified, societal impact investors must find an "*anchor study*", to accurately translate them into economic terms. This is the case for Cellulant, a regional African provider of a mobile payment platform used by banks, along with various companies and governments. In collaboration with the Nigerian Ministry of Agriculture, it repurposed a seed and fertilizer subsidy program that lost 89% of its funds due to mismanagement and high levels of corruption. As a result, the company has set up a mobile phone application that farmers use to retrieve subsidized produce from local traders. This innovation has drastically reduced fraud and corruption and has resulted in the distribution of 90% of the planned aid. The assessment of its economic impact is based on a study of the anchoring of a season's results among all subsidized and non-subsidized maize farmers. Subsidized farmers actually earned an additional $99 as a result of improved maize yields. The authors of this research examined several key variables that could determine the choice of an anchoring study. The first variable is related to the *rigor of the study*, either to systematically evaluate the results of all previous research to infer implications for this new research, or to only present the results of a randomized controlled trial, comparing several groups with and without the selected product or service. Case or observational studies are not as significant as these two types of research. The second variable relates to the *relevance of the study*, that is, the integration of people living in the same conditions (urban, rural, etc.) and with identical income brackets, thus reflecting strong similarities between their personal situations. Moreover, it is preferable that the study be recent or frequently cited in research. The third variable concerns the *use of expert advice in the chosen field*, which may be necessary in cases where there is uncertainty or a lack of reliable research. For example, the authors used the expertise of the Center for Financial Services Innovation in Chicago, when no appropriate research had demonstrated the impact of a particular aid measure on the adoption of regular savings habits for low- and middle-income people, proposed by Acorns, a financial technology company. The results showed that even modest savings would allow these individuals to reduce their use of high-cost payday loans.

Estimates of the economic outcomes of the AlcoholEdu program were derived from an anchoring study on fatality and injury reduction, conducted according to the recommendations of the U.S. Department of Transportation, using a measure called the value of a statistical life (VSL). According to this measure, one death is "worth" $5.4 million. If AlcoholEdu could save 36 lives, it would create a social value of $194.4 million. Researchers at the National Institutes of Health (NIH) have estimated the total cost of a sexual assault at $16,657. The social value of the Haven program could therefore reach approximately $631.3 million, if the number of assaults did not increase. The evaluation of the financial literacy program is based on a study of a similar program for high school students, which showed that there was an average difference of $538 in consumer credit debt between participants and non-participants, all of whom have reached the age of 22 years. Over five years, the interest on this debt was about $81, so if 1.3 million students avoided this situation, the economic value of the program would be $105.3 million. The social impact of these three projects would therefore have an economic value of $931 million over five years.

According to Addy *et al.* (2019), the fourth step is to *consider the risks for societal investments and impacts*, if there is any doubt about using the statistical approaches of the previous steps and social science research, to monetize social and environmental benefits. These risks need to be adjusted according to the social values derived from the anchoring study, to reflect the quality and relevance of the research. This is done by calculating an impact realization index from the totality of the values of six risk categories, which correspond to a 100-point impact probability score. Two components of the index relate to the quality of the anchoring study and how it directly relates to the product or service, and represent 60 points. Anchoring studies are rated best if they are based on meta-analysis or randomized controlled research, rather than observational studies. For example, the AlcoholEdu study scored higher than the Haven study and the financial education program. However, if hypotheses are required to link an anchoring study to the desired impact of a product or service, the risk increases while the score decreases. For example, the financial education program study proves that there is a link between training and reduced student debt, so it deserves a top mark. However, studies of the AlcoholEdu and Haven programs show less clear links. AlcoholEdu postulates that its training will reduce the number of alcohol-related incidents and therefore alcohol-related mortality; Haven's study assumes that training in sexual assault prevention will lead to a *de facto* reduction in sexual assault and its consequences, so grades will be lower. The other four components of the index acknowledge the similarities between the study and the project, and are each rated out of 10. The first component relates to the environmental and social context: are the populations urban and/or rural? The second component takes into account national income: are the populations in the same bracket or not according to the World Bank's determination? The third component concerns the products or services provided: are they identical? Are the users in the same age groups? The fourth component is the future use of the product or service purchased: is it consistent with the intended use or not?

Based on these recommendations, Rise Fund has assigned a percentage probability of impact to AlcoholEdu, Haven and the financial education program of 85%, 55% and 75%, respectively. The risk-adjusted monetary impact then becomes $165,024 million for AlcoholEdu (i.e. 194.4 x 85%), $347,215 million for Haven and $78,975 million for the financial education program, for a total impact of $591,043 million out of $931 million. The Impact Achievement Index does not take into account all the risks that may exist between anchor studies and a company's actual product or service, nor all the threats to impact, but it is likely to evolve positively with new societal innovations specific to each area of activity.

The fifth step is to *estimate the final value of the societal impact.* This concept, derived from finance, gives the value of the project beyond an explicit forecast period and generally represents a large percentage of its total estimated value. Projects from companies with an incremental societal impact are not included (distribution of chlorine tablets for better water quality, etc.), but others may have a long-term impact (installation of solar panels with energy savings and reduction of GHG emissions) and deserve an estimate of their final value. For Rise Fund, this final value depends on the estimated value of the impact in the last year of investment, and a subsequent assessment that the probabilities that the return (those most affected) and the societal value can remain constant for the next five years. If the probabilities are high, companies obtain a discount rate of 5%, that is, the annual residual value decreases by 5%, while if the probabilities are low, they obtain a discount rate of 25%. To calculate the final value of the three EverFi programs from 2022 to 2026, Rise Fund took into account their estimated total impact of $159 million in 2021, assumed that the same impact would be generated in each of the following years, and then discounted it by 20% per year. The final value thus amounts to $477 million and represents the total residual value that Rise Fund adds to the $591,043 million of risk-adjusted impact, over the investment term. This brings the total impact to approximately $1.068 billion.

Finally, the sixth step is to *calculate the social return on each dollar invested,* which differs for different companies and investors. Companies can divide the estimated value of a social and/or environmental benefit by their total investment. For example, say that one company invests $25 million in the production of a line of low-cost eyeglasses for rural residents in developing countries and estimates the social benefits based on increased productivity and income for those residents at $200 million. The eyeglasses thus generate a social value of $8 for every dollar invested (200 / 25 = 8), expressed by the IMM as 8X. As for the investors, they must use the proportion of their participation in the companies in which they are involved to calculate their share of social value. If Rise Fund invests $25 million to acquire a 30% interest in a project that is expected to generate a shareholder value of $500 million, only 30% of that value, or $150 million (500 x 30%), is available, resulting in an IMM of 6X (150 / 25 = 6). So, in fact, Rise Fund invested $100 million for a 50% interest in EverFi's programs, which generated $1.068 billion, or $1,068 million in social value. It can claim $534 million (1,068 x 50%), or an IMM of 5.34X.

4.2. Impact and ethical investment opportunities

IMM has the advantage of allowing a direct comparison of investment opportunities, but it is only a directional indicator and not a precise number, since it depends on the anchor study used to determine it. The steps in its calculation must be transparent, and the help of people who understand all the assumptions can be beneficial in obtaining more reliable figures. In addition, a sensitivity analysis can be used to assess how the IMM may change if the basic assumptions are changed, thus putting the key drivers of social value into perspective. Two important remarks concern the impact investment calculation. The first point relates to the moral issues raised by the monetization of societal benefits and costs. For example, is the impact of an extra dollar of income greater for individuals in an emerging market or for those in a developed market? Should an increase in income be considered an impact independent of a family's past earnings, or only below a certain earnings threshold? When lives are saved, should they be given a monetary value? The VSL varies considerably from one country to another, but should a human life be valued differently simply because of geographic location? The second point is of interest to investors, large corporations, foundations and social organizations, which may use social science reports to estimate the potential impact of a company's product or service. During the 2017 summit of the Global Steering Group for Impact Investment, Sir Ronald Cohen, a pioneer and advocate of impact investing, said that the rapid growth of this sector "will cause a chain reaction in impact creation", accelerating the adoption of impact analysis in day-to-day business operations and processes. Businesses, investors and all those who want more private capital to be used to address pressing societal problems need to prioritize the development of better CSV-based innovation strategies, as well as better methods of assessing societal impact. The aim is to succeed in considering societal impact assurance on an equal footing with financial assurance. Rise Fund has therefore created a new entity to stimulate the comprehensive research and studies required to guide impact investment decisions. As more and more CEOs talk about profit and purpose, the IMM offers a rigorous methodology, to advance the allocation of capital to projects capable of delivering salient societal benefits.

5

Development Strategies of CSV-based Innovative Business Models

Clearly, the levers of the ecosystem (vision, societal project and partnership) play a decisive role in developing societal innovations capable of creating shared value and in facilitating their implementation. According to Johnson *et al.* (2014), business model innovations consist of four interconnected elements that together create and produce value. The first element is the *timeline*. In terms of innovation, is it better to be a first mover or a fast follower? When is an innovation likely to reach the tipping point at which demand rises sharply? When does an entrepreneur need to bring in external managers and when should he or she consider pulling out? The second element relates to *collaboration*. The development of innovations and the creation of new businesses is rarely a solitary task and usually requires fruitful collaboration. These can take many forms: between a company and its customers, between large companies and small start-ups, and even between private companies and social entrepreneurs. The third element is associated with the *nature of the innovation* that the company wishes to develop. According to these authors, managers must find a balance between technological development and market expectations and then determine the relative influence of *product innovations* (the product or service marketed, particularly in terms of functionality) and *process innovations* (the way in which this offering is developed and distributed, particularly in terms of cost and quality). Finally, the fourth element consists of the firm's ability to *make a trade-off between secret and open innovations*. Internal innovation implies that the firm uses its own internal resources (its own researchers and marketing department), whereas open innovation involves a knowledge exchange between firms.

The secret to keeping a business model running and thriving is knowing when it needs to be completely rethought. But according to companies, the integration of this type of strategy can take place at three different periods of their lives. The first concerns companies that have integrated societal missions into their business model from the outset. For example, this is the case for Patagonia, a Californian company created in 1972 by Yvon Chouinard, a climbing enthusiast who offers "eco-designed" clothing designed mainly for mountain sports, and has also decided to donate 1% of the firm's turnover to NGOs specializing in environmental protection (Nicolas 2018). For this category of companies, the societal benefit is so closely linked to the product or service offered that it is hard to believe that the brand can fully survive without this societal dimension. The societal dimension becomes a *de facto* intrinsic component of the culture of the company and its brand. The other two approaches are very widespread and are of interest to all companies that are already in business, but have different original situations. One of them corresponds to companies that wish to anticipate their business models becoming obsolete, by taking a proactive approach and developing disruptive innovations capable of offering new products, with a societal connotation that meets the new expectations of current or potential consumers. The other approach focuses on replicating existing business models and transforming them, to reduce the negative social and environmental impacts produced and to correct risks or shortcomings in the societal field. This type of strategy concerns a significant number of companies, which Bharadwaj and Rodriguez-Vilá (2018) call "emigrants of social responsibility". These companies can use three levers: the *value chain* (analyzing and evaluating the environmental and social impacts of the value chain, and the impact of the environmental and social dimensions on the competitive situation), the *choice of industrial investments* and the *life cycle of products*. In their industrial choices, companies can develop social and/or environmental innovations in products and processes, which can reduce negative societal externalities, while improving their competitive advantage.

5.1. Traditional tools of competitive analysis in CSV-based CSR practices

To better exploit these three levers, it is necessary to apply the classic tools of competitive analysis in CSR practices, based on the creation of shared value (CSV) (Strategor 2013, p. 318). Strategic choices are always made after a strategic analysis phase, in other words, an evaluation and a reflection that precedes decision-making. The sociologist Michel Crosier defines strategic analysis as "a method for bringing problems to light". This analysis makes it possible to diagnose the company's context in a complete and integrated manner, in order to better evaluate the choices available to it, determine how to deploy them and understand the rationality of behaviors. A rigorous strategic analysis approach therefore makes it possible to avoid a certain number of pitfalls that await managers when they want to make strategic decisions. To lead to concrete choices – in order to develop societal strategies based on CSV – the company must provide answers to the following four questions. Will the growing constraints associated with this type of strategy change the structure or dynamics of industries? How will societal issues impact the company's strategic positioning? How will the image and perception of the company by key stakeholders change? How should the societal and economic business models be modified? Repairing a business model is not solely about the choice of industrial investments, such as products and industrial processes, to determine the future societal footprint of the products to be sold. These investments must improve the company's competitiveness and thus its competitive advantage. Yet they must also mitigate the societal risks that its activities may cause in terms of the negative societal externalities produced.

Beyond global approaches, the company is required to address the adverse societal effects that can be caused by the life cycles of products and processes (heavy waste) and need to be reduced in a salient way. These life cycles are becoming a major strategic issue that requires a comprehensive assessment of the nature of their negative effects. This issue assumes that the company analyzes the life stages of products to identify these effects, and thus four criteria are selected. The first relates to the *estimation* and *optimization of material efficiency*, such as the reduction in raw material consumption, the choice of renewable materials, the use of recyclable materials, the elimination of harmful substances, etc. The second concerns the *assessment* and *optimization of energy efficiency*, such as the choice of energy sources with reduced GHG impact, reduction of energy consumption during production and use, and the reduced dispersion of toxic substances. The third corresponds to the *analysis* and *design of sustainable products*, such as the technical lifespan for user needs, repair and maintenance capacity, and the acceptability of technological innovations by these users. The fourth criterion is related to the *analysis of the product's reusability*, such as the recycling of sub-assemblies, components, the recovery of residues, etc. To further optimize the reduction of societal impacts, the company can promote the cradle-to-cradle approach to a circular economy, not a linear economy. The linear economy is based on the belief in infinite raw resources and product cycles that have five chronological stages: materials, production, transportation and distribution, use, and waste. The circular model aims to decouple economic growth, from the extraction and consumption of these primary resources. Product cycles are also composed of five chronological stages: materials, production, transport and distribution, use, materials recycled for new use (life). This model is therefore based on the recovery of the residual value of products at the end of their life and their reintegration into a new cycle of value creation. To make this type of economy effective, many companies develop a strategy of leasing their products to customers, instead of developing a sales strategy. These initiatives allow producers to control the circulation of products throughout their life cycle and thus ensure their automatic return at the end of the life cycle. In the automotive sector, manufacturers are faced with major changes. Some manufacturers recover used vehicles and, depending on their condition, put them back on the market after minor renovations, or dismantle them to extract components for recycling, or to offer spare parts for resale at 60% of their new price. Thus, a large majority of end-of-life vehicles are collected, 80% are recycled and sold to the second-hand (spare parts) and recycled metal markets (Strategor 2013, p. 323).

Nature of activity	Criteria for the societal impact of each activity on the company's value chain
General management	Communication practices, transparency, lobbying
Human resources management	Education and vocational training, workplace safety, social benefits, diversity and discrimination, remuneration policies, dismissals, etc.
Technological management	Relations with universities, ethical research practices: GMOs, product safety, recycling, conservation of raw materials, etc.
Procurement, products and services	Procurement and logistics practices, use materials (furs, animal testing, GMOs), use of natural resources
Inbound logistics	Impact of transport: GHG emissions, traffic congestion
Production goods and/or services	GHG emissions, ecological impact and biodiversity, energy and water use, use of hazardous materials, employee safety
Outbound logistics	Use of packaging, collection, recycling, reduction in GHG emissions (transport, energy, etc.)
Marketing and sales	Misleading advertising, children's advertising, pricing (discrimination between customers, anti-competitive practices, access prices for the most disadvantaged), consumer information, privacy
After-sales services	Treatment of used or obsolete products, treatment of consumables, engine oils or printing inks

Table 5.1. *Analysis of the societal impact of value chain activities (Strategor 2013, p. 319)*

Today, the business world is overwhelmed with ideas, and it has become easy for companies to gather a multitude of new concepts from their employees or external people, such as customers and stakeholders of soft power. The classic ideation process based on crowdsourcing provides access to an overabundance of ideas for new products, services and business models. But managers may lack the method to seize the most promising opportunities, because judgment is the key to progress, not ideation. The company must therefore develop symbiotic partnership relationships with its various stakeholders, such as those in the socio-political sphere, the market and the environment in which it operates. These relationships enable the company to use the classic tools of competition, in order to better study its societal footprint and also to better understand society's requirements, which are now an integral part of strategic analysis. This analysis can be carried out at the level of each of the company's partners, suppliers, subcontractors or subsidiaries, in each country, and has a dual advantage. The first advantage is the analysis of the environmental and social impacts of the value chain, that is, of some of the company's activities that are likely to produce negative societal externalities in a salient way (see Table 5.1).

The second advantage is the assessment of the impact of the social and environmental dimension on the competitive situation (see Table 5.2).

Evaluation criteria	Impacts of the societal dimension on the competitive situation
Factors or conditions affecting inputs	Availability of human resources, access to research institutions, transfer of scientific knowledge, existence of adequate infrastructures
Related or supporting industries	Availability of local raw materials, organizations and access to the necessary industries, effective application of environmental and socially acceptable standards
Conditions of demand	Requirement of local standards for environmental protection, demand for products/services with social and environmental value, potential for a "Bottom of the Pyramid" (BoP) approach
Context of the strategy and competition	Protection of intellectual property, transparency, corruption

Table 5.2. *Assessment of the impact of the societal dimension on competition (Strategor 2013, p. 318)*

5.2. Foundations of business models

After the strategic analysis stage, companies need to consider the nature of the innovative environmental and/or social business model that they need to develop. Creating a business model is usually a specific process that often lacks a framework for exploring new opportunities, which leads to many companies missing out on some of the low-cost ways to radically improve their productivity, which can ensure shared value. Assuming that such a business model requires a set of decisions, the secret to success is therefore to know who makes these decisions, when and why? According to Girotra and Netessine (2015), managers must formulate a strategy that determines how their company's innovation efforts will support the overall business strategy. Often, managers who specialize in executing strategies based solely on competitive advantage have proven to be ill-equipped to think innovatively about the development of innovations that create shared value (financial and societal performance). Moreover, when interesting ideas emerge, such as societal innovations, companies do not have the processes or parameters that would allow them to adopt them. Indeed, CSV-based innovations can be both product- and process-based. "Product innovation includes new products (design, nature of the raw material used as a component, etc.) and services introduced into the organization, while process innovations are defined as new elements introduced into production operations" (Dubouloz 2013), of products, raw materials or product components. Product innovation, which has an internal focus, aims to improve the efficiency of organizational processes (Utterback 1994). It must therefore meet the expectations of market stakeholders (suppliers, customers, investors, etc.) and the socio-political sphere (soft and hard powers), whereas process innovations are focused on the "how", that is, how the work is carried out within the organization (Dubouloz 2013).

The repair strategies of the existing business model can be illustrated by taking into account, the example of the company Brita, which is based on secondary information. Brita was founded in 1966 by Heinz Hankammer, who had the idea of optimizing tap water in an intelligent and practical way. The first products were manufactured by hand in the garden of its founder, and a few years later the company became an innovative leader in the optimization of drinking water[1], by selling tap water filters. In 2005, noting the weakness of the company's "single-product" position, which had been exposed to sluggish growth, the managing director realized that a related market, bottled water, needed to be tackled. He then decided to "repair" the company's value chain by developing other products. "The positioning of filtered water as an environmentally friendly alternative has allowed the company to take over a societal need, which is the reduction of waste, and enter a new market" (Bharadwaj and Rodriguez-Vilá 2018). Several scalable, profitable, growable and inclusive societal innovations have been developed in product offerings, such as water bottles, jugs and water filtering technology, to improve the taste, quality and purity of filtered water, as well as to represent a long-term economic advantage over bottled water. These CSV-based innovations have enabled the company to intelligently strengthen its business by creating related markets that generate growth and profit, while improving its social and environmental

1 Progress report entitled Développement de l'entreprise (2016), available at: https://www.brita.fr/our-vision.

performance and expanding its market. As a result, the brand has shifted its strategy from a focus on water filtration to a focus on water itself (related market), emphasizing the benefits in terms of the social externalities of the product for the customer (health and well-being) and the environmental benefits for society (waste reduction). This strategy has been able to solidly reinforce its competitive advantage in the bottled water market and to create barriers for entry of companies in this sector. Three years later, this positioning enabled the group to increase its revenue by 47%.

PART 2

Analysis of the Different Environmental Innovation Strategies Developed by One Company and their Impact in Terms of CSV

Introduction to Part 2

Since the beginning of the 1990s and the end of strong growth, States, driven by public opinion, have created many laws and agreements in an attempt to deal with the environmental problems caused by industrialization and urbanization. Prior to this period, nature was only of concern to a few idealistic philosophers, such as Jean-Jacques Rousseau in the 18th Century, or the geographer Élisée Reclus in the 19th Century. May '68 was undoubtedly an important date, although it did not lead to a real political decision in environmental terms. Today, the environment is undergoing phenomena (hurricanes, floods, droughts, the melting of Arctic glaciers, rising sea levels, etc.) that threaten populations and businesses in all countries. Climate change and increased pressure on natural resources are increasingly leading to negative environmental externalities. Winston (2017) has identified a set of such externalities. For example, in 2011, Thailand experienced devastating floods that disrupted the supply chains of many companies, including Toyota, which could not be supplied with car parts and lost \$1.5 billion in revenue. The same was true in 2012 in New York City, where Hurricane Sandy produced waves over four meters high and damaged an electrical transformer at Con Edison, plunging Manhattan into darkness for four days, costing the company over \$500 million and other New York companies over \$6 billion. One year later, Typhoon Haiyan – considered the most powerful typhoon in history – ravaged the Philippines, killing more than 6,000 people and causing an estimated \$14 billion in damage. On September 6, 2017, Hurricane Irma devastated the West Indies with winds of up to 360 km/h, and is classified as one of the strongest tropical cyclones ever recorded. Climate change-related disruptions are therefore likely to cripple the core activities of companies in the value chain which directly contribute to the creation of value for them: supply, production, distribution and consumption (Lowitt 2015). In the case of supply, these disruptions may make the availability of raw materials increasingly unpredictable, leading to risks of supply disruptions (e.g. Toyota), price volatility and lost sales. In production, the waste of energy and raw materials can lead to higher product costs. In distribution, extreme weather events can paralyze transport infrastructure (roads and bridges, ports and maritime routes, regional energy networks) and seriously disrupt both distribution networks and retail chains. Lastly, in consumption, the risks may be linked to product inventory shortages, as well as very high financial risks for companies, among other things. Additionally, in recent years, pressures on land and soil have increased considerably. According to the EU Joint Research Centre[1], between 1999 and 2013, almost 20% of the land area under plant cover experienced a decline in soil productivity, that is, its capacity to create biomass for food, agricultural or energy use. Admittedly, this decline varied from one continent to another, with a decline of 37% in Oceania and 27% in South America but only 14% in Europe. This situation was partly due to land degradation, that is, the depletion of soils that is becoming more widespread year on year. When Tibor Navracsics, head of the JRC, released the third edition of the *World Atlas of Desertification*, on June 21, 2018, he said that, every year, an area equivalent to half of the European Union is damaged – over 2 million km^2 – mostly in Africa and Asia. He pointed out that, according to general consensus, more than 50% of the Earth's surface is currently affected by this mechanism, associated with climate variations and human activities and that the phenomenon was growing. The report also points out that it is difficult to quantify this phenomenon because land degradation is not a static concept but an evolutionary process whereby soils exhaust their biological potential and their capacity to support or feed people. Since soil quality is therefore a variable concept depending on its users, the JRC experts proposed an interpretive framework composed of a few parameters, such as biophysical criteria (aridity, water stress, erosion or loss of vegetation) and socio-economic criteria (population density, urbanization, farming practices, livestock farming, standard of living, etc.). In the Pacific Ocean – the largest in the world – particles from a large patch of plastic waste are contaminating marine species which confuse them with plankton. This phenomenon subsequently reaches all levels of the food chain[2]. The "vortex of waste" spreads insidious contaminants composed of more than 90% plastic "ingredients" of 1–5 mm in size, which corresponds to a minimum of 1,800 billion pieces of plastic smaller than grains of rice which cohabit with marine organisms. The "continent of plastics" is really a "soup" of waste. To show the seriousness of the degradation of our planet, a study published on May 4, 2018, carried out by the WWF[3], states that, from May 5, 2018,

1 The Joint Research Centre, also known as the JRC, is the internal scientific service of the European Commission. It carries out research and provides independent, evidence-based scientific research and advice to support EU policy making. This research study was also inspired by an article in *Le Monde,* dated Wednesday July 4, 2018, which published extracts from the presentation of the climate report by the head of the JRC on June 21, 2018.

2 Contaminations, "Le Pacifique, un océan de plastiques", article published by *Le Monde*, September Sunday 9–Monday 10, 2018.

3 Le Hiv Pierre, La France creuse sa "dette écologique", article published by *Le Monde*, May 5, 2018.

France will be living on credit, in a sense – that is, if the country's standard of living and consumption was applied to the whole planet, all the resources that nature can renew in one year would have already been exhausted.

An original and very worrying study, published in *Nature Climate Change*, on Monday November 19, 2018, tackles the problems of cumulative risks due to climate change for the first time. Today, humanity is experiencing the wrath of climate change, but this will increase, given that, by 2100, half of the world's population could be threatened by six major climatic hazards (droughts, heat waves, deaths, famines, shortages, migrations) of maximum intensity all at once if GHG emissions are not reduced in a significant way. The majority of scientists agree that, as the planet warms, the frequency and severity of the various destructive phenomena increase. Today, negative environmental externalities have become a reality, leading companies to become aware of the dangers that climate change can pose to their performance (Porter and Reinhardt 2007). Business risks are of a different nature and because the impact of this change is global, the problems may persist and the damage may become irreversible (Lash and Wellington 2007), for them and for society in general. These threats, which exist in all countries, require companies to fundamentally redefine their environmental strategies and business philosophies in order to create new value based on shared value and to prosper by significantly reducing negative environmental externalities (Winston 2017). Indeed, weather events and the unbridled exploitation of resources can threaten business performance and global prosperity for a very long time. Therefore, every business, whatever its activity and size, must understand the need to factor the reduction of negative environmental externalities produced by its value chain activities and/or the production of positive environmental externalities into its day-to-day management. To this end, companies must adopt a proactive environmental strategy aimed at long-term performance based on both cost reductions and a quest for legitimacy (Berger-Douce 2011), and, beyond that, a strategy aimed at overall performance (Martinet and Payaud 2007), factoring in environmental aspects and the economic opportunities that these can bring. In this instance, they can no longer think of treating climate change solely as a question of corporate environmental responsibility but as a corporate issue because the negative effects of their activities on the climate are now so tangible that the issue of these effects must be better addressed with strategic tools, not with a philanthropic approach (Porter and Reinhardt 2007).

The Decathlon Group has an international reputation and dimension and is considered a major economic and social player in the sporting goods industry. It was established in 1976 in Englos, near Lille, and its low-cost business model is based on the production and sale of a wide range of self-service and low-cost sports products. In 1986, "Decathlon Production" designed and produced its first bike with Decathlon teams and the first international store was opened in Germany. In 1996, it created the first Passion brands (Tribord for water sports and Quechua for mountain sports), and by 2015, it had around 20 of these brands (Domyos, B'twin, Kipsa, Nabaiji, etc.) relating to various sports and leisure activities[4], along with 50 Decathlon product brands. It has also developed nine service activities, including Alsolia (financing solutions), Decathlon Assurances (sports insurance), Atelier (maintenance, repair and customization) and Skimium (ski rental), among others. It continues to expand internationally, having opened its first store in Shanghai (2003) and another in Moscow (2006) to strengthen its presence in Eastern Europe. In 2015, it had 1,031 stores, 300 of which are in France (30%), with 70,000 employees and a presence in 29 foreign countries (Decathlon 2015, p. 3). In 2016, it had 1,176 stores and 45 warehouses and logistics platforms, selling 1,053,937,000 products and enjoying an 87% user satisfaction rate worldwide. Between 2009 and 2016, revenue in billions of euros was on an upward trajectory (see Table I2.1).

Years	**2009**	**2010**	**2011**	**2012**	**2013**	**2014**	**2015**	**2016**
Revenue	5.4	6	6.5	7	7.4	8.2	9.1	9.97

Table I2.1. *Changes in the Decathlon Group's revenue between 2009 and 2016*

Given its international reputation, if the group does not integrate environmental practices into its global strategy in order to either produce positive environmental externalities or significantly reduce the negative externalities that its activities may cause, or if it tries to ignore them, it may expose itself to a major risk in terms of image. This risk may adversely affect its turnover and, therefore, its profit, among other things, because the group may be a prime target for players in the socio-political sphere embodied by both soft power (NGOs, media, activists, etc.) and hard power (regulatory authorities) as well as those in the market. The Decathlon Group has therefore put societal strategies into practice in a two-stage process. The first began in the early 1990s and focuses on ethical values. The second is based on the integration of societal – and more specifically environmental – innovations based on the creation of shared value (CSV), which began in 1992 with the first eco-design packaging products. To better understand the contribution of these two societal strategies, two case studies have been conducted by the author of this book.

The case study is a specific technique of gathering, editing and processing information that seeks to account for the evolutionary and complex nature of phenomena concerning a social system with its own dynamics (Collerette 1996). It therefore seeks to reveal the trajectory followed by the phenomena studied in order to identify their peculiarities (Collerette 1997). In concrete terms, the case study

4 http://corporate.decathlon.com/nos-marques/nos-marques-passion/.

consists of reporting a real situation (identifying the different activities of the Decathlon Group, the sources of strong negative environmental externalities and the different approaches used to reduce these externalities), examining it in context (identifying the nature of the CSR to be developed, using the concepts of ethical values and CSV-based environmental innovations capable of promoting a positive environmental impact specific to the activities of the sporting goods industry), and subsequently discovering and analyzing how the studied phenomena that the researcher is interested in manifest themselves and evolve (understanding how these two forms of CSR emerge has an impact on the reduction of the externalities and on the competitive advantage of the group) (Collerette 1997). These two approaches to CSR are part of a vision to create the meaning (sensemaking) and impart the meaning (sense giving) of these innovations, according to Weick *et al.* (2005). The construction of meaning can be defined as "the activity of an individual who grasps external reality through cognitive elements, their own goals and the emotions and sensations they feel" (Garreau 2009). This section therefore analyzes a case study on ethical value-based strategies, followed by a case study on CSV-based innovation strategies and the impact that they can have on the Decathlon Group.

6

Analysis of Societal Strategies Based on Ethical Values and their Limitations with Respect to CSV

6.1. Issues concerning ethical values

Firstly, Decathlon has developed social practices drawing on the concept of ethical values and, therefore, corporate ethics. The formalization of values is at the heart of the company's discourse. This formalization is a key vector of the company's communication in responding to the pressures exerted by external regulations (Mercier 2000). These regulations come from the financial, product, resource and social markets, which exercise social control over what the company produces and how it does it (Brechet and Desreumaux 2001). For the company, communicating its values is part of a strategy to enhance its image, although this enhancement is difficult to quantify. The effect, in terms of the differentiation that this enhanced image can generate, is not intrinsic, as it assumes that customers are willing to adopt or appropriate these values in their practices and discourse by integrating them into their purchasing acts. This appropriation is not free of constraints. It is therefore useful to shed some theoretical and practical light on the *factors involved in the difficulties of appropriating corporate values*, which effectively limit their capacity to be a probable attribute of differentiation and create shared value (CSV). This research is structured in two parts. The first part is dedicated to theoretical developments with, respectively, the values of the company as an instrument for enhancing its image and as a potential attribute of differentiation to the process of constructing the strategic practice of company's values and the factors making the appropriation of these values by customers uncertain. The second part analyzes the results of a case study[1] in the form of a survey on the strategic practice of the values developed by Decathlon and their appropriation by customers as an attribute of differentiation. It therefore covers the difficulties of the concept of ethical values as a potential level for CSV.

6.1.1. *Values as an instrument for enhancing the company's image*

Very often, the values of a company are implicitly associated with its behavior towards its social and natural environment, and its stakeholders are therefore ethical values for the company. According to Wellhoff (2009), this is just one of the aspects of these values and it is in the field of marketing that we will find the necessary explanations for the other meaning of the word "value" in the company; the values associated with a brand, which will therefore be called "performance values". They are intrinsically linked to the brand identity of the products and the company's personnel in relation to its customers. Kotler *et al.* (2006) consider that brand identity is based, among other things, on the person-centered approach (relations between the brand and its customers) which gives the brand a set of values known as "identity values" to determine its fundamental characteristics. Performance values are associated with ambition, entrepreneurship, competitiveness, innovation and value creation, along with quality, customer satisfaction, know-how and service, etc. (Mercier 2001b; Wellhoff 2009). They are also associated with the four fundamental conditions that structure the successful integration and development of a product on a market. The product must, therefore, specify the company that carries it, create value, know how to enter a market by generating its own ecosystem and share the value it helps to create. Ethical values concern the behavior of the members of the organization and may appear to be essential for creating a culture of trust between managers and stakeholders interested in the company (Mercier 2001b). Etymologically, "ethics" comes from the Greek word *ethos*, which means morals and ways of acting (Debos 2005). Ethics enables a certain number of rules to be drawn up to guide the conduct of individuals in order to distinguish between right and wrong ways of acting (Mercier 1999). Ethical values are the central component of a company's institutional identity (Claude 2003). They are based on a combination of the company's environmental (environmental values) and social (social values) commitments. Social values may, for example, correspond to safeguarding local employment, the fight against all forms of discrimination (ethnic origin, gender, age, disability), working conditions, decent wages, etc. (Claude 2003). Environmental values may, for example, correspond to the avoidance of the use of toxic products in

1 Gasmi, N. (2014). Limites de l'appropriation des valeurs de l'entreprise comme attribut de la différenciation. *Management & Avenir*, *72*, 51–70.

production processes, the recycling of wastewater, the use of renewable energies, the reduction of CO_2, etc. Ethical values result from the company's position in relation to these obligations, that is, the extent to which it intends to exceed the minimum obligations that bind it to its stakeholders and society in general (Johnson *et al.* 2002).

6.1.2. *The company's values as an attribute of differentiation*

According to Lancaster's theory, products placed on the market can be considered as baskets of attributes that provide utility to consumers. Corporate image is one of the major attributes of product differentiation. Differentiation is defined as the act of conferring uniqueness on a good, a characteristic to which customers attach value (Porter 1986). Image is the set of rational and emotional representations associated by a person or group of people with a company, a brand or a product (Decaudin 2003). Image plays a key role in product differentiation because it becomes an ultimate reference point for the consumer (Hebert 1987). Every company seeks to build a strong, positive and distinctive image that is present in spirit (Kotler *et al.* 2006). Corporate values are one of the vectors in the process of this construction (Westphalen 2000). Performance values influencing brand image are the foundation of the company's image. According to Aaker (1994), brand image creates value for the brand and is therefore a major attribute of differentiation for at least four reasons: it helps the consumer process information about the product, it synthesizes a set of characteristics and helps the consumer remember certain points, particularly at the time of purchase, it differentiates the product, positions it, provides reasons to buy it – making the act of buying necessary – and it tends to foster a positive feeling towards the brand through the characteristics associated with its communication. If the company has internalized the "value chain" of its commercial apparatus (it distributes its own products, like the Decathlon Group, for example), the nature of the relationship between the company's staff[2] and its customers is not always clear and has a strong influence on the company's performance image. The performance values symbolize the image of the company that originally proposed an offer to create value for the company and for the customer. An offer creates value for the customer when the benefits they perceive (contribution of the product in terms of improved user-friendliness, simplicity of use, possibility of observing its results, etc.) are greater than the sacrifices perceived (price level, durability, transfer costs linked to the adoption of the product).

---

2 The performance values associated with staff in customer relations are related to: advice, perfect knowledge of the products, courtesy, credibility, reliability, helpfulness, communication (listening), taking care of customers' problems, efficient after-sales service, etc.

The contributions of ethical values in terms of image are two-fold. The first corresponds to the case where these values (symbolized by a social and environmental commitment by the company) will have only positive external effects and no tangible individual benefit for the consumer: the ethical commitment does not bring any tangible improvement to the attributes of the product. This is the case, for example, when the company uses less polluting renewable energy, recycles wastewater, consumes only a small amount of water, improves working conditions, etc. Ethical values only have an impact on the company's institutional image: it is the company's civic image that is valued. The second type involves cases where the ethical values (symbolized by a particularly environmental commitment on the part of the company) bring a tangible individual benefit to the consumer and also generate positive external effects. This is the case, for example, with food companies that sell products produced by organic farming. This commitment is an attribute of products that contribute to improving consumer welfare and also generate a positive external effect for the environment. These are values that improve the quality of the product (enhancement of the company's product image) and its image as a good corporate citizen (positive external effects: respect for the environment). The company's values are at the confluence of two polarities of differentiation: performance values represent the polarity of deepening rational motivations (the fundamental lever of the act of purchasing), whereas ethical values represent the polarity of virtue which provides an expression of the company's social responsibility (the lever for improving the company's institutional image).

6.1.3. *Strategy development through the practice of corporate values*

Since the 1960s, strategy has emerged as a field of research, focused primarily on the study of strategic choices that contribute to competitive advantage (Chanal 2008, pp. 42–50). The fundamental limitation of this classic approach to strategy is that it does not explain how to achieve the results of these choices. It pays little attention to the process approach to strategy (Pettigrew 1992). Thus, since the early 2000s, a strong interest in the research community has developed from the perspective of strategy practice (Strategy-as-Practice). The term "practice" refers to shared routines of behavior that include relationships, norms and procedures for thinking and acting (Chanal and Tannery 2007). In the process of constructing strategy in practice, communication is seen as essential for exposing strategic decisions (Hendry 2000). Communicating these decisions is the first step in putting them into action and creates a certain irreversibility (Chanal and Tannery 2005). Formal strategy communication exercises form a strategic practice (Chanal and Tannery 2007). Two complementary modes of communication symbolizing this practice can be identified. The first corresponds to the constitution of strategy workshops (Chanal 2008, pp. 42–50). This practice takes place during episodes such as board meetings, management seminars, project presentations, consultant interventions or simple discussions (Wittington 2006). Discourse practices are a component of broader practices in organizations that need to be taken seriously (Hendry 2000). Discourse establishes order and builds a vision, imposing "a story" (de Laville and Mounoud 2004). The second is a mode of communication of a visual nature, based on the reporting technique. It is based on the implementation of a set of signs that must comply with certain standards required by the legislator (labels, for example, AB[3]) or considered as such as a symbol of quality (logo of a brand, for example, Audi[4]). These signs concentrate information that enables the players (customers) to make inferences about the company's strategy.

In strategic practice, the notion of ownership is crucial because it enables the impact of this practice to be assessed. Owning the strategy is making it one's own (Abdallah 2007). For de Laville and Mounoud (2004), ownership corresponds to the acceptance and interpretation of a concept or idea. Using the term "appropriation" allows us to insist on the central character of the internalization of the strategic discourse (Abdallah 2007) and of the information conveyed by the reports intended for the internal (employees) and external (customers, etc.) players of the organizations. From the perspective of practice as a direct contribution to the construction of a competitive advantage (Johnson *et al.* 2003), the notion of approach is therefore a central variable. The appropriation of the strategy by the internal and external members of the organization is proof of its integration in their practices and discourse. The effectiveness of a strategy presupposes consistency between three chronological stages, that is, between the formalization of the strategy (generic strategy), the communication of the strategy through the discourse and signals developed by the company (strategy in practice) and the appropriation of the strategy communicated by the players (employees, customers, etc.) in their practices and discourse.

6.1.3.1. *Process of building the generic strategy of the company's values*

The process of building the strategy in practice is always preceded by the formalization of a generic strategy. This formalization corresponds to writing an official text (de Laville and Mounoud 2004). When it comes to the company's values, it is based on the official choice[5] of evocative words or phrases (appearing in

3 *Agriculture biologique* (AB) is a symbol that conveys information about a French company's commitment to the environment.

4 Audi is a symbol that represents a brand with quality products.

5 The choice of values is almost exclusively made by the company's senior management. At best, the operational managers are involved. Staff with no "executive" function are rarely involved in this process, if at all.

the imperative or verbs in the infinitive) summarizing the company's fundamental values. Regnault (2006) points out that when a company defines values, it actually determines what is right or wrong, or what should or should not be done. These values are generally limited to no more than five[6] (Mercier 2001b), to make them easier to remember. The "choice of values" stage (ethics and performance) is a determining factor since values are the vehicle of the company's identity. Companies voluntarily favor the display of ethical values. This preference is explained by the company's desire to prove that it is an institution that implements actions to "correct" market "failures", particularly negative external effects (Daudigeos and Valiorgue 2010), and to improve the social environment within the company. Companies have understood that the behavior of stakeholders, especially customers, is certainly determined by instrumental rationality (criteria based on quality, price, product sustainability, etc.), but that it is also determined by the social environment within the company. However, they are also increasingly sensitive to the way in which the company behaves towards its natural and social environment (criteria based on virtue: ethical values). The privileged display of ethical values is therefore part of a strategy of legitimization anchored in the company's institutional communication (Dimaggio and Powell 1983; Suchman 1995), the use of evocative discourse (Philips *et al.* 2004), and the congruence of the company's values with those deemed appropriate by society (Philippe 2006).

6.1.3.2. *Strategy development process through the practice of the company's values*

In practice, the strategy essentially corresponds to the choice of media used to communicate the formalized values to the company's stakeholders (customers and employees). This communication is based on two complementary formats. The first consists of displaying these values in traditional communication media developed by the company: website, brochures, annual reports, books[7], etc. In order to better explain and disseminate these values, companies opt for coordination instruments such as codes of conduct or a charter of values (Mercier 2001b). The second method should enable the company to translate the (ethical and performance) values chosen into a set of visible signs on the products, in their points of sale and on their website so that customers, when they make a purchase, can make the link with these values or remember them. This technique is decisive, because the customer has no direct link

6 http://www.valeurscorporate.fr/engager-une-demarche-valeurs/formaliser-ses-valeurs/.

7 According to the daily newspaper *Les Echos*, of Friday April 30, 2010, the "book" mode offers two advantages to the company: an opportunity to develop detailed information on the meaning of its values and information that is not associated with advertising, along with information that is perceived as credible by customers.

(contact) with the company (production and sales functions are increasingly outsourced), making the company able to find out how the chosen values are "practiced". In the case of performance values, reporting is mainly embodied by the brand of the company's products. The brand has always played a central role as a source of information for consumers, since the emergence of the modern brand. Since the 1880–1950 era of the beginning of mass consumption, the brand has become the essential signal for structuring and organizing the market, and for the strategic role of the brand in the process of product differentiation (Lipovetsky 2006). The practices of societal (ethical) communication cover a wide range of realities and depend on the targeted stakeholders: company employees, customers, journalists, suppliers, shareholders, NGOs, etc. (Benoit-Moreau *et al.* 2010). Companies often resort to staging the argument of ethical values through media and non-media advertising and, above all, through descriptions mainly represented by labels. A label is a distinctive sign affixed to a product that attests to its conformity with a norm or standard and, in principle, makes it possible to resolve the problem of asymmetry of information between the seller and the final consumer (Caswell 1998). Labeling indirectly develops the principle of raising consumer awareness of the company's ethical behavior (Ballet and Bhukuth 2005), from eco-labels (Organic Agriculture, etc.) to social labels (Trend Setters, Kaleen, Investors in People, etc.). In recent years, ethical brands (The Body Shop, Max Havelaar, etc.) have emerged to make the company's ethical values more visible. These values are also symbolized by the sponsorship activities that the company develops under the "corporate foundation" mode. Unlike corporate social responsibility, which is accompanied by accountability (improving the company's performance), the foundation mode is a free donation without a *quid pro quo* (de La Broise 2006).

6.1.4. *Factors limiting the appropriation of the company's values by customers in their practices*

In the likely process of using values as an attribute of differentiation, the steps by which values are selected and communicated (value strategy in practice) are controlled by the company. However, the stage at which these values are appropriated – a preliminary stage for the effectiveness of this instrumentalization – depends solely on the willingness and ability of the customers to make inferences about these communicated values. The term "inference" refers to the capacity of an information source to convey information on attributes that are not directly related to it (Larceneux 2002). To make these inferences, customers draw on information sources from the media used by the company to communicate its values (company website, labels, brand, formal or informal written/oral discourse, etc.), from those they access when they purchase and repeatedly consume the company's products, and from direct contact with staff. Certain factors may call into question the appropriation of formalized values, as they may lead customers to only pay little attention to information on these values. The theory of the information processing process is therefore called upon to shed light on these factors. Attention, which appears to be a regulator of an individual's cognitive activity (Ladwein 2003), is a subject's ability to sort out what in their environment and within themselves is relevant and what is not (Mialet 1999). The prediction of individuals' behavioral choices is based on the socio-cognitive model, which is based on the interaction between personal, environmental and behavioral factors (Bandura 1986). Personal and environmental factors are the main mechanisms regulating individual behavior (François and Botteman 2002). Environmental factors are considered to be related to the social context (purchasing context, employee behavior, advertising, etc.) in which customers are led to make inferences about values and their personal factors are considered to be related to their cognitions, that is, their thoughts and beliefs used to accomplish one or more tasks (making inferences about values and appropriating them in their practices and discourse). Three types of factors are identified which may limit customers' attention to the process of processing information on values formalized and communicated by the company.

The first is associated with cognitive bias. The term bias refers to the distortions between the way individuals (in this case, customers) should reason to best ensure the validity of their conclusions and the way they will actually reason (Gardair 2007). Cognitive biases have impoverishing, blinkering and rigidifying effects on strategic thinking (Laroche and Nioche 2006). Clients may be exposed to value reasoning biases, which are explained by the use of reasoning based on the salience and availability of value information. Appropriating information, which is of a technical nature (reports, speeches, etc.), implies a whole process of assimilating this information on the meaning to be attributed to the term "values" and its possible link with the company. For example, some customers may have biased reasoning regarding this link, due to the risk that they associate the term "values" with morality. Morality and ethics share normative discourses that aim to regulate our conduct or actions (Comte-Sponville 1994). The objective of the company (especially a private one) is often associated with maximizing shareholder value. This reasoning of value maximization finds its explanation in certain economic studies[8] that limit the role of the enterprise solely to the maximization of that value (profit). The attribution of the term "values" to the company may therefore appear incongruous: values and the company do not go well together. This incongruence can also be explained in some studies on social thinking. Wolter (in Rouquette (2010)) points out that any object of representation lends itself to emotional assessments: it can be considered good or bad, desirable or reprehensible, attractive

8 Friedman, in an article he wrote in 1970 in the *New York Times Magazine*, summarized this approach with the explicit title: "Corporate social responsibility is to increase profits".

or repulsive. In this form of social thinking, the affective component is maximized (a categorical rejection of assigning values to firms), as opposed to the cognitive component, which is minimized (customers do not ask whether the firm has values): this is the nexus effect. This effect reflects an *a priori* refusal to associate the word "value" with the company. Cognitive bias can also come from the cognitive limit of customers regarding the term "company values". This limit supposes that this term does not say much, if anything, to them in their daily life and that it is "not socio-cognitively salient"[9], that is, it does not generate curiosity and discussion for them. This cognitive and affective deficit may result from the lack of opportunity for customers to be exposed to the information communicated by the media on this term, or from their inability to make inferences about the values conveyed by the media.

The second factor is related to motivational biases to which customers may also be exposed in processing information in relation to values. These biases refer to self-defense and self-favoring (the individual seeks to avoid failure) (Gardair 2007). These motivational biases may be explained by the fact that some customers lack the innate mental activity that is specific to the meaning of the message conveyed by value discourse and reporting. They need to create mental activity themselves that responds to the understanding of this message. Clients may not feel compelled to engage in this activity unless they perceive that it can generate tangible private benefit. Instead, their attention will be focused on the information that brings them that benefit. Motivation to process the information conveyed by the various reports may also seem weak: customers may form their attitudes from elements beyond value information, that is, they take this route in a context of low involvement and/or low ability to process this type of information (Petty and Cacioppo 1983). Motivational biases can also be explained by a concern for cognitive economy and by a refusal to enter into information processing that requires time and effort.

Finally, the third factor is related to the gap that customers may perceive between the formalized, communicated values and the values practiced by the company (the company's day-to-day practices and discourse). The values practiced have a deeper and more lasting character insofar as they result from a history, which is what the company relies on most heavily over time (Regnault 2006). In the process of making inferences about values, customers can use the information provided, but the information that they generate as a result of analyzing a situation they have experienced with the company (information from the values practiced) is a key component of this process. The sources of information that influence inference-making therefore come from perceptions, representations or evaluations during

9 This expression is used by Flament and Rouquette (2003), cited by Wolter in Rouquette (2010, p. 61).

repeated experiences of consuming the products, being in contact with the products and the employees at the point of sale or online, etc. (inductive reasoning), and/or by making inferences about the performance of a product based on an attribute (price, quality, etc.) from other known products (deductive reasoning) (Ladwein 2003). As company employees or subcontractors are rarely or never involved in the development of company values, they risk "producing" values in their practices and discourse that do not correspond to those that the company has formalized and communicated. As a result, customers may "appropriate" values that do not correspond to those that the company has desired and formalized.

6.2. Comparative analysis of the values communicated by Decathlon and the values appropriated by customers

> The Decathlon Group has an international reputation and dimension. As a major economic and social player in the sporting goods industry sector, it must be seen to reduce the negative externalities, especially environmental, that its activities can bring about, or produce positive environmental externalities. The group should not be a prime target for actors in the socio-political sphere embodied by soft power and hard power and those in the market. It has structured its societal practices in two stages. The first has drawn on the concept of ethical values since the early 1990s. In order to enhance its image, the group has opted for three ethical values: responsibility, generosity and sincerity, and a value associated with performance, or vitality. A survey was carried out among Decathlon customers to measure the spontaneous awareness of these values, that is, the proportion of customers who are aware of the values communicated and make them their own in their purchasing decisions. The results show that only 40% of customers cite at least one value, and the 30 different values named are broken down into 73% performance values, 10% ethical values and 17% words unrelated to the concept of value. In fact, no value formalized by Decathlon was cited, so if the group wishes to make its values a societal attribute that differentiates its products, customers will not be concerned, as they favor tangible attributes (improvements to the intrinsic qualities of products) and are therefore not part of an eco-responsibility process.

Box 6.1. *Ethical values and the limits of their appropriation as an attribute of differentiation by customers*

Based on the results of a case study, conducted in the form of a survey, a comparative analysis was carried out on the values communicated by the Decathlon Group[10] and the values appropriated by the 322 customers interviewed in one of its

10 Decathlon Production was created in 1986. In 2007, Decathlon had 405 stores in a dozen countries and just under 250 stores in France. Since 2008, Oxylane Group has been the group's new face.

stores (in Quetigny-Dijon). This case study is a technique for formatting and processing information that seeks to shed light on the consideration of ethical values as components of societal practices (Collerette 1996), capable of inducing societal performance and competitive advantage for the company (Collerette 1997). The aim is to identify whether or not there are gaps between the values communicated and practiced by this group and those appropriated (perceived) by its customers. The appropriation of the values formalized by these customers presupposes that they know these values (visibility of the values), accept them (adhere to them) and integrate them as an attribute of differentiation in their purchasing act. The results linked to this appropriation only concern the awareness stage and will enable us to analyze the awareness index of the values formalized in words and communicated by Decathlon to the customers surveyed, and then the probable differences between the values communicated and memorized by these customers. Of the 322 people surveyed, 71.9% practiced a sporting activity very often or quite often, 50.15% were women and 49.85% men, and 78.25% lived in the city of Dijon and its surrounding area. 3.7% had been customers for less than a year, 24.2% for 1–5 years, 29.5% for 6–10 years and 42.6% for more than 10 years (72.1% had been customers for more than five years). As most of these 322 customers were former customers, if Decathlon's values attracted their attention, they were effectively likely to appropriate them (memorize and quote them).

6.2.1. *Ethical values as a substitute for CSR*

The Decathlon Group's commitment to environmental and social missions is based on two types of strategies. The first is limited by the group's managers' choice of four words that are supposed to embody its identity: responsibility, generosity, sincerity and vitality. The ethical values are emphasized (responsibility, generosity, sincerity), while performance values are solely represented by the word "vitality". The preference for ethical values can be explained by a strategy aimed at giving the company legitimacy and enabling it to fit in with society. For the sake of publicity, these values are posted on the group's website[11]. The second strategy relates to the ethical commitment under the term "responsibility" with the words "Our civic commitments" and "Sustainable Development", with the Oxylane Foundation[12] and the Art Foundation having been created in 2005 and a social charter implemented since 2002. The four goals of the Decathlon Foundation are to contribute to the integration of women, men and children through the practice of sport, to support people in vulnerable situations, to encourage the involvement of employees who

11 http://www.oxylane.com.

12 http://www.oxylane.com/index.php?p=4 and http://www.fondations.org/spip.php?article433.

want to commit to solidarity actions, using sport as a vector of integration and to provide assistance in the construction of community projects, the renovation and construction of sports areas, providing sports training and equipment, etc. This strategy is also communicated in the form of signage to make the four values visible in places where customers are present (especially where products are sold). The performance values are those conveyed by the group's various brands. To this end, in 2012, the group had 21 "Passion" brands that refer to the world of sports (Kipsa for football, Inesis for tennis and golf, B'twin for bicycles, etc.) and 12 component brands that refer to technological risks (Novardy for waterproofing textiles, Geonaute for lamps, heart rate monitors, watches, GPS, etc.)[13]. Performance values are also embodied by the store's staff in relation to customers: product knowledge, availability, friendliness, credibility, etc. Labels are used to signal the ethical values of the Decathlon Group: hunting and hiking pants (label: 100% organic cotton), short- and long-sleeved tee-shirts for running (label: 100% organic cotton), football shoes (label: 0% PVC – reduced CO_2 emissions), fleeces (35% industrial waste and 65% plastic bottles), Wed'ze junior ski underwear (label: 100% organic cotton)[14], etc.

The main limitations of the use of the concept of "ethical values" boil down to two factors. The first relates to the risk of perceiving it as a CSR strategy that relegates societal issues to the philanthropy and corporate citizenship departments of the company. This positioning is thus part of a vision where societal issues are not dealt with using the tools of the strategy (Porter and Reinhardt 2007). This approach therefore perpetuates the separation between societal problems and their solutions, which require societal innovations capable of significantly reducing the negative societal externalities produced by the company's activities. The second concerns the difficulty for customers to make inferences about the concept of ethical values and about their management tools represented by the term "responsibility" with the mentions of "Our civic commitments", "Sustainable Development" and "Oxylane Foundation" as elements of differentiation for societal attributes.

6.2.2. *Awareness index of the values displayed by Decathlon among the customers surveyed*

Based on the definition of awareness developed by Kotler *et al.* (2006), awareness of a company's values measures the tendency of customers to mention them, either spontaneously when a value category is stated (spontaneous awareness)

13 Sources: Decathlon website, Quetigny store and *Le Monde Eco & Entreprise*, March 5, 2013.

14 Sources: Decathlon website and Quetigny store.

or in an assisted manner when they are asked if they know the name of the values being mentioned (assisted awareness). The study of spontaneous awareness of Decathlon's values was favored, because the 322 customers interviewed were asked to express their opinions without being assisted with the values they had memorized. Analyzing the results of the awareness index meant studying the proportion of the population of customers who manage to verbally "produce" (quote) the words they associated with the values of this group in relation to the total population of these customers (P = 322). This first population category, P_1, therefore corresponds to customers who claimed to know, and were able to quote, the values they believed were those declared by the Decathlon Group. A second category P_2 is then made up of customers who were unable to quote these values and comprises three sub-populations: sub-population P_{2a} who believed that this group did not have any values, sub-population P_{2b} who claimed to know the Decathlon values but were unable to quote them and sub-population P_{2c} who did not know if Decathlon had values.

The study was able to distinguish between these two populations P_1 and P_2 (see Table 6.1). The P_1 population cited at least one value that it associated with Decathlon and represented 127 customers (39.44%). The P_2 population that did not produce any of the group's values represented 195 customers out of 322 (60.56%). The P_{2a} sub-population that claimed that Decathlon did not have any values represented 19 customers (5.90%), the P_{2b} sub-population that claimed to know these values without being able to cite them represented 102 customers (31.68%) (they had difficulty retrieving them from memory and therefore produce them) and finally the P_{2c} sub-population that claimed not to know if Decathlon had values represented 74 customers (22.98%) (they had no idea whether Decathlon's values existed or not). The first result of this survey study is to highlight one of the key limitations of the likely effect of Decathlon's values in contributing to the enhancement of its image, which is the low proportion of customers (P_1: 39.44%) who managed to produce at least one value. Thus, a very high proportion of customers (P_2: 60.56%) did not pay attention to the values declared by Decathlon and would therefore not be targeted when these values were used as an attribute of differentiation when they made a purchase.

The study did not include questions to identify specific reasons for each of the three sub-sections of the P_2 population (195 customers) for not citing and therefore not paying attention to these values. Nevertheless, certain hypotheses can be put forward (developed above in section 6.1.4), which are specific to each of them. For P_{2a} customers (5.90%) who thought that Decathlon did not have any values, the explanation could be the association they could make between the term "Decathlon values" and morality. For them, attributing values to the company could therefore appear incongruous. This incongruence can also be explained by the nexus effect: obviously, a company cannot have values. For P_{2c} customers (22.98%) who did not know whether the company had values, the term "company values" could be at the crossroads of low levels of knowledge and low levels of affectiveness. This finding meant that they did not hear or heard very little about this term in their daily lives and it therefore did not generate any curiosity or discussion at home. This lack of awareness and affectiveness may be due to Decathlon's inability to make its values known, and therefore to the lack of an effective persuasive communication policy: choice of inappropriate and inaccessible display media for customers, signs used (labels, brands, Decathlon Foundation) symbolizing Decathlon's performance and ethical values that are difficult to identify and understand for customers. This deficit can also be explained by the limited cognitive capacity of this category of customers to make inferences about the values conveyed by the various reports put in place.

Total population P: 322 Decathlon customers surveyed			
P_1: population that produced at least one Decathlon value	**P_2: population that did not verbally produce (cite) any Decathlon values**		
	Population P_{2a}	**Population P_{2b}**	**Population P_{2c}**
127 customers out of 322 (39.44%)	Customers stating that Decathlon has no values: 19 out of 322 (5.90%)	Customers stating that they are aware of Decathlon's values, but are unable to cite them: 102 out of 322 (31.68%)	Customers saying they do not know if Decathlon has values: 74 out of 322 (22.98%)
These 127 customers out of 322 (39.44%) can be the target of Decathlon's value differentiation	These 195 customers out of 322 (60.56%) cannot be a target for societal attributes as a differentiating factor.		

Table 6.1. *Awareness index of Decathlon's values among customers surveyed*

Finally, P_{2b} customers (31.68%) who claimed to be aware of the values formalized by Decathlon but were unable to cite them may have had difficulty associating writing and meaning with this term. The main factor may have been their difficulty in retrieving the precise words expressing these values from memory, that is, activating the semantic representations relating to these words. Producing a word in writing or orally requires the activation of conceptual/semantic representations which are relatively pertinent to the concept of expression and these representations consist of different forms of information, among which the perceptive and functional properties associated with the "object" to be named can be found (Bonin 2003). For this author, naming an object is only possible if, and only if, semantic knowledge about this object is retrieved. Thus, if this sub-population of customers had difficulty activating the words "Decathlon values", it meant that they lacked information to name these words – a lack that can be explained by the lack of understanding of the meaning associated with these words. Memory difficulties when attempting to articulate "Decathlon values" may have also resulted from the inability of these customers to make instinctive inferences about these values, due to lack of motivation and/or cognitive ability to make inferences about the values.

6.2.3. *Discrepancies between the values displayed by Decathlon and those quoted by customers*

Measuring the appropriation of the four formalized and communicated values consisted of identifying the existence of discrepancies between these values and those memorized by the 127 customers who were able to produce at least one of them, using two indicators. The first indicator resulted from the comparison between the number of values that each customer was able to appropriate and the number of values communicated by this group (see Table 6.2).

Number of values declared by Decathlon on its website: four				
Distribution of the number of values cited for 127 customers				
Only one value cited	Two values cited	Three values cited	Four values cited	Five values cited
35 customers (27.56%)	47 customers (37.01%)	35 customers (27.56%)	7 customers (5.51%)	3 customers (2.36%)

Table 6.2. *Distribution of the number of customers according to the number of memorized values*

The results of the survey show a discrepancy between these two numbers of memorized and formalized values. A large majority of customers (82, or 64.57%) could only cite one or two values, only seven (5.51%) could cite four and three (2.36%) cited five. Thus, the cognitive ability of the 127 customers to memorize and produce values mainly varies between two and three, which revealed their difficulty in appropriating the four values declared (standard number) by Decathlon. The second indicator is linked to the comparison between the numbers of the values quoted and communicated. The customers named thirty values, whereas Decathlon only formalized four (see Table 6.3). This result shows an initial very significant discrepancy, which also reveals the difficulty customers had in perceiving the same values associated with Decathlon. It therefore shows that it is difficult to get the majority of customers to integrate a number of values close to the one chosen for the company into their mental lexicon.

Values received (cited) by the 127 customers				
Performance values (associated with the brand and the behavior of store staff): 22 out of 30, or 73.33%.	Quality/price: 37* (29.13%**)	Material/quality: 31 (24.41%)	Price: 31 (24.41%)	Welcoming the customers: 25 (19.68%)
	Product choices: 20 (15.75%)	Skills: 16 (12.6%)	Accessible to all: 15 (11.81%)	Innovation: 13 (10.24%)
	Reliability: 12 (9.45%)	Performance: 8 (6.30%)	Technicality: 7 (5.51%)	Service/Proximity: 6 (4.72%)
	Comfort: 4 (3.15%)	Simplicity: 4 (3.15%)	Serious: 4 (3.15%)	Kindness: 4 (3.15%)
	Team spirit: 3 (2.36%)	Loyalty: 3 (2.36%)	Family: 3 (2.36%)	Reactivity: 1 (0.79%)
	Customer satisfaction: 1 (0.79%)	Safety: 1 (0.79%)		
Ethical values: 3 out of 30 or 10%.	Respect for the environment: 7 (5.51%)	Ecology: 1 (0.79%)	Solidarity: 1 (0.79%)	
Have no value "status": 5 out of 30 or 16.67%.	Sport: 7 (5.51%)	Nature: 3 (2.36%)	Full-on: 3 (2.36%)	Notoriety: 2 (1.57%)
	Few brands: 1 (0.79%)			
Declared values (displayed on the website) of Decathlon				
Performance value (1)	Vitality (can be associated with brand values)			
Ethical values (3)	Responsibility	Generosity	Sincerity	

* Number of times the value was cited; ** percentage of customers who quoted it in relation to the 127 customers.

Table 6.3. *Values cited by customers* and values declared by Decathlon

A second difference is the degree of similarity between the nature of the (ethical and/or performance) values declared by the company and the values perceived by the 127 customers. The 30 appropriate values had very unequal citation frequencies.

Only eight values (all performance values associated with the brand and the behavior of store staff) had a percentage of quotations higher than 10%, four of which were widely named first and second: quality/price (24 times out of 37 first and 11 times out of 37 second), material/quality (17 times out of 31 first and 7 times out of 31 second), price (10 times out of 31 first and 11 times out of 31 second), customer service (6 times out of 25 first and 11 times out of 25 second). The other values are very marginal, produced by a number of customers that varies between 12 and 1. The values cited by customers fall into three categories: words or groups of words associated with performance values (22 out of 30, or 73.33%), ethical values (3 out of 30 or 10%) and values that have no value "status" (5 out of 30 or 16.67%).

6.2.4. *Main factors preventing customers from adopting the values formalized by the company*

Taking these results into account, two causes may explain the difficulty experienced by the 127 customers in appropriating the values formalized by the company. The first relates to the difference between the nature of the values formalized and those cited. Decathlon has favored the display of ethical values and the majority of customers memorize performance values (customer service, quality/price, etc.). This choice by customers can be explained by their inability to access sources of information that would enable them to make inferences about ethical values. The results of a study[15] on the factors influencing the perception of the image of the Decathlon Group confirm this trend. Out of 298 customers surveyed, only 46 (15.44%) and 48 (16.11%) stated that environmental values and social values, respectively, have a strong and very strong influence on the image of the group, while 253 (84.90%) stated their interest in price and 230 (77.18%) in product quality. The interest in performance values could also be part of a social construction process that the 127 customers have regarding values. A social representation is defined as a set of assertions that an individual has about an object (Lassarre and Roland-Lévy 2011). The attitude of these customers towards Decathlon is based on an instrumental rationality: they expect, above all, that the company will offer products that provide them with a tangible private benefit (affordable price, product that allows them to practice their sporting activity comfortably). The second cause corresponds to the tendency of customers to favor information from employee practices and discourses (values practiced daily by store employees) and information about the products of the group's brands (price, quality, etc.) over that communicated by Decathlon. The answers given to the question:

15 This study was carried out in 2012 in the same store as the study on the group's values carried out in 2010.

"Rate each of the four sources of information[16] that influenced you to find out about Decathlon's values from 0 to 3" confirm this observation. Indeed, the results showed that the "communication source", which is controlled and perfectly mastered by the company and is supposed to make the values chosen to embody its identity known, has very little influence (1.13). On the other hand, the other sources of information used by the 127 customers were staff behavior (2.36), skills (2.46) and Decathlon brand products (2.43). These sources (average 2.42[17], well above the theoretical average 1.5, resulting from (0 + 1 + 2 + 3)/4) strongly influence customers in making inferences about Decathlon's values. Customers therefore tend to favor, consciously or unconsciously, the information to which they are exposed during their experiences while consuming the products or being in contact with the store and its staff. As a result, the company has difficulty in "imposing" a pattern of attitudes on the nature of the source of information that should influence them in appropriating the values. Thus, out of the 322 customers questioned, only 127 (39.44%) were able to cite at least one value, but none of them corresponded to those formalized by the Decathlon Group. Therefore, if Decathlon intends to use its values as an attribute of differentiation, none of the customers surveyed would be concerned by this instrument.

6.2.5. *Main limitations of the study*

This exploratory study attempted to provide some practical answers to the difficulties of appropriating a strategy based on Decathlon's values as a probable attribute of differentiation by 332 customers in this group. It nevertheless presents three main limitations. The first is linked to the representativeness of the study sample. From a practical point of view, it was difficult to choose a representative sample of the customers who frequented the store where the survey was conducted: customers with limited availability, instructions from the store manager not to bother the customers, etc. Consequently, the study used only a descriptive approach to the results. The second corresponds to the absence of qualitative questions on the factors that led some customers to assert either that the group had no values or that it had values, but without being able to cite them. The third limitation concerns the notion of ownership of the formalized and communicated values. The variables "memorization" and "differences between cited and memorized values" used to

---

16 The four sources of information offered are advertising communication (source of information chosen by the company), staff behavior, staff skills and Decathlon brand products (sources of "practised" information). Clients are asked to give a score between 0 and 3 (for 0, the component has no influence, 1 little influence, 2 a fairly good influence and 3 a very strong influence) to each of these four sources.

17 The average (2.42) of the "practised value" sources is the result of: (2.36 + 2.46 + 2.43)/3 = 2.42.

measure this notion provided partial information. The nature of the information used to make inferences required in-depth work. A set of qualitative questions could therefore shed light on this appropriation: how do customers make inferences about values? What sources of information have they consciously or unconsciously used to make these inferences? Do they attribute the same meaning to the values they have cited as they do to the company's values? Will they incorporate these values as an attribute of differentiation?

7

Analysis of CSV-based Environmental Innovation Strategies Developed by a Company and their Impact

A company can implement various environmental innovations, which are capable of reducing the negative externalities caused by its activities, producing positive externalities and inducing societal and financial performance.

7.1. Environmental innovations, environmental externalities and competitive advantage

Innovation strategies are recognized as a guarantee of the sustainability of organizations, regardless of their size (Camison-Zomosa *et al.* 2004; Soparnot and Stevens 2007). Innovation is the foundation of entrepreneurship (Julien and Marchesnay 1996) and environmental innovation is therefore an integral part of entrepreneurship (Berger-Douce 2007). The emergence of the field of sustainable (environmental) entrepreneurship is recent and occurs at the intersection of two fields that are themselves relatively new: sustainable development and entrepreneurship (Bres *et al.* 2001). Defining the concept of environmental innovation is an arduous task, as it is dynamic and changes according to the angle of analysis, the nature of the innovation developed (Gasmi and Grolleau 2003) or the sector of activity of the firm. An environmental innovation is defined as any action, or set of alternative solutions, undertaken with the aim of reducing, managing, maintaining, improving or correcting negative environmental impacts, or even preventing damage to the environment and the climate in general (Gasmi and Grolleau 2003; Depret and Hamdouch 2009). An environmental innovation is also defined as a new or improved process, equipment, product, technique or management system that prevents or reduces the negative environmental externalities that may be caused by the company's activities (Arundel *et al.* 2007; Horbach 2008). According to O'Neill *et al.* (2009), environmental innovations can focus on the preservation of nature and communities, as well as on the pursuit of opportunities to develop products, processes and services for economic (the company) and non-economic (general interest) gains. There is therefore a diversity of environmental innovations based on creating shared value (CSV) that a company can develop to provide solutions to the environmental problems to which certain activities in its value chain may be susceptible, significantly reducing negative environmental externalities while improving its competitive advantage. These environmental innovations must have an industry-specific impact in at least one of the five main environmental areas such as energy (avoid waste, save energy, minimize GHG effects), air (minimize carbon footprint), waste (recycle, increase product life, rationalize components, raw materials), water (rationalize, monitor, avoid losses, better manage discharges by preventing pollution, recycle, etc.) and raising the awareness of key stakeholders, such as customers, suppliers, employees and the general public to adopt environmentally friendly behaviors. For example, innovations that are then likely to reduce negative environmental externalities may relate to logistics, building design and operation, products, processes, site consolidation and so on.

Externalities give rise to external effects (positive or negative), which generally refer to relations between agents that do not pass through the price mechanism, that is, they are non-market effects and thus have no monetary counterpart. Environmental externalities correspond to environmental practices perceived as those that generate private costs and collective environmental and social benefits. Their production thus contributes to the well-being of agents other than the adopter (Gasmi and Grolleau 2003). In the case of negative externalities, their counterpart is left to the stakeholders. Positive externalities result from the capacity of innovations to enable the firm developing them to "correct" market "failures" and, in particular, the negative external environmental effects (Daudigeos and Valiorgue 2010) caused by its economic activity. Kapp (1971) defines all these effects as direct or indirect losses borne by third parties or the general public, resulting from a firm's activity. The purpose of environmental integration in the overall strategy of the company is to bring the company to meet the expectations of its stakeholders by internalizing its externalities. As Dejean and Gond (2004) point out, this internalization is therefore part of a process of creating sociological values within the company, modeled on the idea of a "citizen" company. This contractualist view of the internalization of these externalities, which can also be associated with Porter's hypothesis, shows the ideal facet of environmental behavior acceptable to these various stakeholders: innovating to create shared value (CSV) meets a societal need (environmental performance), while generating profit (financial performance) for the company.

Not all innovations have a salient impact in terms of positive environmental externalities and competitive advantage. Indeed, cosmetic innovations (Martinet and Payaud 2007), which are part of an adaptive approach characterized by incremental innovations (Mathieu 2008), are qualified as minor innovations and have a very limited impact on these externalities and on competitive advantage. According to Hart (1995), only major proactive innovations specific to a firm's sector of activity can move the firm forward on the road to sustainable development and competitive advantage. For Eccles and Serafeim (2014), these major innovations imply two conditions on the part of firms. The first concerns the development of innovations that give priority to environmental concerns that are likely to have a real, positive and salient impact on the environment. The second condition assumes that firms focus on the environmental concerns and innovations which are most likely to create a competitive advantage for them. This advantage is only effective if these innovations can "manufacture" "environmental" product attributes that can be a source of differentiation, constitute a source of entry barriers for competitors and improve relations with institutional and market stakeholders (suppliers, customers, investors, etc.). The "environmental" attributes of differentiation will enable the company to offer eco-products that provide utility, that is, individual private benefit to consumers (Lancaster 1996) and collective benefit to society. According to Porter and Reinhardt (2007), in order to assess the strategic opportunity of an environmental innovation, the company's CSR managers must approach it from two perspectives. An "inside out" view consists of understanding the impact of their company's activities on the climate (air pollution, water pollution, etc.), and an "outside in" view consists of understanding how climate change (floods, scarcity of raw materials, etc.) and environmental regulations can influence the company's competitive advantage.

This analysis of CSV-based environmental strategies and a case study focuses on environmental innovations that are part of the "inside out" perspective that assesses the influence of company activities on climate. An environmental innovation is viable if it provides a concrete solution to a concrete environmental problem, but it can also include techniques that are not specific to the environmental field. Depending on the nature of these activities, the distinction between different environmental innovations can be based on various criteria: mode of adoption (voluntary, mandatory), fields of application (products, processes, organization, etc.), intensity of innovation (incremental, radical) and framework of intervention.

7.2. Different categories of environmental innovation and shared value creation

With reference to the "intervention framework" criterion, three categories of innovations are to be distinguished and can produce a specific and significant positive impact on the environment and on competitive advantage: integrated and additive environmental technological innovations, integrated technological innovations that are not purely environmental, and organizational (non-technological) environmental innovations (Gasmi and Grolleau 2003). Two reasons explain our choice to analyze the different forms of innovations and their impact in terms of CSV for the firm. The first relates to certain theoretical insights on the contributions of these innovations to a firm in terms of reducing negative environmental externalities, or producing positive externalities and competitive advantage. To this end, concrete examples of innovations based on secondary information will be presented. The second reason is the use of these innovations as a tool to analyze the case study concerning the Decathlon Group.

7.2.1. *Environmental technological innovations and shared value creation*

Environmental technological innovations that can generate shared value are additive and/or integrated. Each of them may have a specific impact on positive or negative externalities and on the competitive advantage of the company.

7.2.1.1. *Additive environmental technological innovations*

An additive technological innovation is associated with a device that is added to processes or products in order to reduce environmental damage associated with production and/or consumption (Patris *et al.* 2001). Additive innovations are added to existing technologies without modifying the operation of the company: waste treatment, reduction of energy and water losses (Reverdy 2005), waste management and recycling (Depret and Hamdouch 2009) and dispersion or dilution of toxic emissions so as to reduce the intensity of their impact. They do not always require a significant research and development effort. Additive innovations known as "end of pipe" innovations, which are described as curative, make it possible to directly or indirectly mitigate the environmental consequences of production processes. They do not attack the negative environmental impacts that the company's activities may generate at source. They correspond to simple transfers of pollution from one environmental compartment to another, from one place to another, from one stage of the product life cycle to another (Gasmi and Grolleau 2003). Additive innovations modify the production methods that alter the environment in a relatively incremental and tangible way. Their disadvantage is that they promote the transfer of pollution that is recovered by effluent treatment equipment, the pollutants being even more concentrated and having to be treated in turn (Reverdy 2005). There are three types of aqueous effluent treatment methods: 1) discharge into the natural environment after treatment by an autonomous wastewater treatment plant (internal to the industrial site), 2) discharge, generally, after pre-treatment on the industrial site, into a wastewater network leading to a collective industrial or urban wastewater treatment plant before discharge into the natural environment and 3) spreading of effluents on agricultural land (Djelal *et al.* 2008). Often, additive environmental innovations are limited to providing solutions to comply with the constraints imposed by regulatory environmental policies by internalizing the costs induced by these sovereign constraints (Depret and Hamdouch 2009; Oltra and Saint-Jean 2011). Market failure then justifies public intervention to point out to companies the inefficiencies in reducing the negative environmental externalities generated by their activities, and the potential continuous improvements to be made in their production processes or products (Porter and Van Der Linde 1995): this is therefore the technology push effect linked to regulation. In industry, investments in additive technology lead to a reduction in the overall productivity of the company (Coenen *et al.* 1995), due to the increase in production costs that can be generated by the recovery and treatment of physical waste and water without significantly increasing output. However, this type of investment can be a source of competitive advantage for the company, resulting from the improvement of its image as a good corporate citizen which can be brought about by water treatment, waste recycling, etc. (Coenen *et al.* 1995). The image as an intangible attribute and product of differentiation is thus enhanced. This type of attribute, which is not very visible to the customer, can only play its role of differentiation if it is communicated effectively to them.

7.2.1.2. *Integrated environmental technology innovations and shared value creation*

Integrated technological environmental innovations are part of an effort to reduce the adverse environmental effects that can be generated by the company's activities at source. Greenhouse gases (GHGs) may come from one or more activities under the direct control of the company, or from those of its suppliers, distributors of its products and customers (Porter and Reinhardt 2007). If the activities are under a company's control, innovation may relate to logistics, building design and operation, but mainly to the product and processes. Product innovation is aimed at designing new products (nature of the raw material used as a component, functionality, etc.) with the help of specific services introduced into the organization in order to meet the expectations of market demand (Dubouloz 2013). It has an internal focus and aims to improve the efficiency of organizational processes (Utterback 1994). Process innovation corresponds to new elements introduced into production operations (Dubouloz 2013), products, raw materials or product components. This innovation relates to the optimization of work conducted within the organization (Dubouloz 2013). These two categories of innovations are part of an approach that prevents the reduction of inputs, production of pollutants, consumption of energy and water, waste, etc. (Dubouloz 2013). In the case of product innovations, the reduction of negative environmental externalities can relate to the design of products that are sustainable, reusable, recyclable, dismountable, repairable (Patris *et al.* 2001), the reduction of inputs by limiting the number of product parts (waste reduction), the use of 100% biological or recycled raw materials as product components (phosphate-free, chlorine-free eco-products), etc. (Patris *et al.* 2001). For example, in agriculture, some of these integrated innovations can play a key role in reducing negative environmental impacts while improving farm profitability. For example, Jain Irrigation Systems (JIS) in Jalgaon (India) provides irrigation systems to small farms. Indian agriculture is traditionally dependent on monsoons, which have become weaker in recent years, effectively leading to a long-lasting drought that has caused the majority of these farms to go bankrupt, along with increasing debts, which lead some farmers to commit suicide (Haanaes *et al.* 2016). Noting the difficulties linked to this climatic context, JIS decided to invest in micro-irrigation systems. These systems have enabled these small farms to significantly increase their production by optimizing the balance between fertilizers, pesticides and reduced water use (Haanaes *et al.* 2016).

Integrated environmental technological innovations can also be part of a logic that prevents pollution, resource wastage, etc. To this end, some companies, especially multinationals, encourage and help their suppliers to take the environmental dimension into account in their activities. For example, the Cargill and Unilever groups have responded to the destruction of tropical forests and wetlands. These groups have invested and worked with farmers to develop sustainable innovations in the cultivation of palm oil, soybeans, cocoa and other agricultural products: these investments have improved crop yields and seed production for farmers, reduced negative environmental externalities and strengthened the competitive advantage of both companies (Nidumolu *et al.* 2009). Three types of benefits emerge. The first concerns the improved image of these two groups (Cargill and Unilever), which have enabled farm operations to reduce these externalities. The second relates to the security of their supply of raw materials, which do not adversely affect the environment. The third corresponds to improving the intrinsic quality of their products (products composed of GMO-free and pesticide-free raw materials) and to the increase in the production levels of these raw materials (cost reduction). Integrated technological innovations can also concern all systems that use processes involving in-house "recycling" of their effluents – or by-products – that reduce harmful substances in processes (Patris *et al.* 2001), or increase input reduction or substitution (renewable energy). For inputs that produce GHG emissions, Integrated Gasification Combined Cycle (IGCC) technology can be an excellent substitute for traditional pulverized coal-fired power plant methods, as it can reduce GHG emissions through more efficient carbon dioxide capture and storage (Lash and Wellington 2007). The IGCC method also reduces the costs of coal-fired power plants, which are subject to more stringent emission standards, as well as offering low-carbon products. This type of integrated innovation renders some additive innovations unnecessary, as they are part of systems that reduce GHGs at source.

7.2.2. Integrated technological innovations which are not purely environmental and shared value creation

Integrated technological innovations that are not purely environmental are primarily aimed at improving the competitiveness of the firm, but through the effect they cause, they can create shared value by significantly reducing negative environmental externalities or by producing positive externalities while positively impacting the firm's competitive advantage. These innovations are based on new business models that profoundly transform the production process, product design and consumption. In recent years, they have been mainly embodied by the third wave of information technologies, driven by information technology and leading to a revolution in the world of objects (products, industrial equipment, etc.). IT is transforming products into intelligent, connected and integrated objects, bringing radical improvements to their functionality and performance (Porter and Heppelmann 2015). Connected objects share three fundamental elements: physical components (mechanical and electrical), intelligent components (sensors, microprocessors, controls, data storage tools, software, embedded operating systems, digital interfaces) and connectivity (ports, antennas, protocols, networks enabling communication between the product and the operating system external to the product) (Porter and Heppelmann 2016). The first forms of these objects appeared in the field of logistics (Porter and Heppelmann 2016). These objects require technological infrastructure as a tool that creates strong opportunities for optimizing value chain management and improving the organizational efficiency of the company, which forms the basis for any competitive advantage (Porter 2015). Technologies based on intelligent and connected objects can affect all economic sectors by creating ecosystems adapted to each of them. With this type of integrated technological innovation, companies can propose an offer based on service innovation (product–service) by integrating a growing range of services, articulated with the basic offer to propose new functionalities allowing a sustainable use of the product (Lauriol 2009).

Some technological innovations based on computing and connected objects are referred to as hybrid societal innovations. A societal innovation is hybrid if it is likely to simultaneously reduce the negative social and environmental externalities produced by the company's activities, or to induce positive externalities, while improving the company's competitiveness and therefore its profit (Gasmi 2017). For example, in the field of logistics, smart and connected objects have proven their strong impact on GHG reduction. Data generated by these objects and integrated with other information offer the possibility of optimizing vehicle maintenance operations before the component concerned breaks down (change the oil when its level has reached a threshold rather than according to the time elapsed since the last oil change), to check traffic conditions, to provide each driver with an optimized delivery plan (traffic fluidity, shortest route, etc.) (Porter and Heppelmann 2016) or to use new generations of fuel-free transport. For example, the Amazon, Google and DHL groups are developing airborne deliveries by drone: with this concept, the aim is to cover the "last-mile logistics", or the final part of the delivery to the customer[1]. These UAVs enable these groups to significantly reduce GHG emissions from logistics activities (distribution of finished products), which is the most energy-intensive activity when the product is delivered to each customer (reduction of negative environmental externalities), with convenience for customers (speed of service, access to hitherto isolated regions, therefore a competitive advantage) and a positive social impact (ability for the elderly and/or people living in these remote geographical areas to meet their expectations without having to travel and also to help to reduce their social isolation). Other UAVs are used outside a logistic activity when, for example, there is a risk of pollution in coastal areas. They can be used to identify the contours of a recent oil spill in seawater to facilitate the intervention of specialized vessels. These UAVs can therefore occupy an empty observation space, that of an intermediate altitude between the Earth and low Earth orbit observation satellites. UAVs will now increasingly play a key role in reducing the negative environmental and social externalities produced by various economic activities because, as Anderson (2018) points out, they have become objects that "capture reality", that is, they digitize the physical world, both right side up and upside down, by scanning the ground and air. Initially, UAVs were of interest only to photographers, as they have an impressive photographic potential, but their use was later extended to journalism, television, cinema and communication infrastructures (see Table 7.1).

What do companies use drones for?	**%**
Aerial photography	34%
Real estate	26%
Construction and industry	26%
Agriculture	21%
Emergency management	8%
Insurance	5%
What do drone operators want to do which is against the law?	**%**
Night flight	65%
Crowd surveillance	35%
Flight beyond the visual range of the operator	19%
Control from a moving vehicle	9%
Fly above altitude limit	9%

Table 7.1. *Use of UAVs and desired UAV use for operators (Anderson 2018)*

1 Article *Le Monde*, Économie & Entreprise supplement, March 30, 2016.

COMMENT ON TABLE 7.1.– *The sum of the percentages is greater than 100 because some operators work in more than one sector. The main requests for waivers were received by the U.S. Civil Aviation Agency.*

A mini-case study of secondary type information analyzes the nature of the savings that the use of a UAV can bring about (Anderson 2018). For example, a 7.5 hectare site was inspected by UAV and traditional methods with three common tasks to be performed: preparation, execution and data processing. In the conventional two-person approach, preparation took 6 hours, execution 11.5 hours and data processing 2.8 hours, whereas with a single-person UAV, these tasks took 4.9 hours, 0.8 hours and 2.7 hours, respectively. UAVs have therefore resulted in savings in the execution of tasks. Today, UAVs are a sophisticated technology that will increasingly fundamentally transform economic activity, particularly in the logistics sector. Indeed, they are equipped with professional-quality software and are becoming real data collectors that can be used to offer a variety of services. For example, car and truck journeys can be optimized, irrigation equipment can be managed efficiently and water consumption reduced on farms – all of which combine data recorded by humidity sensors and weather forecasts (Porter and Heppelmann 2015; Anderson 2018). From now on, UAVs will be a part of our lives, just as electricity applications have been.

Certainly, the use of UAVs is a strategy that can induce CSV. However, essential information, both private and professional, concerning customers and generated by this mode of transport, may lead companies to exploit and use them without their consent. For a manager whose company uses UAVs, the main question is when to be concerned about ethics. Putting into practice an ethical strategy that includes data security and processing, as well as the cyber resilience of the company's tools, becomes increasingly difficult as the volume of data collected increases. The alternative to the (current) lack of ethics on UAV operations is to develop, according to Gibbens (2018), two strategies that can protect corporate data. One is decisive, linked to the construction of a secure system for the company's network, using three types of actions. The first consists of a scrupulous reading of contracts by managers, as some of them present risks. Indeed, even if companies are in the habit of scrutinizing contracts for their software, those for drones and associated technologies are often neglected or even ignored. The second action is the implementation of domain-specific restrictions and strict rules and practices for laptops and other mobile devices that use USB ports and SD cards. This makes the network more secure with regard to the large volumes of data collected and processed by UAV systems, or else manufacturers have access to and can then share them. There are also systems that can only function fully if data sharing is not allowed. Finally, the third action concerns the monitoring of digital and physical company indicators.

These safety and reliability indicators help the company to understand whether a UAV is functioning properly and whether it is safe. Over time, the company becomes able to identify its weaknesses and detect trends, and can thus prevent potential problems and avoid lasting damage. The other strategy is to ask three main sets of questions. First, regarding the operation of a UAV: do you trust your UAV? Will it perform the tasks required? How accurate is the navigation system, sensors and data produced? How can you ensure that the safety devices will prevent fraudulent use of the UAV by competitors? Second, regarding the data: is it 100% secure? Do you have confidence in the data processing process and in the communications architecture? Are the UAV and its data flows cyber resilient? Third, regarding protection: do your user contracts protect you? Do you trust the user contracts related to your data and networks? How can you ensure that you remain the sole owner of your data? Can you comply with commercial and official data management policies?

In production, intelligent and connected objects have a new potential that transforms the operation of production units where machines are linked in networks. These fully optimized and automated machines can manufacture several parts in one and also detect virtually dangerous malfunctions that could stop other equipment, etc. (Porter and Heppelmann 2016). They enable the company to greatly reduce the risk of producing parts with defects, which are a source of waste. Thus, since 2014, with the creation of 3D industrial printing, the production processes of products have been radically modified. These connected objects offer three major advantages: flexibility (product customization), the ability to produce a set of parts in one piece and the elimination of assembly and storage operations (d'Aveni 2016). For example, the General Electric (GE) group has decided to produce more than 45,000 fuel injectors per year for certain jet engines. However, using printing technology, it can produce a fuel injector, which previously had to be assembled from 20 separately molded parts, in a single run: this reduces manufacturing costs by 75% while at the same time significantly reducing waste (d'Aveni 2016). Intelligent connected products can facilitate quality management, as they allow continuous monitoring of their actual performance. Moreover, they are able to identify and solve design problems (which can generate waste) that tests would not be capable of revealing (Porter and Heppelmann 2016).

Until now, intelligent robots have been static (bolted to the floor, surrounded by partitions so as not to endanger employees, difficult to move) and therefore less flexible. The new generation of these objects is embodied by adaptive robots that are smarter and more collaborative with employees. This type of robot offers five advantages: it becomes a teammate of the employees, allowing them to feel more secure; it relieves the employees by eliminating thankless tasks so that they can devote themselves to less painful high value-added tasks, thus increasing their commitment and personal satisfaction; it considerably reduces the execution time and generates significant savings for the company (competitive advantage) (Nikolaidis *et al.* 2015); it reduces negative environmental externalities (waste reduction, etc.); and it improves the use of certain functions, such as management control, logistics, etc. (Nikolaidis *et al.* 2015) by exploiting all the information collected daily in relation to each of these functions. This type of innovation, which is essentially primarily aimed at improving the competitiveness of the company, therefore leads to a significant reduction in the negative environmental externalities previously produced by its activities and a positive social effect for employees (reducing the drudgery of work). This is also the case of the sharing service offered by the company Smoove[2]. To reduce maintenance costs, increase product life and minimize the risk of theft, it has equipped its bicycles with chain-less transmissions, puncture-proof tires and padlocks. These various positive contributions are aimed at improving the tangible attributes of the product (durability, comfort of use and cost reduction for the customer) and, therefore, the competitive advantage for the company. In addition, this technology allows the reduction of negative environmental externalities that are due to the use of this type of product, with the reduction of waste from used tires. According to Iansiti and Lakhani (2015), "the industrial Internet, which is based on the ubiquity of digital connectivity where most of the information work is digitized by the user of the connected laptops and mobile devices, has made it possible to digitize and connect tasks, processes, machining and service operations that were previously comparable". "Technological innovations based on intelligent and connected objects or on the industrial Internet, which are not specifically designed as investments dedicated to the reduction of negative environmental externalities produced by the company's activities", correspond, as Sanchez and McKinley (1998) and Boiral (2004) point out, to "technological innovations related to the more or less unintentional contingent factors on the reduction of these externalities". The positive environmental impact results from the capacity of these technologies to strongly reduce inputs (the monobloc part thus reducing the consumption of several parts, energy and waste), to increase the life span of products, etc. This type of innovation offers a triple advantage: improvement of the company's competitive advantage (flexibility, reduction of costs linked to the sharp reduction in the number of parts, reduction in production time), positive impact for employees (reduction in the arduousness of their work) and reduction of negative environmental externalities (reduction of waste, raw materials, water and electricity consumption). These positive social and environmental impacts improve the image of the company as an institution.

2 Smoove is a French company created in 2000, which designs, produces, monitors and maintains self-service bicycle systems and complementary bicycle services.

7.2.3. *Organizational environmental innovations and shared value creation*

While technological innovations, which have been the subject of most research, are widely accepted (Keupp *et al.* 2011), organizational innovations are described as "emerging" (Damanpour and Aravind 2012). Organizational innovation is the first term used to define non-technological innovations (Dubouloz 2013).

There is often little interest in organizational innovations in general. This can be explained by the fact that they are developed in intra-organizational contexts that do not refer at all to entrepreneurial behavior, and that they also have the character of internal innovations and are therefore less visible (Fayolle and Hernandez 2007). Organizational innovations cover a wide range of things, such as innovations in practices, administrative processes, organizational structures (Alänge *et al.* 1998) or new ways of organizing the architecture of the activities of the business value chain, or industry, of the firm in such a way that the operational efficiency of this chain is improved.

The business value chain is composed of the succession of inter-organizational linkages of activities necessary to create an offer, from raw material suppliers to end customers (Johnson *et al.* 2014). Operational efficiency consists of carrying out value chain activities with fewer inputs and GHG emissions than one's competitors (Porter 2015), thus improving environmental performance (reducing negative environmental externalities) and the company's competitive advantage.

The distinction between technological innovations and organizational innovations relates to the cost and the nature of the benefit (economic and environmental) that they can provide to the firm. In theory, organizational innovation would be less costly and more difficult to evaluate than technological innovation (Rogers 1995) as it is difficult to protect and its implementation may cause significant disruption to the firm (Alänge *et al.* 1998).

Three types of organizational innovations can be proposed. The first innovation consists of identifying the activities of the company that generate strong negative environmental externalities, subcontracting them to companies with specific skills or making improvements internally to reduce these externalities. In the case of outsourcing, companies must be flexible to react quickly to changes in competition "imposed" by the imperative of taking environmental issues into account. They must therefore externalize aggressively to gain efficiency while preserving their basic competitive skills to stay ahead of the competition (Porter 2015). Internally, companies can also, for certain activities, such as transportation, replace one or more resources, for example, cars using diesel with hybrid vehicles or using flex fuel (bioethanol), whose engines consume less energy and emit few GHGs. They can also develop maintenance programs (cars, trucks, boats, etc.) that meet regulatory deadlines, choose schedules with less traffic, short transportation routes, opt for loads that can lead to a reduction in GHG-reducing energy consumption, etc. (Lowitt 2015). Sometimes, an organizational innovation associated with an original idea such as avoiding turning left at an intersection can, according to Winston (2017), reduce waiting time at intersections and vehicle fuel costs. By implementing this idea, the US-based UPS group saved 30 million liters of gasoline a year. All these various logistics-related innovations induce a synergy of shared value creation by strongly reducing the negative environmental externalities that this type of activity can produce while simultaneously improving the competitiveness of the company.

The second organizational innovation concerns the closer links between production sites and those of suppliers, distributors and customers. This can greatly limit externalities: reducing transport-related GHGs (reducing the number, duration and distance of journeys), waste (capacity for cooperation between production and marketing activities and those of suppliers, to reduce the causes of non-conformity of components, products, raw materials, etc.) and so on. This type of innovation can also improve the performance of the company and thus its competitive advantage. This advantage may result from cost reductions due to lower fuel consumption (and therefore lower prices), fewer delays in the delivery of products to customers and, more generally, improvements to the operational efficiency of the company's activities and to its image as a good corporate citizen.

The third organizational innovation involves assessing the degree of vulnerability arising from the increased costs associated with the negative environmental externalities that may be generated by suppliers' activities (Lash and Wellington 2007). To avoid this risk, the company should source from suppliers that do not use vital raw materials from geographical areas threatened by climate change or boycotted by consumers because of their negative impact on the climate (Lowitt 2015), and instead select those that use organic or recycled raw materials, define valid codes of conduct for production (treatment and disposal of waste, wastewater), evaluate the waste and reuse of materials, energy and water use, etc. (Lash and Wellington 2007). The company can also extend its efforts to reduce negative environmental externalities to downstream partnership relationships (customer companies: B to B relationship). This is the case, for example, with the relationship developed by the company Jain Irrigation Systems, which specializes in the production of agricultural equipment, including micro-irrigation systems, with its small farmer customers in the Indian state of Maharashtra. Noting that most of its customers did not have the financial resources to purchase its micro-irrigation systems, nor the means to resort to external financing, Jain Irrigation Systems decided to help them to apply for government subsidies, to use its systems efficiently and to commit itself to purchase a portion of the crops produced at a reasonable price and then resell them (Haanaes *et al.* 2016). This symbiotic cooperation between Jain

Irrigation Systems and its customers has reduced negative environmental externalities (optimizing the fertilizer–pesticide balance and reducing water and energy consumption), improved positive social externalities by enabling these farmers to make a living from their business (better yields and safety due to product sales to Jain Irrigation Systems) and improved company performance. With its traditional customers, a company can also establish an action plan to reduce the negative impact of the use of its products, that is, create an incentive to sort and bring used products to its sorting centers for recycling, provide advice on how to use the products better and thus increase their life span, etc.

8

Analysis of Specific Environmental Innovation Strategies to Each Activity of the Decathlon Group

Since 1992, after developing CSR strategies based on ethical values, the Decathlon Group has integrated societal strategies into its global strategy, based on the creation of shared value (CSV). The group has set up a "materiality map" to identify the relevance criteria of its activities that generate (directly and indirectly) strong negative environmental externalities. Decathlon has determined three categories of these activities by measuring CO_2 emission rates: products and production (55% CO_2), transport, including the travel of employees, customers and products (33% CO_2), and the operation and construction of sites (buildings) (12% CO_2). The group has used three types of innovations to significantly reduce these externalities and improve its competitive advantage. These are additive and integrated environmental technological innovations, integrated technological innovations that are not purely environmental and primarily organizational environmental innovations. Less costly organizational innovations have their limitations, however, as they are difficult to evaluate, difficult to protect and invisible to customers. The development of innovations has led to a steady reduction in GHG emissions, except for product and production activities, which are steadily growing, and an increase in sales of eco-products and diversified after-sales services, as customers are becoming increasingly eco-responsible because they are very satisfied with the product offerings. Moreover, this positive balance is due to the establishment of relationships based on trust, as well as on a collaborative partnership with stakeholders in the socio-political sphere and the market. This approach is part of a contractualist conception of societal practices.

Box 8.1. *The key role of synergistic innovation strategies in reducing negative environmental externalities generated by Decathlon's activities*

This second case study focuses on CSV-based environmental innovation strategies and is a continuation of the ethics-based strategies of the first case study. Its singularity is to show that the Decathlon Group has greatly evolved and improved its societal strategies. This evolution is mainly due to the implementation of societal innovation strategies, capable of significantly reducing the negative environmental externalities of its activities; or producing positive externalities and environmental attributes for product differentiation, while improving the competitiveness, and therefore the competitive advantage of this group. In order to analyze the process of putting these strategies into practice, this study uses a research article published in the *Revue de l'entrepreneuriat* (Gasmi 2020). Only information based on secondary data, primarily from the first two sustainable development reports – published on the group's website in 2013 and 2014[1] – and, in addition, from the 2015 and 2016 sustainable development reports.

Three main factors explain the use of this data. The first is related to the difficulty of accessing the so-called "primary" information to identify the environmental activities and innovations concerned, and the impacts produced. The second relates to the wealth of raw information contained in the first two sustainable development reports. Finally, the third is the challenge posed by this research on raw information concerning the environmental innovations developed by a large international group, such as Decathlon, and the impact they may have. The purpose of the case study is to give meaning (sense-making) to these innovations and to disseminate them (sense-giving) (Weick *et al.* 2005).

The process of constructing this sense is organized in four chronologically logical steps. The first consists of knowing the key phases of the environmental commitment based on the group's CSV, and the second enables identification of all of its activities, specific to the sporting goods industry, producing negative environmental externalities. The third analyzes the different forms of innovation developed in each of these activities: integrated technological innovations, organizational innovations, etc. The fourth step is to collect all the information on each of these innovations, to analyze the nature of the negative environmental externalities they could reduce, or the positive externalities created, and the impact they may have had in terms of competitive advantage for this group. The summary of information from these four steps and the analysis of the results of this case study are structured by the author of this research.

1 http://corporate.decathlon.com/Nus-connaitre/chiffres-cles/.

8.1. Analysis of the Decathlon Group's environmental policy based on CSV

The environmental innovation policy of the Decathlon Group, based on CSV, was tentatively launched in 1990 by recruiting a single researcher; since 2015, however, about 50 people have been working in its research center, Decathlon SportsLab. The research programs focus on innovations that improve existing products and then that create new ones, allowing an average of 40 patents to be filed each year. In order to better develop innovation strategies, capable of adapting its products to the expectations of its various key stakeholders, Decathlon's R&D is based on a co-creative or collaborative approach. This collaborative approach enables it to integrate all internal and external stakeholders likely to play a positive role in defining these innovation strategies, in order to offer products that meet customer expectations in terms of acceptable group behavior.

Internally, management of the sustainable development innovation strategy is structured around two teams (Decathlon 2015, p. 11). The first is made up of a Decathlon leader (in charge of the sustainable development strategy with the Shareholders' Committee) and a sustainable development leader (who defines the sustainable development policy according to the guidelines proposed by the sustainable development team and employees, etc.). The second team is made up of two steering committees: a committee of representatives from the group's various activities (logistics, production, design, etc.) whose role is to provide a cross-functional perspective on the proposed sustainable development strategies, and a Shareholders' Committee, in charge of validating the strategies and objectives proposed by the Decathlon leaders. This strategy of integrating a group of middle managers into the formulation of environmental strategies is part of a vision of sharing top management leadership with these managers (Chan Kim and Mauborgne 2014). This sharing of leadership can lead to positive internalities for employees and thus strengthen trust with their superiors. The notion of "internality" relates to the fact that there is a social value in an individual with an internal explanation (Louche *et al.* 2006). Externally, the Decathlon Group integrates market stakeholders (customers, sports enthusiasts, subcontractors considered as business partners) (Decathlon 2015, p. 13), who are involved in all stages of product design. These stakeholders prevent the group from being exposed to certain competitive risks if its products do not meet customer expectations, in terms of reducing the negative environmental externalities produced by its activities. Decathlon has also involved its soft power stakeholders (NGOs, federations, education and research, local communities, CSR experts) in the formulation of environmental innovation projects that generate shared value, through participation as employees, members of committees, directors, etc. (Decathlon 2015, p. 13).

This association is a lever for reinforcing the legitimacy of the group's activities. It has also initiated a collaborative strategy with the various regulatory authorities (European Commission, Ministry of Ecology, local authorities) to share information and participate in standardizing work and forming methodological recommendations (Decathlon 2015, p. 13). In this way, it wants to avoid pressure and potential legal risks (Crifo and Forget 2014). This approach of integrating stakeholders from the socio-political sphere and the market is part of a contractualist conception (Jensen 2002) of social and environmental practices. To make the creation of shared value operational, Decathlon set up two platforms – Openoxylane in 2014 and Decathlon Creation in 2015 (Decathlon 2015, p. 48) – which enables its stakeholders to propose innovative ideas by intervening in all phases of product development: defining essential characteristics, choosing colors, materials, determining the design, proposing the name, evaluating the fairest price, etc. In addition, to stimulate sustainable innovation, each year the group organizes the Green Awards, which rewards the best initiatives in terms of sustainable development or social responsibility. In 2014, two packaging projects – a logistics and real estate project in Russia, and a customer–stakeholder event, "Gr'In Day", entirely dedicated to sustainable development – were awarded prizes (Decathlon 2015, p. 27). In 2016, at the Decathlon Innovations Awards (DIA), eight innovations were produced (Table 8.1), three of which were developed with the expertise of Decathlon's internal R&D department, SportsLab: notably, the Kalenji K-Only system, designed after a three-year collaboration between the brand, the R&D center and the Luxembourg Institute of Health (LIH). Quechua's mattress, which has a rapid inflation and deflation system, won first prize.

Innovations							
Ziplayer by Artengo	Kalenji K-Only System	Air Seconds Mattress by Quechua	B'twin U-Fit fork (on RR520)	Ski Boost 300 Archtec by Wed'ze	BFast Glasses by Nabaiji	Legging Shape Booster by Domyos	Fouganza Be Connected
Average scores							
5	4.31	4.14	4.04	4	3.78	3.7	This product has been withdrawn from sale

Table 8.1. *Decathlon Innovation Awards (Decathlon 2016, pp. 47–49)*

Social actions	Economic actions	Environmental actions
Design: product safety, quality and durability	Accessibility of product prices for customers, with the smart cost approach	Design: multi-criteria analysis of product life cycles, use of renewable, recycled or recyclable raw materials, product design and packaging, etc.
Production: improvement of working conditions, employee safety, supplier requirements, working hours, etc.	Free sports facilities	Production: continuous assessment and improvement of the environmental impacts of Decathlon sites, development of more environmentally friendly manufacturing processes and strategic partnerships
Logistics: management of products, unsold goods (recovery, recycling, donation, etc.)	Pilot projects for fair pay for production workers	Logistics: reducing the distance traveled by products, maximizing the container filling rate, the least environmentally damaging mode of transport, the environmental performance of logistics platforms, etc.
Commerce: organization of local events boosting the network of local sports associations	Fairer prices, accurate information on product attributes, etc.	Trade: optimization of existing energy performance, eco-construction, sorting and recovery of waste products and promotion of soft mobility (renewable energies, energy storage, smart city, etc.).
Users: encouragement to practice sport, product safety, transparent information, etc.	Information on the use and durability of products	Users: display of product performance, reparability of products by users and in the Decathlon workshop and sale of second-hand products

Table 8.2. *Levers developed by the Decathlon Group in terms of sustainable development to reduce the negative effects produced by its activities (Decathlon 2016, pp. 10–11)*

Innovation has enabled the group to integrate 2,800 new products into the Decathlon range each year. As the innovation strategy is based on crowdsourcing, the group has, for the first time, organized Hackathlons, which are very successful with its teammates and other external participants. "Hackathlon" is a variant of a hackathon – a contraction of the terms "hacker" meaning to modify, tinker with and "marathon", a long and arduous run. In the computer world, this concept corresponds to "commando operations" that test ideas and then produce application prototypes in a limited time (Autisssier *et al.* 2018). The Decathlon Creation crowdsourcing platform now offers trials to its members. The design teams focus on innovations that are primarily functional and based on CSV, in order to surprise and satisfy their customers. The challenges of CSV for the Decathlon Group focus on three pillars: social, environmental and economic actions (Table 8.2).

8.2. Analysis of the contributions of Decathlon Group's environmental innovations

Decathlon Group's innovations are not limited to improving the quality of conventional product attributes (comfort, quality, price), which are a fundamental lever in the purchasing act for customers, but include innovations that contribute to significantly reducing the negative environmental externalities that can be generated by certain activities in its business value chain. The first innovations with a positive environmental impact initiated by this group were developed in 1992, with the first eco-design product packaging. In 2006, an "eco-tool" was developed to quantify the environmental impact – global warming, water and energy consumption, eutrophication and depletion of resources – of products, and the first products with an eco-design approach were introduced in stores under the Passion Domyos brand.

In 2007, the first store with an environmental dimension was built in France and a process created to account for the carbon emissions of products. This approach enabled the group to identify four sources of direct and indirect GHG emissions related to the activities of the Decathlon network: raw materials (cultivation and extraction of materials), production (energy, waste, direct air emissions), transport (employee and customer travel, goods transport) and Decathlon sites (energy and air conditioning leaks, purchases and services, waste, building construction, IT equipment, machines, furniture and fixtures). In 2008, a network of environmental leaders was created (around 30 employees trained in the group's environmental approach) for the Passion brands and industrial processes, and in 2009, the group developed the first environmental display tests of product impacts for customers. In 2011, an independent third-party organization conducted the first environmental certification of any Decathlon store and, at the same time, it established 10 "for our environment" initiatives with the aim of reducing GHGs by 15% by 2020: managing waste, developing renewable energies, supporting the life of products, encouraging customers to take action, eco-designing products, reducing the impact of car parks, integrating stores into their environment, optimizing store energy, minimizing the impact of supplies and giving products a new lease of life. In 2013, the first annual report on sustainable development was published and, in order to draw up the first assessment of GHG emissions generated by its activities, the group identified four possible sources: energy, waste, transport and production (Table 8.3). In 2014, these emissions amounted to 4,519,000 metric tons of carbon equivalent CO_2 (Decathlon 2014, p. 15).

Energy	Waste	Transport	Production
1,000 kWh of electricity: 550 kg CO_2 eq.	1 metric ton of paper not recovered: 850 kg CO_2 eq.	1,000 km of employee business travel driven by car: 255 kg CO_2 eq.	1 kg of conventional cotton: 19 kg CO_2 eq.

Table 8.3. *GHG emissions expressed in kilograms of CO_2 (Decathlon 2013, p. 29)*

This initial assessment has enabled the Decathlon Group to put in place a "materiality map" (Eccles and Serafeim 2014), that is, to identify criteria for the relevance of activities generating (directly and indirectly) strong negative environmental externalities. Relevance is the fact that a company, which does not take into account the nature and sources of externalities specific to its activities, can only have a small impact on reducing these externalities and on its financial performance. Decathlon has thus outlined three categories of activities that generate externalities measured in CO_2 emissions, for which it has been able to develop innovations that are likely to significantly reduce them: activities related to products and production (55% CO_2), transport, including employee and customer travel, products from production countries to storage and sales stores (33% CO_2) and operations, and construction of Decathlon sites (buildings) such as sales stores, warehouses, international headquarters offices, brand sites and production offices (12% CO_2) (Table 8.4). In 2014, the Decathlon Group published its second annual report. It was able to improve upon the reduction of GHG emissions in activities related to transport, operation and construction of the sites, but saw a sharp increase in the actual production of products due to the increase in sales.

However, the balance sheet of GHG emissions, resulting from Decathlon's activities, shows that these GHGs are decreasing year on year. To reduce the negative environmental externalities generated by these three categories of activities, the Decathlon Group has implemented various forms of innovations, specific to each of them. Thus, the following three sections analyze these CSV-based innovations, which they can generate in terms of positive externalities produced or negative externalities reduced, while positively impacting the group's competitive advantage. The different names for these innovations have been attributed by author of this work.

<table>
<tr><th colspan="5">Distribution of CO_2 emission rates according to Decathlon's activities in 2013</th></tr>
<tr><th>Product and production activities[2]</th><th colspan="3">Activities related to transport</th><th rowspan="2">Activities related to site operation and construction</th></tr>
<tr><td rowspan="2">55%</td><td>Customer travel: 22%</td><td>Employee travel: 4%</td><td>Product transportatio n: 7%</td></tr>
<tr><td colspan="3">33%</td><td>12%</td></tr>
<tr><th colspan="5">Distribution of $CO2_2$ emission rates according to Decathlon's activities in 2014</th></tr>
<tr><th>Product and production activities</th><th colspan="3">Activities related to transport</th><th rowspan="2">Activities related to site operation and construction</th></tr>
<tr><td rowspan="2">67%</td><td>Customer travel: 17%</td><td>Employee travel: 3%</td><td>Product transportatio n: 6%</td></tr>
<tr><td colspan="3">26%</td><td>7%</td></tr>
<tr><th colspan="5">Breakdown of CO_2 emission rates according to Decathlon activities in 2015</th></tr>
<tr><th>Product and production activities</th><th colspan="3">Activities related to transport</th><th rowspan="2">Activities related to site operation and construction</th></tr>
<tr><td rowspan="2">74%</td><td>Customer travel: 14%</td><td>Employee travel: 2%</td><td>Product transportatio n: 5%</td></tr>
<tr><td colspan="3">21%</td><td>5%</td></tr>
<tr><th colspan="5">Distribution of CO_2 emission rates according to Decathlon's activities in 2016</th></tr>
<tr><th>Product and production activities</th><th colspan="3">Activities related to transport</th><th rowspan="2">Activities related to site operation and construction</th></tr>
<tr><td rowspan="2">71%</td><td>Customer travel: 18%</td><td>Employee travel: 2%</td><td>Product transportatio n: 4%</td></tr>
<tr><td colspan="3">24%</td><td>5%</td></tr>
</table>

Table 8.4. *Distribution of GHG (CO_2) emission rates (Decathlon 2013, 2014, 2015, 2016)*

2 The impact of the products takes into account the extraction of raw materials, production, use and end of life of Decathlon Passion brand products (66%) and products of other international brands (8%).

8.3. Environmental innovations related to product and production activities

Product- and production-related activities generate the highest negative environmental externalities in the Decathlon Group's value chain (Table 8.4). For example, for a cotton T-shirt, both production activities and use of raw materials alone generated 33% and 27% of the GHG emissions, respectively, or 60% overall (Table 8.5).

Life cycle	Production	Raw materials	Use	Distribution	Transport	End of life
Environmental impact	33%	27%	19%	12%	7%	2%
	60%		40%			
On average, a T-shirt produces 7.2 kg of CO_2, which is equivalent to operating a filament bulb for 150 hours						

Table 8.5. *Environmental impacts of the life cycle of a cotton T-shirt (Decathlon 2014, p. 25)*

To reduce these GHG emissions, Decathlon has developed innovations that can, in summary, be classified as integrated and organizational technological innovations.

8.3.1. *Integrated technological innovations related to products and processes*

Integrated technological innovations concern products and processes. For Decathlon, the "product" technological innovations are aimed at improving the efficiency of organizational processes (Utterback 1994) and are a response to the expectations of potential customers who are sensitive to eco-products, whereas "process" innovations relate to how work is carried out within the group (Dubouloz 2013) to design and manufacture more than 20 eco-products.

These products are divided into two categories (Table 8.6). The first category is made up of products mainly resulting from innovations related to the use of environmentally friendly raw materials as components. This is the case, for example, with items made with 80% recycled yarn for the Mc Elioffel T-shirt, 100% organic cotton for the athlete T-shirt and 65% recycled polyester (a lightweight component from recycled plastic bottles) for Quickhiker Ultralight tents along with a kit for repairing broken hoops, which increases the product's lifespan (Table 8.6). The second is based on the process dimension of the innovations and relates to the process used to obtain the environmentally friendly raw material as a component in certain products, for example organic cotton.

Categories of articles	Revenue by sport activity	Environmental actions
Product innovations: use of environmentally friendly raw materials as product components		
Underwear	Wed'ze Junior Ski (skiing)	100% organic cotton
T-shirts	Athlete T-shirt (running)	100% organic cotton
	Kapteren TSD Comfort T-shirt (running)	70% recycled polyester
	Deefuz Kapteren T-shirt (running)	70% recycled material
	Domyos T-shirt (soft gym, yoga)	100% organic cotton
	Mc Elioffel T-shirt (rugby)	80% recycled yarn
Shirts	Arpenaz Quechua shirt (hiking)	70% organic cotton
Polar	Polar Forclaz 50 by Quechua (hiking)	Yarns made of 100% recycled plastic bottles from 2016 onwards
Shoes	Football shoes cap 100 leather 700 (football)	0% PVC, reduced CO_2 production (leather and rubber)
	Kipsta F300 Sala shoes (football)	
	Namib 100 shoes (hunting)	30% recycled material
	Namib 50 shoes (hunting)	Since 2010, water consumption has been reduced by 50%
Boots	Sabotins Inverness 50 (hunting)	0% PVC, decrease in CO_2 production (leather and rubber)
Pants	TZ 50 pants (fitness)	50% to 70% recycled polyester
	Baggy Kapteren (running)	50% recycled polyester
	Pants Namib 50 to 200 (hunting)	100% organic cotton
	Arpenaz Quechua pants (hiking)	100% organic cotton
Tights	Kapteren tights (running)	30% to 70% recycled content

Tents	Quickhiker Ultralight with kit	65% polyester textile from recycled plastic bottles and a kit for repairing broken hoops
Snowshoes	Snowshoes (hiking)	40% reduction in CO_2 production since 2010
Process innovations: limiting the use of raw materials and water consumption in the product production process		
Backpacks	Arpenaz 10 Quechua bag (hiking)	Designed with only one seam: less material used, less production time (less expensive) and more bags for distribution
Tents	Quechua	Designed with a combination of colored yarn with neutral yarn: 75% reduction in water consumption since 2016
Mattress	Quechua	Rapid inflation and deflation system (2016)

Table 8.6. *Environmental innovations having a direct impact on products*

In 2014, the Decathlon Group established itself as one of the five best cotton companies in the world as a result of having participated in the Better Cotton Initiative (BCI) program since 2012. BCI is a non-profit organization which, through its cooperation with a multi-stakeholder group of organizations, has been able to define the best way to develop sustainable cotton cultivation under the name "Better Cotton"[3]. This initiative was then extended to many other raw materials (Fouilleux and Goulet 2012). The BCI program aims to promote more sustainable management of cotton by developing integrated technological innovations that allow better management of water consumption, more judicious use of chemicals and improved working conditions[4]. Compared to conventional cotton cultivation, a study carried out by Decathlon in the state of Gujarat (India) shows that these innovations have generated significant gains: a 3% increase in yield, a 17% reduction in water consumption and a 30% reduction in the use of chemical fertilizers and pesticides. Prior to 2013, the shares of BCI and recycled cottons were insignificant (613 metric

3 http://bettercotton.org/about-bci/who-we-are/.
4 http://www.oxylane.com/better-coton-initiative/.

tons), whereas in 2014 they reached 4,271 metric tons (Decathlon 2014, p. 29). In 2016, Decathlon decided that 100% of the cotton used would gradually be produced in a sustainable manner from 2018 to 2020 (Decathlon 2016, p. 52).

These integrated technological innovations in the production process for such raw materials reduce negative environmental externalities at source. They can generate two types of "environmental" attributes that differentiate products and thus generate a competitive advantage for the company. The first attribute, qualified as intangible, is linked to the collective benefit (general interest) that the use of these materials as components of the product can bring (reduction of water consumption by 60% compared to conventional cotton, reduction of the risk of pollution, because this cotton is cultivated without chemical fertilizers, pesticides or GMOs)[5]. This positive effect on the environment enhances the (civic) image of the group as an institution. The second attribute is related to the individual private benefit that the use of these raw materials can generate for the customer, because the intrinsic qualities of the products are improved. This is the case, for example, with Domyos T-shirt products with 100% organic cotton – a fabric that does not irritate the skin (comfort) and retains its durability after numerous washes (guarantees the durability of the cotton and therefore of the product). The combination of product and process innovations can also bring about a positive social impact for the customer (fabric of the product that protects from possible skin problems, hence a gain for social security) and a competitive advantage for Decathlon. This combination of innovations is described as a hybrid: it simultaneously reduces negative environmental and social externalities while improving product differentiation and therefore the group's competitive advantage (Gasmi 2017). Decathlon has also developed integrated technological innovations on another form of "process" involving the dyeing of fabrics, which leads to a reduction in raw material consumption and the consumption and pollution of the water used. This process consists of combining a colored yarn with a neutral yarn: all of the yarn spools are dyed, without using water. This technology has significantly reduced water consumption by 75% (130 million metric tons of water are saved, the equivalent of 44 Olympic-sized swimming pools per square meter of fabric, and as many thousands of liters of unpolluted and non-spilled water) (Decathlon 2014, p. 30) and has reduced production time and costs while improving the integrity of the product. These fabrics were used in 2016 in Quechua tents.

8.3.2. *Organizational environmental innovations*

Two categories of organizational innovations have been identified as associated with the merger of Decathlon's upstream and downstream sites and the development

5 http://www.decathlon.fr/tee-shirt-manches-courtes-bio-id_8238316.html.

of service activities. These innovations do not have a direct impact on the intrinsic characteristics of the product, but have a positive impact on the environment and the competitive advantage of the company.

8.3.2.1. *Organizational innovations related to site reconciliation and processes*

Organizational innovations, which bring together certain manufacturing sites for products, suppliers and customers, are aimed at optimizing the operation of Decathlon Group's business value chain architecture. These innovations are defined as new ways of organizing production, R&D, marketing, supplier activities, etc., which are related to human resources and which aim to improve the efficiency of the organization (Edquist *et al.* 2001). In 2014, this local production and sales strategy was being developed in Brazil (29.8% of products manufactured and sold), China (89.6%), Russia (2.2%) and India (28%) (Decathlon 2014, p. 57). Decathlon planned to manufacture 80% of its products with 100 suppliers. Bringing sites together can generate three types of benefits. The first concerns the group's ability to be more responsive to the environmental issues specific to each region of the world where Decathlon is present and also to offer products that better meet the expectations of local markets. For example, with a simple technical tool supplied to the Decathlon India teams from the B'twin teams of Decathlon France, they designed and manufactured the Mybike, adapted to the needs and budget of Indian customers. These bikes are 40% cheaper than the model sold before the French and Indian teams collaborated. The second results from the reduction in packaging costs used in the export of products, transport, etc., which can further strengthen the price competitiveness of products on local and export markets. Finally, the third advantage is linked to the creation of direct or indirect jobs in the country of production. The increase in the working population may lead part of the Indian population, which until now has been relative non-consumers of Decathlon products, to become real consumers, thus presenting an opportunity to increase the group's market share in India and also in exports. These three advantages are a source of competitive advantage for the group in the countries where the sites are being brought together. This rapprochement also allows Decathlon to significantly reduce negative environmental externalities: reduction of waste (reduction of the causes of non-compliance observed at certain subcontractors) and reduction of GHG emissions (reduction of distances and therefore of transport times between suppliers and producers). Bringing sites closer together can also facilitate the process of raising awareness among distributors and customers about the challenges of reducing the negative environmental impact of their activities, as well as among suppliers by training them to reduce the negative environmental externalities that their activities can generate.

The second form of organizational innovation that Decathlon has also developed effectively combines a technological product and process innovation with an organizational innovation. It is therefore an integrated technological innovation with no direct link to the environment, as in the case of the Arpenaz 10 Quechua backpack (Decathlon 2014, p. 23) for hiking (Table 8.6).

This bag is produced with a single seam, and the process used is based on a folding technique that allows it to be made with only two pieces of fabric that are then sewn into one piece. This hybrid societal innovation based on CSV has a positive impact on the environment and, by generated effect, reduces raw material use, water consumption, manufacturing time (less energy consumption) and increases the quantity of bags to be transported in a truck (fewer transport routes, etc.). It offers comfort to the customer (positive social impact) while reducing costs (improved competitive advantage).

8.3.2.2. *Service-based organizational innovations*

Organizational innovations can also have an impact on the reduction of negative environmental externalities generated by product- and production-related "service" activities.

Four types of service-based innovations are likely to directly or indirectly increase the use and better end-of-life treatment of products (Table 8.7).

The first type of service, called "Trocathlon", is a free activity which is especially dedicated to second-hand products. It allows Decathlon customers to drop off certain sports items that have already been used (skis, bicycles, fitness or riding equipment)[6] at its stores. This service thus feeds the second-hand products sector and encourages the recycling of used components. The owners of these products then have a strong chance of selling them and recovering the full price of these repaired products, knowing that no commission is asked of them. Decathlon also mobilizes its expert staff to check equipment safety points upstream, better present sports items, help define the price and support sales. The products are then displayed in tents set up outside stores in the car parks. The "barter" system is an action which is part of a form of collaborative and circular economy and has a triple positive impact. The first is of an environmental nature: longer use of the product and reduction of "solid" waste through the recycling of certain components (circular economy). In addition, support at the end of product life can also be provided by joining the various eco-organizations (recycling channels for the various products on sale in French stores), by collecting and recycling hunting cartridges in stores, etc.

6 http://www.oxylane.com.

The second impact is of a social nature. It is a question of giving purchasing power back to customers who can thus acquire another new product by paying in part with "Decathlon vouchers". The third impact, for Decathlon, consists of creating a competitive second-hand sports goods market. This advantage is the result of differentiation based on products that are still in good working order and meet the expectations of a market segment consisting of people with limited means who can buy cheaper second-hand sports goods in this way.

Types of innovations	**Features**	**Types of positive environmental externalities**
Trocathlon	Deposits by customers of second-hand products (bicycles, skis, fitness and riding equipment, barely or no longer in use). Double sales per year: third week of October and March	Longer use of the product, reduction in solid waste
Corrective actions	Repair, destruction, management of in-store product recalls	Extended product life, recycling of used products
Eco-cheques	Bicycles, bicycle accessories, maintenance	Energy savings, sustainable mobility
Encouraging customers to take action	Fostering respect for the environment among customers	Participation in "Vital sport" sporting events: practicing sport, discovering the richness and fragility of the environment
	Development of the eco-cheque principle	Possible purchases of certain green products (bicycles, their accessories, services)

Table 8.7. *Service activities and positive environmental externalities*[7]

The second service is based on a set of corrective actions allowing certain products to extend their useful life. To this end, customers are invited to bring back or return their defective products to Decathlon stores. The goal of this action is also

7 *Idem*.

to remove those faulty items and to recycle them. In 2014, the corrective actions put in place made it possible to reduce negative environmental externalities by repairing items (10%), destroying others (5%), managing customer recalls in stores (5%) and returning items to warehouses (80%). Of the items returned, 50% were destroyed, 25% were repaired and 25% were returned to suppliers. Thus, out of 800 million items sold, 180 quality corrective actions concerned 3 million products, that is, 0.375% (the products concerned are those belonging to Decathlon brands and other international brands). The repair activity can have a positive impact on the environment because it limits the number of products thrown away, while improving understanding of how products work – to discourage customers from returning them to store – by making a website[8] for the Passion brand and making Oxelo's YouTube channel available to customers to ensure they can make better use of these products.

The third type of "service" innovation concerns the implementation of an "eco-cheque" policy. The eco-cheque is a benefit in kind, in the form of vouchers for the purchase of environmentally friendly products and services. In the case of Decathlon, customers can purchase bicycle products and other accessories and services related to bicycles[9]. The list of products and services that can be purchased with eco-vouchers is updated every year.

Finally, the fourth service is related to the organization of sporting events. In 2014, 622 "customer–actor" events were organized in France, with the participation of 190 stores (Decathlon 2014, p. 36). For example, the Vital sport event is based on a dual concept: enabling customers to discover and learn about different sports disciplines and respect for the environment. To this end, the organization of *La Belle Rando* allows customers who are travelling to discover their local natural environment, its richness and fragility, with guides. It is also an opportunity to strengthen the links between Decathlon and local sports associations.

8.4. Environmental innovations related to site construction and operation

The construction and operation activities of the sites in the Decathlon network are linked to sales stores, warehouses, international headquarters, brand sites, offices for basic functions (production, sales, marketing, etc.) and buildings for support activities (human resources, procurement, R&D, etc.). These activities are sources of negative environmental externalities and are also affected by specific innovations

8 http://support.geonaute.com/.
9 http://www.decathlon.be/community/fr/Ntre-entreprise/use-your-eco-checks-check-decathlon/.

capable of reducing these externalities. In 2014, Decathlon will have 44 warehouses and 884 points of sale, 103 of which will be created in the same year. Three categories of organizational innovations developed by Decathlon must reduce these negative externalities resulting from the failure to optimize energy, the consumption of water and reduction of waste.

8.4.1. *Organizational innovations related to energy optimization*

In 2014, average energy consumption of a store was 145.5 kWh/m^2/year while the average energy consumption of a warehouse was 71.2 kWh/m^2/year (Decathlon 2014, p. 39). This consumption can be optimized by using four types of organizational innovations. The first concerns driving forward and providing information on the importance of this optimization by conducting an awareness campaign among employees of various Decathlon stores, located in the same country. This is aimed at creating a collaborative network to synergistically exploit their skills in order to reduce the negative externalities produced by energy consumption. This is the case, for example, of a Decathlon employee in the UK who has built a network of "Green Keepers" to provide local stores with solutions that can reduce this consumption.

The second type is the development of an energy management process. The aim is to ascertain the level of energy consumption, in real time, in order to allow employees to be alerted when consumption peaks. Decathlon Italy is thus gradually equipping its stores with this technology, enabling the alerted employees to be reactive.

The third type of innovation consists of integrating the environmental dimension at source, in other words, from the very beginning of the construction project for new stores, warehouses and production sites, by certifying them High Environmental Quality (*Haute qualité environnementale* or HQE). Since 2011, every new building constructed (including stores and warehouses) has been certified HQE. In November 2014, a new international base camp to house the mountain brands Quechua, Wed'ze and Simond was inaugurated in Passy in the heart of the Mont Blanc valley. The HQE label has targeted landscape integration as a priority, with 66% green spaces and green links for bicycles and pedestrians. Site management included optimizing energy performance (large triple-glazed openings, insulation, natural light) with a choice of environmentally friendly materials, optimizing water management, recycling 100% of construction site waste, etc. The project was managed in accordance with the HQE label. To further reduce GHG emissions, two new warehouses were certified (BREEAM certification is the longest-established system for assessing and certifying the environmental performance of buildings), in 2014 in Rouvignies, France (HQE) and Betonka,

Russia making a total of five certifications. In 2014, 9.21% of the square meters of owned and operated stores were certified, that is, 35 sites[10], representing 6.47% of the m² and 24 more sites than in 2013. Decathlon also uses renewable energy sources in France, such as wind power (Calais) and solar power (Istres), while in Belgium, five stores are equipped with solar panels covering between 20% and 25% of each store's energy needs. In addition, Decathlon designs LED signs that reduce energy consumption by a factor of five.

Finally, the fourth type of organizational innovation concerns the implementation of corrective actions to modernize existing facilities such as air conditioning and heating equipment, thus reducing their consumption. These include, for example, the replacement of old rooftops (monobloc air conditioning and heating) with High Energy Performance (HEP) type units or the use of free cooling. Free cooling consists of cooling the building without air conditioning by using the outside air during the day, the temperature of which is lower than that of the inside air, and at night by evacuating the heat stored during the day. These various organizational innovations reduce greenhouse gas emissions by optimizing energy consumption (positive environmental impact) in sales outlets and other buildings. They also have a positive social impact for employees and customers (cooling of buildings without air conditioning) and a reduction in the cost of energy consumption that can be passed on to customers in the form of lower prices, all while improving the group's image and thus the competitive advantage of the group's products.

8.4.2. *Organizational innovations related to waste and water*

Decathlon Group has identified four types of waste generated by its own sales stores and warehouse sites: sorted paper and cardboard (48%), mixed waste (46%), sorted plastics (3%) and others (wood, scrap metal, textiles, etc.) (3%) (Decathlon 2014, p. 41). To reduce and recycle all these wastes, Decathlon has implemented three forms of organizational innovation. The first concerns the internalization of waste sorting and recycling operations that lead to waste being transformed into raw materials as components of new products or given a second lease of life. By 2011, 90% of stores would be sorting cardboard waste, with 42% sorting plastics and recyclable bicycle containers. In Western Europe, Decathlon Belgium has developed the most efficient waste management by sorting 75% of these three types of waste and also by recovering aerosol cans, inner tubes and metals. In Russia, the certified warehouse in Betonka has the highest waste sorting rate (98%) of all its stores. As a result of these various actions, the sorting rate in stores, and especially in

10 This number was re-evaluated at the end of 2014 (Decathlon 2014, p. 39).

warehouses, increased sharply, by 56% and 46%, respectively, in 2013 and 2014, and by 86% and 88% in 2013 and 2014 (Decathlon 2014, p. 42). The second form of innovation is part of an awareness campaign for employees and customers to reduce waste. Thus, at the entrance to French stores, several bins are used to sort batteries and electrical and electronic waste, which Decathlon then sends to sites equipped to recycle them properly (Decathlon 2014, p. 42). In October 2014, the proceeds from the cash bags from Decathlon stores in Spain enabled the financing and organization of a beach clean-up campaign to raise awareness of environmental issues among customers and employees. It also presents an opportunity to create partnerships with local institutions, such as the Ministry of Sustainable Development and other associations. Finally, the third form of organizational innovation is linked to increased construction of multi-storey car parks and concrete store floors that reflect light. These innovations limit maintenance costs (no need to change carpets, savings on cleaning), reduce urban sprawl and the consumption of arable land, and preserve landscapes. The optimization of water consumption management is the result of two types of organizational innovations. The first concerns the effect that the construction of multi-storey car parks can have by limiting the number of waterproofed surfaces, in order to reduce the amount of rainwater to be managed by the community if it links to the public network or Decathlon sites themselves. The second results from the installation of green roofs allowing rainwater to be recovered by means of two tanks of 20 m^3 each, to supply the toilets and automatically supply water to certain stores.

The various organizational environmental innovations in the optimization of energy, water and waste reduce negative environmental externalities and can also be a lever for competitive advantage for the company. Indeed, despite the lack of impact of these innovations on the intrinsic qualities of the products and their lack of visibility for the customer, they can nevertheless bring two benefits to the company. The first relates to the reduction of unit costs due to the reduction in water and electricity consumption and the recovery of certain waste as product components. The second benefit results from the various positive environmental externalities that can be generated by these innovations which, through their induced effect, can improve the "environmental" image of the company as an institution.

8.5. Environmental innovations related to transport

Storage and transportation of products are two important activities in the commercial development of a sporting goods company like Decathlon. Transportation-related activities are a major source of GHG emissions. In fact, in 2014, 26% of these emissions resulted from customer travel (17%), employee travel (3%) and product transportation (6%) (Table 8.4). In the same year, CO_2 emissions per item delivered in Europe (transported from the country of production to the stores) amounted to 353 g. Two categories of organizational innovations have been identified based on the actions that Decathlon Group has developed to reduce these emissions: organizational innovations aimed to bring the sites in the Decathlon network closer together and the substitution of modes of transport.

8.5.1. *Organizational innovations related to site reconciliation and packaging design*

The first organizational innovation is based on bringing together Decathlon's production sites, its suppliers, distributors and customers, and is a major source of GHG emission reductions. This reduction is the result of optimizing the distances traveled by people (customers, employees) and trucks transporting goods (products, raw materials, etc.) as well as fuel consumption, tire wear, etc. For example, to reduce emissions from stores located in Russia, local employees have adapted their logistics network to the geography of the country, which has seven time zones and no less than 1,000 km between the Moscow distribution platform and Decathlon stores. Thus, to optimize the route and transportation time for products, regional platforms have been opened near the most distant stores and loaded trucks leave from Moscow to reach them. In 2014, this type of organization made it possible to reduce distances traveled by 1 million km, that is, 1,500 t of CO_2 not released into the air (Decathlon 2014, p. 43). The second organizational innovation is based on the design of packaging boxes that optimize truck loads and the storage of certain products. For example, the Decathlon research team has worked on a new way of assembling B'twin bikes which involves changing the size of the cardboard boxes used: these are smaller, not as tall and therefore easier to handle. This new design has made it possible to transport 50% more bikes in the trucks, which means more items can be shipped per m^2, and therefore, the number of trucks and journeys can be reduced (Decathlon 2014, p. 44). The average loading rate per truck between large import and distribution warehouses is therefore 49.05 m^3 or 12,504 items per truck. Decathlon was able to ship 1,259 items/m^2 in 2014 compared to 1,165 items/m^2 in 2013. In Zaragoza, the warehouse increased from an average filling rate per truck of 49 m^3 to 52 m^3 in 2014, representing a 7.6% increase on the previous year (Decathlon 2014, p. 44). In France, the Bouc-Bel-Air warehouse and the stores in its distribution area have innovated in terms of the height of truck loads, enabling them to carry 40% more boxes. The stores have invested in trolleys to load more boxes, and logistics organization has been reworked by reusing containers such as plastic bins for transporting goods. Optimizing the transport and storage of items in the warehouses has a positive impact on the environment (reduction of GHG emissions) and is a source of competitive advantage for Decathlon, as a result of the improvement to the quality of its environmental image and a sharp reduction in transport and storage costs.

8.5.2. *Organizational innovations related to modes of transportation*

Transport is an intermediate consumption service and is an auxiliary to production activity; the demand for transport can only be understood in relation to the nature of the mode of production activity, in particular its technical and spatial structure (Didier and Prud'homme 2007). Freight transport consists of two modes: oversea and overland. Overland transport corresponds to all land transport modes, that is, road, river and rail. It is often intended for intracontinental freight transport and has developed considerably since the opening of borders in Europe. Oversea transport concerns international maritime and air transport. It is intercontinental, and its flows are controlled through hubs where goods transit. The choice of transport mode that optimizes the reduction of GHG emissions depends on the transport infrastructure developed by the countries in which Decathlon's stores and warehouses are located, its suppliers and distributors, and the ability to develop alternatives to road transport. For example, in countries where infrastructures exist that can accommodate multimodal platforms, Decathlon sets up "large import" warehouses. In Europe, 11.5% of products are transported by train or barge[11]. In 2015, Decathlon will have two logistics platforms in Spain and four in France, two of which are located in the Nord-Pas-de-Calais region (Rouvignies and Dourges). Rouvignies (specializing in the logistics of small-volume items, particularly textiles) was established in 2013 and is Decathlon's largest continental multimodal platform, delivering to 23 of the group's regional warehouses throughout Europe. This platform, which also boasts an e-commerce activity (7% of the group's total business), has become an e-commerce zone in Houplines for high-volume items such as fitness equipment or bicycles that were previously outsourced to a Belgian service provider. Rouvignies was chosen because of its strategic geographical position for logistics activity. Indeed, its location on a site of almost 20 hectares, as well as its proximity to ports and motorways, allows the products of suppliers (India, Sri Lanka, China and Thailand) to be delivered by sea, and for Decathlon products to be delivered by motorway[12]. In addition, if the Seine–Nord Europe Canal were created, the group would eventually consider making deliveries by inland waterway too, in order to meet the need for additional logistics capacity to better cover Northern Europe. For logistics flows coming from Asia, Decathlon has long worked with a shipping company committed to a continuous improvement model, in order to benefit the environment. The shipping company has done this by investing in a fleet of boats that will reduce its fuel consumption and by communicating its environmental performance to Decathlon every year. In Russia, in order to reduce the negative environmental impacts generated by the activity of transporting items from the production area to the distribution area, Decathlon has chosen (for certain

11 Post-carriage from the port to the large import warehouse; three out of seven warehouses are located near the ports.

12 *Le Journal des Entreprises*, Nord-Pas-de-Calais, 2 December 2014.

Quechua brand products) to use the Trans–Siberian Railway, which connects Russia from Asia to Europe and is seven times less damaging to the environment than air transport and is twice as fast as boat transportation. These alternative innovations also serve to reduce GHG emissions and transport costs, which can translate into a competitive advantage in terms of price. Decathlon also uses other levers to reduce these emissions. For example, Decathlon stores reserve parking spaces for carpooling in order to reduce the number of cars for shopping (Wallonia, Belgium); they recruit salespeople living close to their workplace (Grenoble); and they encourage the use of carpooling and self-service bicycles (Villeneuve d'Ascq) and so on. These various transport-related organizational innovations have been able to significantly reduce the environmental impact of products delivered to stores in Europe (Table 8.8).

Nature of evolution	g CO_2/art (2013)	g CO_2/art (2014)
From production countries to Europe	323	232
Large-scale import warehouses (Europe) to distribution platforms	101	49
From distribution platforms to stores (European scope)	84	72
Total	508	353

Table 8.8. *Environmental impact of products delivered in Europe in g CO_2/article (Decathlon 2013, 2014)*

8.6. Main positive impacts resulting from the various environmental innovations

The first impact of the innovations developed by Decathlon Group corresponds to the increase in sales of eco-products. Between 2010 and 2014, the growth of these sales was 7.2% (2010), 9.4% (2011), 10% (2012), 10.5% (2013) and 10.3% (2014) (Decathlon 2014, p. 25). If these sales are explained by conscious purchasing actions by customers, they are evidence of the existence of a demand which is responsive to eco-products. To ensure that customers can enjoy their products for as long as possible, Decathlon uses its network of 1,000 workshops around the world, and 20 regional workshops in Europe, to provide a wide range of after-sales services (maintenance, repair, customization). In 2016, its workshops became omnichannels by providing access to spare parts and components via their website (Decathlon 2016, pp. 64–65). The second impact is on customer satisfaction, which is proving to be consistently high. In fact, two surveys were conducted in 2015 and 2016 by the group, soliciting customer opinions on four criteria (customer service, recommendation rate, satisfaction rate, negative evaluation rate), using scores out of 5 or percentages (Table 8.9).

Evaluation criteria: scores or %	**2015**	**2016**
Customer service	4.42/5	4.38/5
Referral rate	92%	91%
Satisfaction rate	88%	89%
Negative valuation rate	6%	6%

Table 8.9. *Assessment of the level of customer satisfaction (2015 and 2016)*

The various CSV-based innovations for the three activities that are at the root of strong negative environmental externalities thus show the ideal facet of Decathlon Group's activity: generating attributes based on improving the intrinsic quality of its products (improving the company's financial performance), while creating collective benefit (general interest) and improving the company's environmental performance (Porter and Kramer 2011; Pfitzer *et al.* 2014).

PART 3

Analysis of Social Innovation Strategies Based on CSV and their Impact on the Company and Society

Introduction to Part 3

In the past, companies were rarely considered actors of social change, but with CSR, social practices have become real opportunities to create shared value (CSV). In other words, to reduce the negative social externalities produced by their activities, or to produce positive externalities while strengthening product differentiation through social attributes that improve their competitive advantage and stakeholder relationships (Gasmi 2014, 2017). The correlation between social progress and commercial success is becoming increasingly marked. Thus, if companies, regardless of their size or sector, do not take into account social issues within their general strategy, if their activities produce negative social externalities that they try to ignore, or if they do not produce positive externalities, they may expose themselves to a major risk in terms of their company image. This risk can also be costly in terms of profit, turnover, etc., as these companies may become a prime target for NGOs and the media. This is the case, for example, with Nike, against which several lawsuits have been brought by human rights activists on the working conditions in the factories of its subcontractors, known as sweatshops (Gasmi and Grolleau 2005). Limiting the integration of the acceptable dimension of corporate behavior to external stakeholders (customers, suppliers, the state, NGOs, etc.) is therefore, according to Dupuis (2007), only "an instrument of stakeholder theory focusing on the institutional dimension of the company". The company should therefore not develop innovations just to satisfy market stakeholders (consumers, investors, etc.). It must also expand them for the benefit of employees and, as Kramer and Pfitzer (2017) point out, it must stimulate progress in all regions of the world, in order to contribute to a decrease in poverty, pollution and disease, and thus to an increase in collective benefits for society. The treatment of social issues must be seen solely as a CSR issue, and must therefore be approached with strategic tools, as opposed to using a philanthropic approach (Porter and Reinhardt 2007). The study of social innovations and the impact they can have, in terms of creating shared value, is based on a research article published in 2017[1]. Social practices are defined as a set of actions or innovations undertaken to directly or indirectly reduce negative social impacts and/or maintain or improve the quality of life of employees, their families and society at large (Johnson *et al.* 2014), or to create economic models capable of offering products to poor populations. To provide an overview of the relationship between social innovations (organizational and institutional) and social transformations, it is necessary to consider at least two fields of research, that of economic development and that of social development, where the notion of innovation has become inescapable, mainly since the 1980s (Kline and Rosenberg 1986; Osborne 1994). The reference to the term innovation, which is one of the "most widely used words", means it has become the "bearer of a positive outlook" (Cros 2002) and that it corresponds not only to the transition from one development model (in crisis) to another emerging one, but also to one of the specificities of this new model. Formerly, innovations were seen and negatively perceived as a source of "creative destruction" with regard to jobs (Rogers 1995). In the field of science and technology, and subsequently in the field of economic development, innovations have become established in research and public policy, mainly through the notions of innovation processes and systems (Lévesque 2005). Today, according to this author, the almost constant reference to innovation is not a simple fad (transition), but a model, one of the most striking characteristics of which is that it makes relatively constant and continuous use of innovation in both economic and social development.

This section, which deals with social innovation, represents the second pillar of CSR, and focuses on organizational and managerial innovations that are likely to provide social responses to the legitimate expectations of certain key stakeholders within a company. Social innovations are synonymous with the creation of social value by responding effectively to society's needs in terms of health, nutrition, assistance to an ageing population, housing improvements, etc. (Porter and Kramer 2011). This concerns all populations as a whole – regardless of age or whether they have a decent income – as well as company employees.

1 Gasmi, N. (2017). Innovations sociales et création de valeur partagée au sein des entreprises. *Vie & Sciences de l'Entreprise*, 204, 96–112.

9

Foundations of Social Innovations for Consumers

A company can practice different forms of social innovation in order to create shared value for itself and for some of its various stakeholders: low-income consumers, poor populations, populations with decent incomes and so on.

9.1. Social innovations for low-income consumers

Aware that a low-income clientele exists, many companies have invested in business models capable of satisfying their needs, by creating low-cost, lower-quality products and services. Historically, the low-cost model was born in Germany, at the end of World War II, with the creation of the Aldi chain of stores. It then developed in the 1970s in the United States in the air transport sector with Southwest Airlines, then in Europe in 1995 with EasyJet, as a result of the deregulation of European airspace. This made it possible to reduce prices in order to attract customers for whom the cost of air travel was unaffordable (Ben Slimane and Di Cioccio 2013). It has spread to sectors as different as the automobile, retail banking, insurance, fitness and distribution sectors, among others (Ben Slimane and Di Cioccio 2013). This is the case with Lidl for distribution, Kiabi and Primark for textiles in Europe and Market Basket for distribution in the United States. Similarly, Free offers a low-cost service that Xavier Niel, the company's founder, describes as a social service, since it is based on lower communication network access costs and helps contribute to the reduction of social and informational inequalities.

Objective	Maximizing profits through better access to goods and services	
Value proposition		
Choice of beneficiaries	**Quality of goods and services**	**Scope of the offer**
All consumers can purchase the low-cost offer.	Lower than that of the traditional model of the company, in order to avoid a cannibalization effect of its market shares compared to the traditional offer.	Goods and services offered at low prices.
Sources of offer value		
Terms and conditions and motivation	**Partnerships and reputation**	**Innovations**
Terms and conditions: reconfiguration of the value chain production to reduce costs. Motivation: absence of employee motivation within the company.	Partnerships: possible co-creation with for-profit organizations. Reputation: potentially quite damaged.	Product-oriented innovations.

Table 9.1. *Key features of the low-cost model (Yunus* et al. *2015)*

In the car industry, the majority of manufacturers have produced low-cost cars, such as the Volkswagen Beetle, the Mini Cooper, the Citroën 2CV and the Renault Logan. For these manufacturers, these products are designed for the so-called "budget" markets. The low-cost model is considered the most widely used strategy for fighting poverty effectively and represents a phenomenon of sustainable consumption (Bourcieu 2013), characterized by unprecedented growth that should continue in the coming years (Rivière *et al.* 2017). It refers not only to a commercial or production strategy, but also to a business strategy (Lendrevie *et al.* 2009). It is based on a number of specific features such as the simplification of supply (reduced quality), price reduction and thus a lasting and drastic reduction in costs (Table 9.1). The firm must then necessarily take these specific features into account by rethinking its approach to markets and its value chain so that it can control the reduction in costs, thus leading to a significant and lasting drop in sales prices. The low-cost positioning is based on the triptych of cost advantage, volume and differentiation strategies for products and services, and oversimplification by stripping them of all their secondary attributes in order to focus on a simple but necessary value promise for the customer. For companies that are able to articulate these three elements, the value created by differentiation necessarily involves a balance between the low costs it has generated and the positive perception that customers have of the value that the offering has created for them. The cost advantage is the linchpin of this business model's strategy. It therefore requires a company to develop organizational innovations or new ways of organizing the architecture of the activities of its business value chain, so that the operational efficiency of this chain is improved. The value chain comprises a succession of inter-organizational links of activities necessary to create an offer, from raw material suppliers to end customers (Johnson *et al.* 2014). Its operational efficiency is only effective if these activities are carried out in less time and with fewer inputs and costs than for traditional competitors (Porter 2015).

Drawing on the work of Rivière *et al.* (2017), four basic activities directly related to the product (supply) are involved: procurement, design, production and marketing. In the case of procurement, operational efficiency consists of reducing the number of suppliers, wholesaling orders and developing lasting and stable relationships with selected suppliers. With design activity, R&D spending is limited. For marketing and sales, the reduction in costs is due to the low price of supply, which plays a role in advertising and leads to a rationalization of marketing expenses with the involvement of customers, thus with the transfer of tasks. These transfers are specific to each field of activity. For example, in air transport, the tasks transferred by EasyJet are booking, ticket printing, free boarding, etc. Finally, for production, cost reduction can be generated by four strategies. The first concerns the strategies of rationalization and standardization of the means of production with the reduction of training, operating and maintenance costs, optimized use of resources, automation of production and therefore a reduction in personnel costs. The second is linked to an aggressive outsourcing policy (outsourcing of activities external to the core business). The third strategy involves relocation to countries where so-called "institutional" externalities are positive for the company in terms of cost reduction (low costs of wages, raw materials, energy, etc.). The fourth strategy consists of encouraging staff to be versatile and flexible. The low-cost approach has met with some success because it meets the high expectations of customers who want to have more for a lot less. It also acts as a challenge to traditional businesses by indirectly forcing them to justify their value proposition to customers. However, this model gives rise to abuses and controversies, as in the case of Ryanair, which is often accused of violating labor laws or receiving illegitimate airport subsidies. It would, however, be wrong to equate it with a pure gimmick based on failure to comply with the rules of law or on the short-sightedness of consumers. Paradoxically, low cost does not stand out by basing its model on low-cost production[1]. In fact, some other

1 E. Combe is Professor of Economics at the Skema Business School and Vice-Chairman of the Competition Authority. He wrote, "Low-cost is a great incentive to become more competitive" in *Le Monde*, Économie & Entreprise supplement, September Sunday–Monday 24, 2018.

companies also do so, such as smartphone operators (Samsung, Apple, etc.) and firms in the sporting goods industry (Nike, Adidas, etc.). Other companies offer discounts, price slashes and sales without these reductions being considered low cost.

Through the social role that low-cost model companies can boast, they conceal their primary purpose, which is the creation of value (profit) for the shareholder. This model is therefore exposed to an ethical dilemma. On the one hand, it certainly allows consumers with modest incomes to have access to low-cost and lower-quality products. On the other hand, it offers this type of product with an inevitably drastic reduction in costs, which is often achieved through poor working conditions and social dumping. In his work, Fletcher (2013) shows the perverse social effects of low cost. The author points out that "only 30% of the staff working for Ryanair, for example, are paid employees, which explains the difficulty in enforcing labor law and maintaining minimum social guarantees". Moreover, "the company is registered in the Irish Commercial Register, which makes it pay its social security contributions in Ireland. Dozens of different employment contracts are signed by sub-contracting recruitment agencies, mainly for the provision of services (for pilots). Ryanair has been convicted several times in France for 'concealed work', 'illegal employment of flight crew' and 'illegal lending of labo'". Other examples of perverse effects concern the companies Lidl and Free. In the TV program *Cash Investigation*, which was broadcast on France 2 on September 26, 2017, an investigation looked into the working conditions of the employees of these two companies. In the case of Lidl, conditions were very harsh and were even said to be harmful to their health: many of them were forced to take time off work due to tendinitis or back problems. They were also under constant pressure from their managers to meet the quotas imposed. Some employees "had to lift around 8 metric tons of parcels every day". One manager even resorted to humiliating discourse: "If I come and the store is badly run, I promise that you and I will see each other every week. It's going to be a bloody mess [...]. You're going to lose one to two weeks' pay a month because I'll lay you off for six days at a time and you're going to die". According to Moati[2], "We shouldn't be pleased that competition is driving prices down. The roll-out of discounted prices is conducive to household purchasing power that can hardly be based on income dynamics; the proliferation of discounted offers shows the exhaustion of a consumption model and the need to renew it". This author adds that it is more necessary than ever to reorient market offers in the direction of

2 P. Moati is Professor of Economics at Paris Diderot University and co-founder of the *Observatoire société et consommation* (ObSoCo). He wrote, "L'économie du prix cassé est aux antipodes des défis de notre époque" (the low-cost economy is the opposite extreme of the challenges we are facing) in *Le Monde*, Économie & Entreprise supplement, September Sunday–Monday 24, 2018.

"good consumption". "Low-cost has its place, but whoever sacrifices everything in order to cut costs concentrates the value proposition on essential useful effects and optimizes its production by eliminating unnecessary cost centers". To legitimize themselves, many large groups have tried to enter low-cost markets. However, these initiatives were quickly perceived as risky and harmful for them in terms of image. In 2008, Danone launched a range of low-cost yoghurts in France (eco-pack of six yoghurts for the price of one euro). The public's reaction was to suspect this group of wanting to make profit at the expense of the poor and Danone had to abandon this product range in 2010 (Yunus *et al.* 2015). To distinguish itself from low cost, which often focuses on innovations in design and processes, the social business model is part of an approach of disruptive innovation.

9.2. Social innovations for the well-being of the poor

9.2.1. *Characteristics of the BoP (Bottom of the Pyramid) social business model*

The issue of poverty does not just concern emerging countries, but developed countries too. In the United States, more than 15% of the population or 45 million citizens are officially considered poor by the Census Bureau. In Japan, they account for 16% of the population. In the European Union, more than 120 million citizens are considered to be at "risk of poverty or social exclusion" according to Eurostat data from December 2012 (Yunus *et al.* 2015). Often, it is government grants and subsidies and NGOs that try to provide solutions to the problem of poverty. The market theory approach can provide an alternative to such solutions. According to this approach, it is up to companies to take over by developing economic models that can significantly reduce poverty, while making a profit. Generally speaking, companies in developed countries are more interested in low-income populations using the low-cost model than in very poor populations. There was therefore a need to create social innovations based on socially responsible business models (social business) in order to offer products and services to markets that meet the needs of these poor people (Porter and Kramer 2011; Pfitzer *et al.* 2014). Prahalad (2004) suggests that major international groups should focus on the 4 billion people who live on less than $2 a day[3], otherwise known as the Bottom of the Pyramid (BoP). To this end, he proposes implementing social innovations to design products and services based on a price/performance ratio that can divide the prices corresponding to those in the Western world by 200. The concept of social business is different from that of traditional low cost. It has been developed in developing countries, with

3 The CSR-BoP investment is above all a response to vital social needs in the areas of health, malnutrition, water, electricity, communication, etc.

three fundamental characteristics that have the following objectives: a social impact that takes into account all forms of poverty, management that is similar to that of the company, which must therefore be sustainable and not make a loss, and profits made that are not paid to shareholders, but reinvested in the company or used for a possible reimbursement of the amounts initially injected by investors (Yunus *et al.* 2015). Social innovations associated with CSR-BoP are often the prerogative of large companies and consist of developing socially responsible investments (SRI) that target markets for people living in extreme poverty (Martinet and Payaud 2007; Porter and Kramer 2011; Pfitzer *et al.* 2014). These markets are often neglected as they are considered economically unviable.

Social business models only generate social returns on investment, and companies determine upstream which consumers are eligible for their offer. The target is very broad. This is the case, for example, with poor people who do not have a telephone (SFR), have a housing problem (Bouygues), are over 60 years old (Essilor), have to use their car to find or keep a job (Renault[4]), and poor families with a child aged between 6 and 24 years (Danone) (Yunus *et al.* 2015). Social business can also be the source of important positive opportunities that can generate long-term business benefits for the company. It is therefore part of a market-based approach that needs to repair the limits of modern capitalism, where the classical entrepreneur must also be a social entrepreneur. Thus, to think that "the market can reduce poverty is to believe that entrepreneurs and existing businesses must work to make capitalism inclusive, whereas today it only serves to exclude the poor, who are kept out because the offers of existing businesses and institutions are not adapted to their reality" (Ben Slimane and Di Cioccio 2013).

Interested companies therefore place their commitment in a strategic outlook which, according to Hamel and Prahalad (1989), does not consist of playing better than the competitor (low-cost model) but of changing games, to its advantage. Indeed, social business is concerned with offering quality products and services to avoid stigmatizing poor consumers; the latter are placed at the heart of the reflection and not the products, so the idea of profit is expressly discarded. Stakeholders, especially those in the soft power sector, have a positive perception of the approach of companies investing in so-called BoP markets and thus enable them to build new relationships of trust with those stakeholders. Social business is considered by the major international groups as an effective lever for investing in these markets

4 For example, Renault has chosen to work with the Wimoov associations, Fastt (*Fonds d'action sociale pour le travail temporaire*, French Social Action Fund for Temporary Work) and Udaf (*Unions départementales des associations familiales*, French Departmental Unions for Family Associations).

without them being suspected – by the public or NGOs – of being those that exploit poverty to make a profit. According to Payaud and Martinet (2010), "the role and effects of CSR-BoP question prejudices about poverty and the suspicion of a private contribution to the fight against poverty" (Table 9.2).

Objective	**Improving access to goods and services representing basic necessities according to a sustainable model**	
Value proposition		
Choice of beneficiaries	**Quality of goods and services**	**Scope of the offer**
The company that creates this type of social model determines the selection mode of the consumers concerned.	Identical to the traditional model in order to avoid stigmatizing poor consumers.	Goods and services offered at affordable prices.
Sources of offer value		
Terms and conditions and motivation	**Partnerships and reputation**	**Innovations**
Terms and conditions: reconfiguration of the value chain distribution to successfully reach the beneficiaries of the offer. Motivation: strong employee motivation.	Partnerships: co-creation is possible with associations whose objective is to provide social welfare. Reputation: strong positive image with soft power stakeholders.	Environmentally friendly and customer-oriented innovations.

Table 9.2. *Key features of the BoP social business model (Yunus* et al. *2015)*

Yunus *et al.* (2015) point out that "poverty is not created by the poor"[5]. CSR-BoP practices show the desire, willingness and ability of these poor populations to get involved in their local area. According to Pfitzer *et al.* (2014), to create companies that are both socially responsible and profitable, managers must take into account six mutually reinforcing elements: integrate a social objective, rigorously define the social need, measure the social and financial value, set up a semi-autonomous innovation structure specifically dedicated to social business, develop

5 Interview conducted by *Le Monde*, Économie & Entreprise supplement, November Sunday 5 and Monday 6, 2017.

partnerships with external actors (NGOs, local communities, etc.), capitalize on one of their historical activities and obtain government support. CSR-BoP social innovations can be technological or organizational in nature, and they depend on the positioning of the company in relation to the social issues of its sector. The managers of companies that make major advances in addressing these issues in a profitable manner are those who see them as their *raison d'être*, that is, they are part of their culture (Pfitzer *et al.* 2014). Within the range of for-profit CSR innovation strategies, Payaud and Martinet (2010) point out that "CSR-BoP appears to be the most advanced form".

9.2.2. *Analysis of different forms of BoP social business innovations*

Some practical insights into the effect that the social business model can have on poor people and the companies concerned are provided by three examples of innovations created by the major groups: Coca-Cola, Novartis and Nestlé. Secondary information conveyed by these innovations demonstrates the capacity of this business model to generate profit and proves its social role with regard to disadvantaged people (Pfitzer *et al.* 2014). The following three main factors explain the use of this information: it is difficult to access primary information to analyze the social business models developed by these companies; the raw information contained in the examples studied provides practical insights into BoP innovations and the effects they can produce to reduce poverty; and the author of this book wishes to structure the analysis of this information himself by giving it meaning (sense-making according to (Weick *et al.* 2005)), in terms of positive social externalities generated for poor populations and improving competitive advantage for these groups.

In the case of the Coca-Cola Company, in 2008, its subsidiary Coca-Cola Brazil launched the Coletivo initiative. After a six-month study, the group drew up a business plan that included collaboration with local NGOs. The project aimed to create training programs for young people in difficulty, focusing on retail and entrepreneurship. These programs would then work with a Coca-Cola distributor on specific improvements in inventory management, promotions and merchandising, with the ultimate goal of increasing Coca-Cola sales to the Brazilian middle classes (Pfitzer *et al.* 2014). This project,[6] launched in 2009, is a socially responsible, sustainable and profitable investment. More than 50,000 young people have been trained, 30% of whom have gone on to obtain their first job at Coca-Cola or at one of its distributor partners (small businesses or large corporations such as Walmart and

6 This project has since been extended to more than 150 low-income communities throughout Brazil.

McDonald's). For Coca-Cola, in two years, the volumes sold, and the profitability of this project was satisfactory (Pfitzer *et al.* 2014). This example shows that this form of innovation can generate three types of impact. The first is of a social nature; the semi-autonomous structure in charge of the societal project has created value for people in economic difficulty to access products adapted to their needs and has also enabled these people to get an education, a job, and beyond that, dignity. The second is related to the economic viability of this project by creating value for the company (profit). Finally, the third impact concerns the improvement of the public image that this type of CSR-BoP innovation can generate for the whole group to which this structure belongs. The improvement of the group's image is an intangible attribute that can only strengthen the differentiation of its products and thus its competitive advantage.

The second project, Arogya Parivar[7], was implemented in 2006 by Novartis in India. It aimed to provide essential medicines to millions of the poorest people in rural parts of the country who typically do not have access to healthcare. After conducting market research, Novartis selected medicines in 11 disease areas from its portfolio and set them at affordable prices (smaller packaging, fewer tablets) and then deployed a network of local distributors. To ensure a reliable supply, it recruited and trained hundreds of local educators to teach people how to improve their health and get medical attention. The success story of this initiative is of course due to lower prices, but also to the ability to effectively distribute the drugs to the targeted populations by developing partnerships with local distributors (Pfitzer *et al.* 2014). Given the scale of the investment required in relation to the low price level, it was decided that the Arogya Parivar project would be placed under the aegis of its social affairs group, which operates with seed funding from the parent company and has its own management and management procedures. As a result of this strategy, the project was profitable after 31 months, and 42 million Indians in 33,000 rural villages have benefited from Novartis medicines. The Coletivo initiative shows that investment in social business is a source of improved health for poor people and profit for the company.

Finally, the third case study concerns Nestlé, which in 2010 initiated a project on malnutrition in India. The group's researchers found that 70% of children under 3 years of age and 57% of women suffered from anemia. They visited 1,500 poor households to find out more about their eating habits and how they cook. As a result of this survey, Nestlé introduced innovations to improve the nutritional characteristics of Masala-ae-Magic and Maggi Rasile Chow products through a spice blend enriched with micro-nutrients (iron, iodine and vitamins). These

7 *Arogya Parivar* means "healthy family" in Hindi.

products, aimed at very low-income consumers living in the slums of Dharavi in Mumbai, are sold at the price of three rupees. This pricing policy, coupled with delivery-related innovation, has enabled Nestlé to sell 138 million of these products in the space of three years. Indeed, the group has used existing or newly created non-profit distribution channels to cover as many of the worst affected areas as possible (Pfitzer *et al.* 2014). This project reaffirms the economic and social role of the CSR-BoP model.

9.2.3. *Benefits and outlook of CSR-BoP*

These three examples show that innovations based on BoP social business can bring about four major benefits. The first is social in nature, as poor people can access quality products at low prices in a dignified way. The second is to enable the company to sell products that can generate profit and thus have the possibility of recouping the funds invested if it so wishes. The third relates to improving the social and public image of the groups within society in general. This improvement can strengthen the intangible differentiation of these products. The fourth concerns the motivation of employees who have a strong sense of belonging to groups that are not limited to the creation of value (profit) for the shareholder, but who are also interested in the benefits they bring to society, especially to poor populations. This motivation may also result from a strong sense of the usefulness of their participation in the creation of shared value, whereas they are often less involved when shareholder satisfaction is the only goal (Yunus *et al.* 2015).

Today, many global problems, ranging from inequality to global warming, are of such magnitude that solutions to address them require private sector expertise and scalability. When adopting strategies of shared value, companies inevitably encounter obstacles. None can act alone, as each is part of an ecosystem in which societal conditions may hinder markets and restrict the productivity of its suppliers and distributors. Public policies are also subject to their own limitations, while cultural norms exercise a strong influence on demand (Kramer and Pfitzer 2017). In order to make the most of the opportunities offered by the social business model, companies must place their societal strategies in a collaborative perspective, in other words, integrate the various stakeholders capable of playing a positive role, such as governments, NGOs, local communities, suppliers, competitors and experts (Kramer and Pfitzer 2017). This collaborative or co-creation approach enables companies investing in this type of social model to better identify and adapt their social innovation policy by providing concrete responses to societal issues. Thus, the Action Tank, created in 2010 by HEC, consists of the spheres of society/business/enterprise and poverty includes companies such as SFR, Essilor, Danone, Bouygues and Renault, which are led to work in partnership with associations to define consumer eligibility criteria (Yunus *et al.* 2015). Co-creation or co-innovation is part of an open approach to the manufacture of an innovative social strategy that consists of encouraging the company not to close in on itself, but to open up to other innovative ideas from its various stakeholders. Collaboration takes place at all stages of product design and/or distribution: defining the essential characteristics, choosing environmentally friendly materials and processes that reduce water, electricity and waste, reducing the drudgery of employees' work, evaluating the fairest prices, developing services (advice, training), etc. With this open approach, the implementation of societal strategies is part of an entrepreneurial approach in which market and social control stakeholders are considered as institutional entrepreneurs, and employees as intra-entrepreneurs.

9.3. Social innovations for all consumers

Among the diversity of social innovation strategies, two of them can provide specific effective responses to the nutrition needs of the general population and the health needs of people with disabilities. In the case of nutrition, the American group Dow Chemical introduced an innovation in 2005 that makes it possible to significantly reduce the negative social externalities generated by some of its products, while improving its competitive advantage. This group launched Nexera sunflower and rapeseed seeds, which are used in the production of cooking oils; these seeds boast three major advantages (Pfitzer *et al.* 2014). The first is that they produce twice the oil yield per hectare compared to soybeans. The second is related to improving the shelf life of these oils and their heat resistance, allowing client food companies to reduce their costs. Finally, the third advantage corresponds to the reduction of saturated fatty acid levels (lower than those of competing products) and the absence of trans-fatty acids. This type of social practice effectively creates two attributes of product differentiation (oils) that generate competitive advantage, and therefore financial performance for this firm. The first is a tangible attribute providing a private individual benefit to the customer (shelf life, resistance, cost reduction). The second is an intangible attribute stemming from the use of these seeds, which has a positive effect on society in terms of the related reductions in certain diseases (reduction in cholesterol, obesity, etc.) and, therefore, in social security expenditure. In this case, it is the social image of the company and, as an induced effect, that of the brand of its products that are valued.

In the healthcare sector, Winter and Govindarajan (2016) focus on creating a competitive product for emerging markets. According to these authors, a group of engineers from the Massachusetts Institute of Technology (MIT) in Cambridge, United States, found that 40 million people with disabilities worldwide, mostly in rural areas, are not equipped with wheelchairs. The engineers collaborated with local companies that manufacture traditional wheelchairs, as well as with users from emerging countries who presented their needs and criticisms. The subsequent wheelchair prototypes were tested in East Africa, Guatemala and India, and user feedback has led to the creation of the LFC (Leveraged Freedom Chair) which will be manufactured in India and offers several benefits. The LFCs allow fatigue-free travel of up to five kilometers per day over all types of terrain (good, rough, muddy, sandy), as they are propelled by two levers driven by the movements of the upper limbs, at different speeds depending on the position of the hands, so the users act as a power source and gearbox. The extended wheelbase between the front and rear wheels and safety straps at the feet and chest ensure personal safety. Their streamlined shape and reduced width make LFCs lighter for use in homes. Since some components are identical to those of a single-speed bicycle, maintenance can be carried out in any local workshop that sells bicycles. The price of LFCs is limited to about US$250; therefore, they can be purchased or subsidized by NGOs, government agencies, etc. Due to the success of LFCs, users in the United States and Europe have been interested in purchasing them. MIT has partnered with the Continuum design studio in Boston to use a reverse innovation that will allow the LFC (specific to emerging countries) to be perfected in order to adapt it to developed markets. The GRIT Freedom Chair was created also taking into account feedback from Western test users. An associated start-up, Global Research Innovation and Technology (GRIT), has been manufacturing it since 2015 and sells it for around $3,300 in the United States, less than half the price of competing products. The GRIT-FC has additional advantages, as it is more sophisticated (anti-corrosion coating, digital control), its movements and durability are improved, and the easy removal of the backrest, wheels and footrests with one hand makes it foldable so that it can be put into the trunk of a car. This case study is based on two synergistic innovations that generate four positive impacts. The first is associated with both tangible (improved seat quality) and intangible (improved image of companies as institutions) attributes that can increase the competitive advantage of their products. The second shows that the products designed are efficient and correspond perfectly to the expectations of people with disabilities in emerging and developed countries. The third offers these populations the possibility of moving freely inside and outside their homes. The fourth corresponds to their social dimension, that is, the reinforcement of the socialization of these populations, their autonomy, their possibility to work, etc.

10

Analysis of Various Managerial Innovations Likely to Motivate Employees to Engage in their Work

In recent years, the majority of companies have been developing social and environmental innovations to reduce the negative externalities induced by their activities or to produce positive externalities. Employees can be proud of their company when it implements social practices for its external stakeholders, but they will not understand why it does not invest in social innovations that can provide well-being to them and thus competitiveness to the company. This situation, which risks disrupting the cognitive equilibrium of employees, can generate tacit resistance by limiting their level of commitment to their work to the strict minimum of the formal contract. This rationalization (Joule and Beauvois 2014) is a psychological process that can lead employees to adjust their efforts to the detriment of the organization's interests. Chan Kim and Mauborgne (2014) show that this situation of rationalization is very prevalent in companies and point out that most executives (senior managers) admit that one of their major challenges consists of "bridging the yawning gap between the potential of the people (middle managers, employees) they lead and the talent and energy that these same people actually deploy at work". According to these authors, a study by the Gallup Institute entitled "State of the American Workplace" (2013) showed that 50% of employees are content to "just do their hours", while 20% express their dissatisfaction in a counterproductive way by negatively influencing their colleagues, by not coming to work or by driving away customers through their negligence. Gallup estimates that the latter costs the US economy $500 billion a year. The gap between the talent of these managers and the energy they deploy can result from the lack of a motivational environment that provides little or no incentive for them to engage voluntarily in their work. To avoid this rationalization situation, companies need to develop a set of specific complementary managerial innovations so that each of them can be a source of motivation to encourage employees to invest themselves in an optimal way in their work.

The first managerial innovations appeared in the 1980s, based mainly on Total Quality Management (TQM), using a set of tools, such as quality circles, among other things, and knowledge of human nature, assuming that employees will thus be able to do better quality work. Liedtka (2019), in a study of 50 social innovation projects, found that there is another approach, based on design thinking, which can get employees on board, involve them in the generation of ideas, release their creative energy, give them a sense of security and thus improve their work processes. Design thinking helps to eliminate prejudices and behaviors that hinder innovation. Drawing on the work of this author, three main steps are essential for successful social (managerial) innovation. The first step is to *define the challenges of the innovation* by finding the best solutions to the problems of employee motivation, reducing the risks and costs that it may entail, and obtaining the support and participation of employees in the ideation process. The second step concerns *managing resistance to change* by coaching employees at the beginning of this process so that they have no doubts or questions. Indeed, their actions are often habitual and difficult to change, so very clear safeguards are needed to help them. As there is no innovation without action, these employees must therefore feel psychologically secure to better participate in the ideation process in order to progress in a confident manner in discovering the positive contributions of the innovation that will meet their expectations. The third step is related to *the very process of idea generation*, in order to produce a managerial innovation capable of inducing motivation for employees to become voluntarily involved in their work. This process involves giving meaning to the innovation project, understanding its possible positive impact, and then identifying and selecting solutions that comply with the specific criteria for innovation.

This problem of managerial innovation is crucial in developed countries, as companies are increasingly faced with the need to move from a knowledge-based to a people-based economy. Over the course of the 20th Century, these countries moved from industrial to knowledge-based economies. The 21st Century is another pivotal period of transition towards human economies, which will have important consequences for the management of companies. According to Seidman (2018), human economies "are defined according to the type of work that individuals do in them; for example, the industrial economy replaced the agricultural economy when individuals left farms for factories; then, the knowledge economy moved them out of farms and into office buildings". Today, the value added by employees has also changed: instead of using their muscles, companies must instead use their brains. The know-how and analytical skills that used to make employees indispensable in the knowledge economy no longer give them an edge over machines.

Four different categories of managerial innovations can be developed by the company to motivate employees to get involved in their work and are complementary, likely to produce a synergy leading to positive internalities for the employees, an improvement in their performance and, therefore, in that of the company. The notion of internalities corresponds to the fact that an individual has a social value that has an internal explanation (Louche *et al.* 2006). The first category relates to management based on organizational ethics, the second category concerns the power that the higher purpose can have on the company, the third category relates to teleworking and, finally, the fourth category is about the role that feedback and respect can play in the process of motivating employees.

10.1. Social innovation based on organizational ethics and its impact on employee engagement

The notion of commitment must concern all employees and therefore constitutes a central lever in the process of appropriating management tools related to strategic decisions in daily practice (de Vaujany 2006). The theory of commitment (Kiesler 1971; Joule and Beauvois 1998, 2014) is often used to promote social change (Louche and Lanneau 2004), which is likely to create an interpersonal relationship of trust between the employees of a company and thus to encourage voluntary commitment to their work. Commitment could be described as the link that exists between the individual and his or her behavioral acts and a continuous, non-dichotomic variable (Kiesler 1971). According to Joule and Beauvois (2014), the notion of commitment implies two findings. First, only actions commit us: "we are not committed by our ideas, feelings, or inner self" but by our affective behaviors, and therefore by our actions that others can or could observe. Second, "one can be more or less committed through one's actions." The link between an individual and his or her behavior is not governed by the law of all or nothing: depending on the circumstances, one can be strongly or weakly committed. Commitment is not an internal psychological variable; it cannot be equated with professional involvement or attachment (Charles-Pauwers and Commeiras 2002). It is the product of situational conditions (Louche and Lanneau 2004), which are grouped into two categories: *size* and *reasons for the action* (Joule and Beauvois 1998). For the size of the action, strong commitment may result from certain key factors (Joule and Beauvois 1998, 2014; Girandola and Joule 2008). Indeed, an action performed in a public context that excludes any guarantee of anonymity is more engaging than an action performed in an anonymous context, even though it is explicit rather than ambiguous, when it is heavy in consequences or very costly (in money, time, energy, etc.). The reasons for the action correspond to the characteristics of the internal and external contexts in which the action is performed. External reasons associated with promises of rewards or threats of punishment disengage or distort the link between an individual and his or her actions, whereas internal reasons ("I behaved freely") tighten it (Joule and

Beauvois 1998, 2014; Girandola and Joule 2008). When an individual, responsible and free of their actions, decides to act, they activate a psychological pressure that will push them to try to accomplish what they have committed to (Gueguen *et al.* 2011). The internal reasons are linked to the determining role that the nature of the management practiced by the company can play.

10.1.1. *Foundations of organizational ethics*

"These foundations are based on guiding principles that must be timeless, have intrinsic value, require no external justification and represent the backbone of the company's fundamental ideology". Collins and Porras (1996) point out that "ideology defines the sustainability of an organization, i.e. a constant identity that transcends product or market life cycles, technological revolutions, industrial managerial trends or current leaders". Corporate ethics should respond to a need to moralize the company's employees (Postel and Rousseau 2008), to draw up a certain number of rules governing the conduct of individuals (employees) in order to distinguish between the right and wrong way of acting (Mercier 1999). The institutionalization of ethical values as a management mode is a strategy for legitimizing the company (Dimaggio and Powell 1983; Suchman 1995), both inside (employees) and outside (customers, etc.) the company. Internally, ethical values concern the behavior of members of the organization, and they may appear to be indispensable. It can also help to create a culture of trust between managers and employees (Mercier 2001a). They are a lever for creating meaning, unifying and making all of the company's messages consistent. The purpose of ethics is to define how the company should operate (Johnson *et al.* 2014) and to provide a framework for certain deviant behavior (dishonesty, partiality, conflicts, etc.) by members of the company (Weaver and Treviño 1999; Maxwell and Farmer 2013). Ethics is also recognition at work. The ethical discourse that promotes the idea that this recognition is a question of human dignity and social justice and not merely a question of organizational performance (Brun 2000) is a real lever for mobilizing employees to commit to their work. Ethical practices promote respect for the psychological contract that binds the employee to the company. A psychological contract refers to the set of beliefs that an individual develops, within the framework of an exchange agreement, between themselves and another individual or organization (Rousseau 1989; Morrison and Robinson 1997). This contract is defined as a set of tacit agreements between employees and managers of an organization, and, more specifically, of mutual promises and obligations between them (Robinson and Rousseau 1994). This contract therefore implies expectations that are not found in a formal employment contract (Lemire and Sabat 2005). The social influences likely to influence psychological contractualization are not limited. Frechet (2007) distinguishes two categories of influence: organizational culture and organizational justice. Organizational culture corresponds to "a set of postulates developed by a given group as they solve problems in terms of adapting to their external environment and internal integration" (Girard 2007). It is based on ethics and thus becomes a lever for HR management practices. These practices, which constitute a strategic internal resource, are important in the value creation and organizational process (Tremblay *et al.* 2005). The strategic role of these practices is their influence on employee mobilization. The choice of ethical values as a central component of the organizational culture comes into play in the composition of the psychological contract. At the same time, this choice positively influences organizational justice, and therefore the construction and appreciation of this contract. Typically, within the framework of organizational behavior, three types of justice are identified: distributive, procedural and interactional (Cropanzano *et al.* 2001). Distributive justice is perceived as material or socio-emotional retribution received by the employee; it is associated with fairness in the evaluation of allocation outcomes (Nasr *et al.* 2009). Procedural justice refers to the perceived processes that lead to a decision, while interactional justice refers to the quality of the treatment a person receives in their interpersonal relations with authority (Frechet 2007; Nasr *et al.* 2009). Both categories of influence have an impact on the way a person (employee) receives and interprets a promise (Thomas *et al.* 2003) from the hierarchy. The trust that can be generated by governance based on organizational ethics can strengthen the psychological contract of employees. This contract can be an intrinsic motivator for employees to engage in a process whereby they can make the most of their skills – a commitment that can only further enhance the financial performance of the company.

10.1.2. *Process for implementing management based on organizational ethics*

This success is conditioned by the involvement of middle managers, which is decisive and justified by four factors (Floyd and Wooldridge 1996). First, they are a potential source of information on *changes in the strategic position of the organization*. Their knowledge and experience of the realities of the organization and its markets is generally superior to that of most senior managers. Second, they *generate ideas about this type of management*, allowing them to select values and the ethical document as a management tool, owing to their proximity to the operational activities. Third, they can act as *translators of this document* by explaining to other employees how the document should be internalized in specific contexts in order to make it their own in their work. Fourth, their daily contact with employees or customers gives them the ability to *adjust the process of putting organizational ethics into practice*. The integration of middle managers and operational employees into this process is thus considered an ethical action. This process consists of conducting formal and informal discussions together on the meaning accorded to organizational ethics. These discussions should go from the individual (employee) to the organization and include sincere introspection to determine the values that are central to employees (Collins and Porras 1996). Values are first and foremost an individual and therefore deeply personal concept, whereas corporate values must be defined as a collective "object" and have the capacity to be constantly embodied by all the members of the company. Drawing on the work of Pfeffer and Sutton (2007), the ethical values to be chosen should not be based on truths considered inescapable or on preconceived ideas[1], but on proven facts. All businesses have an identity. This identity is not a pure managerial construction produced by the affirmation of values by senior managers or by communication managers. Rather, it is a narrative construction resulting from a narrative whose episodes are provided by real action (Reitter and Ramanantsoa 2012). The values to be chosen must therefore be linked to reality and to the facts experienced and felt daily by the company's employees, and also to a synthesis of the social, environmental and managerial activities actually practiced (or desired to be practiced) by the company. At a company level, values exist, even though the company has not developed any approach to formalize and communicate them. They are values that structure the behavior of employees without them being aware of it and represent informal daily ethical practices; a set of implicit ethical values shared until now within the company, resulting from a history and transmitted over time. Managers and operational employees should therefore not only focus on the formal dimension of ethics, which offers only a limited vision of organizational ethics (Hireche 2004), but should also take into account the informal ethics that are expressed in behaviors, which underlie relationships and which are also decisive (Mercier 2003). To do this, managers must recognize and identify the informal and formal work situations in which these practices apply and whether or not they pose problems. Taking these problems into account should not be neglected, because ethical practice also means taking into account gestures with others (Girard 2004), going beyond prescriptive discourse in favor of a practice committed to action. Values must not be subordinated to the injunctions of the communicating power generated by the words that are supposed to embody them. Rather, they must "mean" values with which all members of the company can identify, which are essential to their well-being: honesty, impartiality, transparency, social utility, trust, respect, etc. (Maxwell and Farmer 2013).

To enable the various exchanges to positively affect the attitudes of all company employees towards practical management based on ethical values, persuasive oral and/or written managerial speeches will be developed to help raise awareness of the internal and external advantages inherent in implementing this type of management. These arguments can be based on two techniques of influence: *legitimacy* and

1 In choosing values, truths considered inescapable and/or received ideas can, for example, correspond to the imperative of values to have a strong communicative power based on evocative words and a strong image.

rationality (Robins *et al.* 2006). Legitimacy-based arguments consist of discourses that explain the imperative for the company to build the legitimacy of its institutional identity – an identity based on reconciling social and environmental responsibilities towards its external stakeholders (customers, NGOs, suppliers, etc.), and on practical management through ethical values towards its employees. With persuasive rationality, these speeches must convey logical arguments and factual evidence of the benefits that this type of management can bring to employees. The function of the company's ethical values, when perceived by employees as credible, is to reduce internal conflicts and to give meaning to individual commitment and cooperation (Reitter and Ramanantsoa 2012), etc. Thus, if middle managers believe that the arguments of the persuasive rational discourse presented are correct, they will adhere to the company's project (ethical values as a mode of management) (Dupré 2014) and will find it easier to convince their subordinates to adopt these values in their daily practice. These values can, for example, be a synthesis of ethical practices in human resource management which, according to Tremblay *et al.* (2005), are related to hiring, development and management of competencies, reward practices, sharing and transparency of information. They will only be operational if they are set out in an ethical document[2] such as a code of ethics. This code should guide or facilitate the process of appropriation of practical management by values (de Vaujany 2006), and represents the rules, duties and obligations that govern the company's activity and serve to frame internal behavior in order to avoid any ethical conflict between the organization and its external stakeholders (Mercier 2000). To formalize this ethical code, managers can draw inspiration from the ethical documents developed by certain companies for their own reflection[3].

To facilitate its understanding and implementation by all employees, this code may be accompanied by written statements explaining the meaning to be given to each of the values summarizing management practices. For example, *ethical hiring practices* may be based exclusively on the criteria of competence, empathy and orientation towards others, pro-social values and avoidance of discriminatory criteria (ethnic origin, gender, physical appearance, etc.), yet also encourage internal promotions. For *skills development* and *management practices*, the company must show its willingness to establish a long-term psychological contract with employees. *Ethical practices of information sharing* and *transparency* encompass all

2 Various possibilities are available to the company when choosing the name of the ethical document: *credo*, ethical code, company project, rules of behavior, rules of conduct, code or guide of ethics (Mercier 2000).

3 In 1994, French companies such as Framatome, Groupe Lagardère and Renault organized their reflections by taking the example of the ethical policies of companies from English-speaking countries (Mercier 2000).

organizational practices used to disseminate information downwards and also receive information from below (Tremblay *et al.* 2005). This sharing plays two important roles in transmitting, clarifying and considering expectations (Rondeau *et al.* 1993). On the one hand, it is part of an organizational dialogue process. According to Groysberg and Slind (2014), this dialogue can be based on four attributes: *intimacy* (getting closer to employees to create emotional closeness), *interactivity* (promoting dialogue), *inclusion* (extending the role of employees) and *intentionality* (explaining decisions to obtain employee consent). On the other hand, this sharing can be perceived by employees as an act of trust by managers towards them.

Organizational ethics is, of course, a fundamental lever for getting employees to be committed to their work. But we must ensure that the words *ethical values* retain the intensity of their effect on a practical level. If these words have no effect on the behavior of senior managers, they have no substance, and since companies are political systems, hypocrisy would become inevitable at the level of all internal and external stakeholders and employee cynicism would increase. In this case, the assumption that individuals only act in their own self-interest applies to these hypocritical managers, who are perceived as such even when they put forward other motivations. However, a recommendation can reinforce innovations based on organizational ethics, which takes into account the need for sincerity by developing a higher purpose approach to the business. To this end, directors, investors, employees and other stakeholders are increasingly encouraging managers to propose a purpose that complements organizational ethics.

10.2. Managerial innovation based on the higher purpose of employee involvement and commitment

The second innovation relates to this purpose and can be complementary to organizational ethics, thus representing a source of motivation for employees by devoting their skills and energy to their work. Companies then tend to base their culture on the power that this higher purpose can exert on them. According to Quinn and Thakor (2019), "this purpose does not consist of developing a strategy that clearly defines how the company creates economic value, but it considers the positive consequences of the active involvement of employees in the company". It is intrinsic to the quality of working life (QWL). Companies often adopt a purpose in the wake of a crisis that forces top managers to question their ideas about employee motivation and performance, and to try out new approaches. However, it is pointless to wait for a difficult situation to happen before taking an interest in a potential objective aimed at improving QWL. The "cynical" transactional approach to employee motivation can overcome any major obstacles to adopting this purpose and thus make it part of a proactive approach. Drawing on the work of these authors, eight recommendations can help companies put a higher purpose into practice.

The first *challenges the classic approach embodied by agency theory*. According to economists, all employers are faced with the problem of the "principal–agent" relationship, that is, the company–employee relationship. The principal (employer) and the agent (employee) are bound by an employment contract. If the agent becomes unwilling (able to rationalize his or her effort) because of a perceived insufficient level of salary and supposedly inadequate working conditions, he or she will only provide a certain amount of work, that is, less than he or she is capable of. The effort represents a personal cost, and the agent will only exercise it in an optimal way if the principal puts in place contractual incentives and control systems that will counter the rationalization of his or her commitment to his or her work. The classic transactional approach therefore leads to a lack of optimal employee commitment, which is the opposite of the power that a higher purpose may have over these employees.

The second recommendation concerns the discovery of the nature of this higher purpose and the impact it can have in terms of employee commitment. This purpose cannot be invented, because it already exists, but it must be discovered by taking a real interest in employees, by empathizing with them, by feeling and understanding their deepest needs. This goal is not a matter of economic relations, but of a more ambitious managerial discourse, in order to better define how employees are going to invest themselves, to give meaning to their work and to arouse their willingness to become deliberately involved in the company. To better define this concept of a higher purpose, Quinn and Thakor (2019) conducted a study in the form of a survey by interviewing business leaders, including Gerry Anderson. When Anderson became president of DTE Energy[4], this purpose was not part of his process of developing a strategy defining how the company would create economic value, that is, making its objective of creating long-term value for its shareholders well known, because Anderson did not have a more ambitious vision. Prior to the financial crisis in 2008, surveys had shown that DTE employees were not very committed to their work – a finding that Anderson attributed to their inability to change their old habits, that is, to rationalize their intelligence and creativity. After the crisis, many companies realized that middle managers needed to be more involved. To find a viable solution to his problems, Anderson met Joe Robles, a member of the DTE board of directors, who took him on a tour of his group's call centers. He was amazed to discover positive and fully engaged employees working together and dedicated to their customers. Robles remarked that "the most important task of a

4 DTE Energy is a power generation company headquartered in Detroit, Michigan.

leader is to bring people in line with their purpose". Anderson then made a video that expressed the higher purpose of the company (Robles' idea) by showing some of the employees and managers in action and thus explained the contribution of all employees' work to the well-being of the community: workers, teachers, doctors and so on. The energy produced by DTE was needed by the company. The employees were the first to react positively by giving their CEO a standing ovation, and the unions were moved. In this way, they discovered that their work made sense. The higher purpose of the company is therefore to show that the company and the work done by the employees contribute to the needs of the community, customers, shareholders, etc.

The third recommendation corresponds to considering the *need for sincerity*. This sincerity becomes necessary when a company proclaims a purpose and values, whereas the words "ethics" or "organizational ethics" have no effect on the behavior of senior managers and sound hollow. Employees and other stakeholders may perceive their company as a political system where hypocrisy is inevitable and the purpose becomes harmful to them and the company.

The fourth prescription is therefore *transforming the sincere message into a permanent message* that explains the higher purpose of the company as long as the senior managers remain in place.

The fifth is related to *stimulating individual learning*. In classic economic logic, the motivational elements are external (sanctions, rewards); however, when the company adopts a higher purpose, managers gradually perceive that learning and progress become powerful drivers, because in a motivating environment, employees want to think, learn and evolve.

The sixth recommendation proposes *transforming middle managers into leaders driven by purpose*. It has a real impact, because motivating and involving employees requires middle managers who are fully aware of the company's purpose, support it and lead with it in a strong and moral manner. This approach goes beyond what the majority of companies expect from their managers with organizational ethics.

The seventh is *convincing employees of the major advantages of the purpose*. As soon as managers and supervisors have integrated the purpose of the company, they must help front-line employees to link it to their daily tasks by showing them that they are also part of the process. In this way, the purpose will better permeate the company's culture, which will be better able to shape behavior, even in the absence of managers.

Finally, the eighth recommendation deals with *liberalizing positive energies*. All firms have a pool of generally untapped agents of change that Quinn and Thakor

(2019) called *positive energy networks*. The people involved are talented, optimistic, purposeful, easy to spot and trustworthy. The role of these networks is to stimulate other employees and to support each stage of cultural change. The power of the company's higher purpose leads to positive results in terms of employee engagement in work and thus increased competitiveness for the company, but only if it is effectively communicated.

10.3. Social innovation based on teleworking and employee engagement

Work is recognized as fundamental for social integration. It is an opportunity to share experiences with other employees and to get involved in activities whose aims go beyond individual interest. Beyond its economic dimension linked to employment, "work makes it possible to acquire a social status that determines one's place in society, thus strengthening one's social identity" (Vézina *et al.* 2001). Work also promotes personal identity and development (self-actualization), which reinforces self-esteem and confidence in one's abilities (De Bandt *et al.* 1995). Socially active individuals have greater confidence in others and feel more in control of their environment, thereby strengthening the social capital of a community (Bélanger *et al.* 2000).

According to Bloom (2015), "to increase company productivity, more employees must be allowed to work at home". New information and communication technologies have enabled this form of work organization to become a viable alternative to traditional offices, reducing costs for employees (travel expenses) and for the company, while at the same time generating positive environmental externalities (Turetken *et al.* 2011). For example, in 2008, Deloitte LLP reduced its costs by $30 million by redesigning workspaces and reducing energy consumption by restructuring its offices to accommodate its mobile workforce (Meinert 2011). Similarly, the AT&T and IBM groups have implemented major teleworking initiatives that have led to savings of $550 million and $700 million, respectively, and to the satisfaction of employees choosing to telework up to three days a week (Nidumolu *et al.* 2009). The free use of telecommuting can have an effect beyond that of reducing GHG emissions and transportation costs. It can also be perceived by employees as an act of autonomy and responsibility and thus be an intrinsic motivator for voluntary engagement in their work. According to Berinato (2018), Nicholas, professor of economics, and Liang, co-founder of the Chinese online travel agency Ctrip, asked the volunteer staff of the agency's call center whether or not they wanted to work from home for nine months. Half of the volunteers were able to work from home while the other half were assigned to the office as a referral group. At the end of the study, the answers to the questionnaires and the detailed collection of each other's performance revealed that the teleworkers felt happier, more attached to the company and, above all, were more productive than those who stayed at the office. The company saved $1,900 per employee during this experiment. This author believes that one-third of the productivity improvement was induced by a calmer environment, which is more conducive to the accomplishment of assigned tasks (telephone calls), whereas in the office, employees are more distracted. However, if telework is imposed by the company, it can generate psychosocial risks, due to professional isolation and the high level of autonomy required. These risks may also manifest themselves in the form of uneasiness, intrusion of the professional sphere into the private and family sphere, etc. The combination of social innovation based on organizational ethics and innovation relating to voluntary work arrangements (teleworking) can strengthen the psychological contract leading to increased confidence in interpersonal relations between employees and their hierarchy. Employees with a well-established social life – who are older, married, etc. – tend to opt for teleworking.

10.4. Managerial innovation based on the role of feedback and respect in the employee motivation process

Folkman and Zenger (2018) conducted a feedback study to understand whether employees prefer receiving compliments or suggestions that might enable them to improve their work. They surveyed 899 people, 49% of whom were US residents, on their perception of feedback. Two categories of feedback emerged. The first is positive feedback consisting of compliments, encouragement or praise. The second is corrective feedback consisting of suggestions for improvement, encouragement to apply new or more effective methods, and remarks to highlight what has not been optimally achieved. The results of this study "show that a significant proportion of employees (57%) expressed a preference for corrective feedback while a minority (43%) said they preferred compliments or recognition". As for "feedback that could improve their performance and advance their career, 72% of participants opted for corrective feedback". Feedback is certainly perceived as a positive act; however, according to these two authors, the way of formulating it is fundamental. For example, *92% of employees accept negative feedback*, if it is adequately conveyed and if it is effective in helping to improve their performance. People who are reluctant to give negative feedback were found to be the least willing to receive it. "The correlation between a person's level of self-confidence and their preference for negative feedback is therefore quite strong". The perception of feedback also varies across generations. All participants are reluctant to give negative feedback, but Generation X is less opposed to it than Generation Y. In general, the need for feedback – positive or negative – increases with age. The conclusion of this study reveals a very clear paradox: "Most employees believe that constructive criticism is essential to their career development and want to receive it from their managers". However, managers are less motivated to engage in this type of exercise, even though their ability to give constructive criticism, especially corrective criticism, is a key factor in their leadership. Feedback is therefore perceived as a form of recognition by employees. This recognition can have a positive impact on these employees in terms of self-esteem, self-confidence, relations between colleagues, and in terms of attraction, proximity and interpersonal relations with hierarchical levels.

Brun and Dugas (2005) distinguish four types of recognition: *existential recognition* (being recognized as an individual), *work practice* (being valued as an employee capable of commitment), *investment in work* (making efforts) and *results* (performing tasks competently and producing results). Management by values also concerns the informational ethics that the company and its employees must have with its external partners (customers, suppliers, etc.). According to Porath (2018), "in order for company employees to be involved and committed, senior managers must show them respect, yet one employee in two does not feel respected". This author points out that, according to some studies based on secondary information, employees who are treated with respect by their managers are 56% more likely to say they are in good health and feel good, have 1.72 times more feelings of trust and security, 89% more pleasure and satisfaction at work, 92% more concentration and sense of priorities, and attribute 1.26 times more meaning and value to their work. Respecting employees means giving them the chance to learn and develop personally, to blossom and therefore to exist.

Spreitzer and Porath (2015) investigated the causes that lead employees to consistently high performance. They found that "happy employees produce more than unhappy ones, show up at work every day, are less likely to quit, go beyond what is expected of them, attract people who are as dedicated to their tasks as they are, are full of energy but know how to avoid burn-out [and] are described as long-term committed long-distance runners". To understand what it means to be happy at work, these authors and their research partners at the Centre for Positive Organizational Scholarship at the Ross School of Business looked at the factors associated with the performance of individuals in organizations. They found that the term most appropriate for employees who are happiest in their jobs is fulfillment. Fulfilled employees are not only satisfied and productive, but also participate in creating the company's future and their own. Across all sectors and all types of jobs, they perform 16% better overall (according to their managers), experience 125% less burnout than their colleagues (according to a self-assessment), are 32% more committed to their company and 46% more satisfied with their work. Thus, these researchers have identified two main components of fulfillment. The first is associated with "vitality", that is, the feeling of being alive, passionate and enthusiastic. Vital employees create energy for themselves and their colleagues. The second relates to "learning", that is, the personal development that can be cultivated by acquiring new skills. Learning can confer technical advantage and expert status, and set in motion a virtuous circle where employees who increase their skills are likely to believe in their personal development potential. These two qualities must be the source of a synergy of complementary skills, so one is unlikely to be sustainable without the other. To help their employees to develop, firms can offer four managerial recommendations: give employees the ability to make decisions, share information with them, minimize incivility and provide feedback on their performance.

Putting these four diverse managerial and organizational innovations into practice requires the creation of an environment that is tolerant of failure. The success of a managerial and organizational innovation mission capable of generating motivation for employees to engage freely in their work implies that it is likely to lead to a decrease in the waste of the company's resources and an increase in its productivity.

Conclusion

This book has attempted to provide a body of information and clarification on the need for leaders to develop societal strategies based on creating shared value (CSV). Despite the opportunities[1] offered by these strategies, many companies still ignore them today and continue to focus exclusively on the pursuit of profit. To meet these mega-challenges, all players in society at large must act together, especially those companies that have the financial, material and innovative capacity to fundamentally redefine their strategies, activities and business philosophy, capable of creating shared value in order to prosper.

In the field of theory, certain levers can motivate companies to develop societal strategies based on CSV. Thus, companies with a strategy and activities linked to a proactive societal approach understand how climate change and potential resource scarcity affect their entire value chain, and will be better prepared to stay ahead of their competitors and contribute to building a more prosperous world. CSR practices associated with a contractualist vision promote these strategies, as they have the capacity to strengthen the competitive advantage of companies while reducing the negative social and/or environmental externalities produced by their activities, or producing positive externalities. One incentive lever corresponds to improved relations with socio-political stakeholders (soft power and hard power) and another to securing the company's competitive position in imperfect markets. In addition, an overriding strategic role can be played by the elements of an ecosystem to make companies more resilient, more inclusive and create sustainable shared value with approaches based on vision, the societal project and partnerships (Winston 2017). However, companies must remain the main actors in their CSR programs, as only they can understand their capacities, their competitive positioning or the societal compromises to be made (Porter and Kramer 2010).

1 See Table 2.1.

The societal strategies developed by the Decathlon Group were the subject of two case studies carried out at different periods. In the first study, the group's ethical commitment to environmental and social missions is based on the choice, by managers alone, of four relevant and evocative words that are supposed to embody its identity and that customers should appropriate in their purchasing decisions. There are three ethical values, associated with responsibility, generosity and sincerity, but performance values are represented by only one: vitality. The preference for ethical values can be explained by a strategy of legitimization of the company and alignment with society, which is associated with the mentions of "Our commitments as citizens", "Sustainable Development", the Oxylane Foundation[2] and Art Foundation, created in 2005, and the implementation of a social charter, since 2002.

The second case study looks at societal innovation strategies based on the CSV principle and the impacts they can produce for Decathlon and society in general. Environmental issues are a source of opportunity to develop innovations that are likely to significantly reduce the negative environmental externalities generated by its activities and/or to create positive externalities, and to be a lever of competitive advantage. Innovations specific to the production and sale of sporting goods are related to products and production, to the operation and construction of the Decathlon network sites and to transport. There are additive and integrated environmental, technological and organizational environmental innovations that improve the company's overall performance (financial and societal). In terms of competitive advantage, some generate individual private benefit for the consumer and a collective benefit, while others only induce a collective benefit and a possible cost reduction, but have no impact on the improvement of the intrinsic quality of the product. This study has highlighted two important strategic insights. One insight shows the pre-eminence of a set of diversified organizational innovations over only two types of integrated technological innovations (for product and production activities) in significantly reducing negative environmental externalities. The other insight concerns the widespread use of organizational innovations to "produce" "environmental" attributes that will be a source of product differentiation and therefore competitive advantage. These innovations would be less costly than technological innovations, in theory, but they are more difficult to implement, evaluate, protect and enhance on the market because of their invisibility for customers. The group has embedded its CSV strategies in a process that requires a clear understanding of the trade-offs between financial, societal and, especially, environmental performance. This process involves focusing on the most important environmental issues inherent in its business sector, identifying relevant issues that have a strong impact on overall performance, assessing their relevance with

2 Sources: http://www.oxylane.com/index.php?p=4 and http://www.fondations.org/spip.php?article433.

evidence of their positive economic impact, the collective interest produced and prospectively adjusting to emerging societal issues (Eccles and Serafeim 2014). With forward-looking adjustment, the group can anticipate the nature of sports eco-products and future competitive societal innovations in products, processes and business models and secure its competitive advantage. In addition, an effective communication strategy addresses institutional and market stakeholders with activity reports on the societal practices developed, and customers with four distinctive logos with a rating from A to E, displayed on Passion brand products (Decathlon 2015, p. 50). Finally, the group's low-cost positioning is based primarily on drastic cost reduction to sell products at low prices. Decathlon works with suppliers often located in developing countries, some of which may not respect the local standards. In this scenario, the company can risk possible boycotts, mainly initiated by soft power actors denouncing such behavior.

Social innovations include organizational and managerial innovations that can provide social responses to the legitimate expectations of some of the company's key stakeholders. Companies invest in business models that can meet these expectations and lead to commercial success, corresponding to two categories of CSV-based innovations. The first is specific to low- or moderate-income populations and is linked to a low-cost model (Aldi, EasyJet, etc.) based on cost advantages, volume strategies, differentiation, and simplification of products and services, in order to focus on a simple but necessary value promise for customers. The second innovation is based on a social business embodied by CSR-BoP (Coca-Cola, Novartis, Nestlé, etc.) and enables poor populations to have access to high-quality, low-cost food or health products, as well as to potential training or jobs, while maintaining their dignity. Social business is part of a market-based approach that must repair the limits of modern capitalism, with a classic entrepreneur who must also be a social entrepreneur. The effectiveness of both economic models presupposes the creation of an ecosystem specific to each of the innovations, which can identify and promote opportunities by positioning these strategies as part of a collaborative outlook with local governments, NGOs, local communities, etc., thus adapting them to the concrete problems specific to each country.

Social innovation strategies also concern employees. They can bring about motivation to lead them to voluntarily commit themselves to their work in order to avoid a situation whereby they rationalize their effort, which can result from a non-motivational environment. Commitment is a lever in the process of appropriating management tools related to strategic decisions in daily practice (de Vaujany 2006), especially as companies in developed countries are evolving towards a human economy that requires the exploitation of employees' brains rather than their muscles.

Four categories of managerial and/or organizational innovations are likely to influence employees and produce a synergy that leads to positive internalities, an improvement in their performance and therefore in that of the company. The first innovation concerns management based on organizational ethics, which is based on timeless intrinsic guiding principles. These ethics play a role in the development of a certain number of rules that positively guide employee conduct, including the creation of a culture of trust between managers and employees (Mercier 2001a), and also in recognition at work, which is a matter of human dignity and social justice. The second innovation is concerned with the potential power of the higher purpose over the company, which recognizes the skills and energy of employees in their work and forms part of a proactive approach. This purpose involves taking a real interest in their deepest needs, better defining how they will invest themselves, giving meaning to their daily tasks and recognizing that they want to think, learn and evolve, using sincere and consistent messages (Quinn and Thakor 2019). The third innovation is organizational in nature and related to teleworking, as, according to Berinato (2018), to increase productivity in the company, more employees must be allowed to work from home. This alternative leads to a reduction in costs for employees and the company (travel, workspaces, energy consumption), while inducing positive environmental externalities with the reduction of GHG emissions (Turetken *et al.* 2011). If the use of teleworking is free, it may be perceived by employees as an act of autonomy and responsibility, but if it is imposed, it may generate psychosocial risks due to professional isolation, intrusion of the professional sphere into the private and family sphere, etc. (Turetken *et al.* 2011). Finally, the fourth managerial innovation takes into account feedback and respect. Positive feedback consists of compliments and encouragement, while corrective feedback consists of negative remarks, suggestions for improvement, incentives to apply new or more effective methods. In general, employees prefer corrective feedback that can advance their career, provided it is properly formulated and conveyed. They perceive feedback as a form of rebirth, which can be existential, of their practice or investment in work, or of their results (Brun and Dugas 2005). According to Porath (2018), only one in two employees feels respected by senior managers, experiences well-being, a sense of satisfaction and attributes more meaning and value to their work. In fact, a high-performing employee is very fulfilled in their work.

The contemporary economy has been extraordinarily efficient in making available a large number of consumer goods and services that meet the basic aspirations of people in Western countries. However, in recent years, many companies have been forced to moderate their excessive pursuit of profit and to focus more on their employees, customers, communities and the environment. Practicing CSR on the sidelines is no longer enough in light of the unsustainable growth of inequalities, the growing evidence of the devastating effects of climate change, and the growing awareness among investors of the conflict between short-term profitability and sustainable development. This is pushing more leaders to understand that they must adopt both financial and social objectives, thus changing the business model of their company. However, Battilana *et al.* (2019) point out that their qualitative and quantitative research on CSR has shown that firms are quick to abandon their societal objectives in their quest for profitability. These objectives correspond to a dual mission, described as hybrid management, which is at the heart of the firm and based on four levers. These concern the setting and monitoring of societal objectives alongside financial objectives, the structuring of the company to effectively coordinate social and commercial activities, the recruitment and socialization of employees to ensure that they adhere to the dual mission, and the exercise of leadership within the framework of this mission. The joint activation of these levers helps companies to develop and perpetuate a hybrid culture. This approach thus gives managers the tools to manage the tensions between societal and financial objectives as soon as they emerge.

References

Aaker, D.A. (1994). *Le management du capital de marque.* Dalloz, Paris.

Abdallah, C. (2007). Production et appropriation du discours stratégique dans une organisation artistique. *Revue Française de gestion*, 33(174), 61–76.

Achabou, M.A. and Dekhili, S. (2013). Luxury and sustainable development: Is there a match? *Journal of Business Research*, 66, 896–903.

Acquier, A. and Gond, J.-P. (2007). Aux sources de la responsabilité sociale de l'entreprise : à la (re)découverte d'un ouvrage fondateur : Social Responsibilities of the Businessman d'Howard Bowen. *Finance contrôle stratégie*, 10(2), 5–35.

Addy, C., Chorengel, M., Collins, M., and Etzel, M. (2019). Calculer la valeur d'impact, une manière factuelle d'estimer les bénéfices sociaux et environnementaux. *Harvard Business Review*, 33, 78–86.

Adner, R. and Kapoor, R. (2017). Comment vous assurer que votre écosystème est prêt pour les technologies les plus récentes. *Harvard Business Review*, 22, 41–48.

Aggeri, F. and Labatut, J. (2010). La gestion au prisme de ses instruments. Une analyse généalogique des approches théoriques fondées sur les instruments de gestion. *Finance contrôle stratégie*, 13(3), 5–37.

Alänge, S., Jacobson, S., and Jarnehammar, A. (1998). Some aspects of an analytical framework for studying the diffusion of organizational innovations. *Technology Analysis & Strategic Management*, 10(1), 3–19.

Anderson, C. (2018). Les drones au travail : le marché disruptif des véhicules sans pilotes est en plein essor, voici comment y trouver sa place. *Harvard Business Review*, 28, 42–54.

Arundel, A., Kemp, R., and Parto, S. (2007). Indicators for environmental innovation: What and how to measure. In *International Handbook on Environment and Technology Management (ETM)*, Marinova, D., Phillimore, J., and Annandale, D. (eds). Edward Elgar, Cheltenham.

d'Astous, A. and Legendre, A. (2009). Une étude exploratoire de quelques antécédents de la consommation socialement responsable. *Revue française de marketing*, 223(3, 5), 39–51.

Autissier, D. and Metais, E. (2016). *Transformations digitales*. Eyrolles, Paris.

Autissier, D. and Moutot, J.-M. (2013). *La boîte à outils de la conduite du changement*. Dunod, Paris.

Autissier, D. and Moutot, J.-M. (2015). *Le changement agile*. Dunod, Paris.

Autissier, D., Raynard, T., Vandangeon, I., and Hureau, J.-P. (2014). *Les réseaux apprenants : une démarche d'accompagnement du changement dans la relation de service à la SNCF*. Eyrolles, Paris.

Autissier, D., Moutot, J.-M., and Lip, P. (2015). *Agir en mode Delivery*. Eyrolles, Paris.

Autissier, D., Johnson, K.J., and Moutot, J.-M. (2016). L'innovation managériale : rupture ou évolution du management. *Question(s) de management*, 13, 25–33.

Autissier, D., Johnson, K.J., and Moutot, J.-M. (2018). *L'innovation managériale*. Eyrolles, Paris.

d'Aveni, R. (2016). Cette révolution est en marche, et elle va avoir un impact sur votre mode de fonctionnement et votre stratégie. *Harvard Business Review*, 13, 29–37.

Ballet, J. and Bhukuth, A. (2005). Les labels sociaux et la lutte contre le travail des enfants : un mode de régulation éthique controversé. *Workshop Commerce international et normes sociales*. Université Montesquieu Bordeaux IV, Bordeaux.

Bandura, A. (1986). *Social Foundations of Thought and Action*. Prentice-Hall, Englewood Cliffs.

Baron, D.P. (2001). Private politics, corporate social responsibility and integrated strategy. *Journal of Economics and Management Strategy*, 10, 7–45.

Baron, D.P., Harjoto, M., and Jo, H. (2008). The economics and politics of corporate social performance. Research document, Stanford Graduate School of Business, Stanford.

Battilana, J., Pache, A.-C., Sengul, M., and Kimsey, M. (2019). Les clés d'une gestion hybride réussie, *Harvard Business Review*, 34, 66–75.

Bélanger, J.-P., Sullivan, R., and Sévigny, B. (2000). *Capital social, développement communautaire et santé publique*. ASPQ, Montreal.

Bénabou, R. and Tirole, J. (2010). Individual and corporate social responsibility. *Economica*, 77(305), 1–19.

Benoit-Moreau, F., Larceneux, F., and Parguel, B. (2010). La communication sociétale : entre opportunités et risques d'opportunisme. *Décisions Marketing*, 59, 75–78.

Ben Slimane, K. and Di Cioccio, C. (2013). Les limites de l'approche low-cost dans la réduction de la pauvreté. *Entreprendre & Innover*, 18, 93–100.

Berger-Douce, S. (2007). Les stratégies d'engagement sociétal des entrepreneurs. *Revue de l'entrepreneuriat*, 6(1), 53–71.

Berger-Douce, S. (2011). Le développement durable, un levier d'innovation pour les PME ? *Revue française de gestion*, 215, 147–166.

Berinato, S. (2018). Que sait-on du lien entre la solitude et le travail ? – Tour d'horizon des dernières théories sur la force des relations sociales. *Harvard Business Review*, 30, 60–63.

Berry, M.A. and Rondinelli, D.A. (1998). Proactive environmental management: A new industrial revolution. *Academy of Management Executive*, 12(2), 38–50.

Bharadwaj, S. and Rodriguez-Vilá, O. (2018). La mission sociale comme avantage concurrentiel. *Harvard Business Review*, 27, 68–77.

Bloom, N. (2015). Pour augmenter la productivité, laissez plus de salariés travailler de chez eux [Online]. Available at: https://www.hbrfrance.fr/magazine/2015/01/5933-pour-augmenter-la-productivite-laissez-plus-de-salaries-travailler-de-chez-eux/.

Boiral, O. (2004). Environnement et économie : une relation équivoque. *VertigO – la revue en sciences de l'environnement*, 5(2), 22–29.

Boiral, O. and Joly, D. (1992). Stratégie, compétitivité et écologie. *Revue française de gestion*, 89, 80–85.

Bonin, P. (2003). *Production verbale des mots. Approche cognitive*. Édition de Boeck, Paris.

Bourcieu, S. (2013). Le low-cost : modèle économique des années frileuses ? *L'Expansion Management Review*, 1(148), 10–19.

Brechet, J.P. and Desreumaux, A. (2001). Le thème de la valeur en sciences de gestion : représentations et paradoxes. *Revue sciences de gestion*, 28, 217–245.

Bres, L., Raufflet, E., and Fillion, L.J. (2001). Développement durable et entrepreneuriat. *Cahier de recherche*, 5.

Brun, J.P. (2000). La reconnaissance : une responsabilité digne d'être partagée. *Colloque travail. Reconnaissance et dignité humaine*. Quebec.

Brun, J.P. and Dugas, N. (2005). La reconnaissance au travail : analyse d'un concept riche de sens. *Gestion*, 30, 79–88.

Buisson, B. and Hyungseok, D.Y. (2018). Innovation de la recherche à l'entrepreneuriat, quelles sont les conditions de la réussite ? *Harvard Business Review*, 28, 15.

Camison-Zomosa, C., Lapiedra-Alcani, R., Segarra-Cipres, M., and Boronat-Navarro, M. (2004). A meta-analysis of innovation and organizational size. *Organization Studies*, 25(3), 331–361.

Capron, M. and Quairel-Lanoizelée, F. (2007). *La responsabilité sociale d'entreprise*. La Découverte, Paris.

Carrigan, M. and Attala, A. (2001). The myth of the ethical consumer: Does ethics matter in purchase behaviour? *Journal of Consumer Marketing*, 7(18), 560–577.

Caswell, J.A. (1998). Valuing the benefits and costs of improved food safety and nutrition. *Australian Journal of Agriculture and Resource Economics*, 42, 409–474.

Chamorro-Premuzic, T. (2018). Les cinq caractéristiques des innovations qui réussissent. *Harvard Business Review, Hors-Série*, October–November, 64–67.

Champagne, C. and Payette, A. (2005). *Le groupe de codéveloppement professionnel*. Presses Universitaires du Québec, Quebec.

Champniss, G., Wilson, H.N., and MacDonald, E.K. (2015). En quoi l'identité sociale de vos clients influence leurs achats. *Harvard Business Review*, 10, 92–101.

Chanal, V. (2008). Stratégie en pratique. In *Management, fondements et renouvellements*, Schmidt, G. (ed.). Sciences Humaines, Auxerre.

Chanal, V. and Tannery, F. (2005). La communication de la stratégie ou l'art de persuader. *Revue française de gestion*, 6(159), 165–186.

Chanal, V. and Tannery, F. (2007). La rhétorique de la stratégie : comment le dirigeant crée-t-il un ordre pour l'action. *Finance contrôle stratégie*, 10(2), 97–127.

Chan Kim, W. and Mauborgne, R. (2014). Vos salariés sont-ils entièrement investis dans la réussite de votre entreprise ? Voici comment libérer les talents et les énergies. *Harvard Business Review*, December–January, 42–68.

Chanteau, J.P. (2009). La "responsabilité sociale de l'entreprise", quelques enjeux d'économie politique internationale. *Colloque EPI*. Poitiers, France.

Charles-Pauwers, P. and Commeiras, N. (2002). L'implication : le concept. In *L'implication au travail*, Neveu, J.-P. and Thevent, M. (eds). Vuibert, Paris, 43–59.

Charreaux, G. and Desbrières, P. (1998). Gouvernance des entreprises : valeur partenariale contre-valeur actionnariale. *Finance contrôle stratégie*, 1(2), 57–88.

Chelli, M. (2011). Choix stratégiques dans le champ de mesure de la performance durable. In *Management durable au cœur des organisations*, Moncef, B., Carbone, V., and Solerot, M. (eds). Hermes-Lavoisier, Paris, 59–88.

Chesbrough, H. (2003). *Open Innovation – The New Imperative for Creating and Profiting from Technology*. Harvard Business School Press, Brighton.

Claude, J.F. (2003). *Le management par les valeurs*. Liaisons, Paris.

Coenen, R., Klein-Vielhauer, S., and Meyer, R. (1995). Integrierte Umwelttechnik und wirtschaftliche entwicklung. Büro für Technikfolgenabschätzung beim Deutschen Bundestag, Report, 35.

Collerette, P. (1996). Études de cas (méthodes des). In *Dictionnaire des méthodes qualitatives en sciences humaines et sociales*, Mucchielli, A. (ed.). Armand Colin, Paris.

Collerette, P. (1997). L'étude de cas au service de la recherche. *Recherche en soins infirmiers*, 50, 81–88.

Collins, J.C. and Porras, J.I. (1996). Building your company's vision [Online]. Available at: https://hbr.org/1996/09/building-your-companys-vision.

Comte-Sponville, A. (1994). *Valeur et vérité*. PUF, Paris.

Coriat, T.B. and Weinstein, O. (1995). *Les nouvelles théories de l'entreprise*. Eyrolles, Paris.

Crifo, P. and Forget, V.D. (2014). Pourquoi s'engager volontairement dans la transition énergétique ? Enseignements de la littérature sur la responsabilité sociale et environnementale des entreprises. *Revue d'économie industrielle*, 148, 349–381.

Crifo, P. and Mottis, N. (2011). L'investissement socialement responsable en France : opportunité "de niche" ou placement "mainstream" ? *Annales des mines – gérer et comprendre*, 104, 14–25.

Cropanzano, R., Byrne, Z.S., Bobocel, D.R., and Rupp, D.E. (2001). Moral virtues, fairness heuristics, social entities, and other denizens of organizational justice. *Journal of Vocational Behavior*, 58, 164–209.

Cros, F. (2002). L'innovation en éducation et en formation : topiques et enjeux. In *Les logiques de l'innovation. Approche pluridisciplinaire*, Alter, N. (ed.). La Découverte, Paris, 213–240.

Cross, R., Rebel, R., and Grant, A. (2018). Surcharge collaborative – trop de travail en équipe épuise les employés et sape la productivité. Voici comment l'éviter. *Harvard Business Review*, 25, 48–54.

Damanpour, F. and Aravind, D. (2012). Managerial innovation: Conceptions, processes, and antecedents. *Management & Organization Review*, 8(2), 423–454.

Darby, M.R. and Karni, E. (1973). Free competition and the optimal amount of fraud. *Journal of Law and Economics*, 16(1), 67–88.

Daudigeos, T. and Valiorgue, B. (2010). Les limites du traitement marchand de la Responsabilité sociale de l'entreprise. *Revue française de socio-économie*, 6, 65–86.

De Bandt, J., Dejours, C., and Dubar, C. (1995). *La France malade du travail*. Bayard, Paris.

Debos, F. (2005). L'impact de la dimension éthique dans la stratégie de communication de l'entreprise : la nécessité d'une communication responsable. *Revue Communication & Organisation*, 26, 92–103.

Decathlon (2013). Rapport Développement Durable 2013 [Online]. Available at: http://developpement-durable.decathlon.com/documents-et-rapports/rapports/.

Decathlon (2014). Rapport Développement Durable 2014 [Online]. Available at: http://developpement-durable.decathlon.com/documents-et-rapports/rapports/.

Decathlon (2015). Rapport Développement Durable 2015 [Online]. Available at: http://developpement-durable.decathlon.com/documents-et-rapports/rapports/.

Decathlon (2016). Rapport Développement Durable 2016 [Online]. Available at: http://developpement-durable.decathlon.com/documents-et-rapports/rapports/.

Decaudin, J.M. (2003). *La communication marketing. Concepts, techniques, stratégies.* Economica, Paris.

Dejean, F. and Gond, J.P. (2004). Responsabilité sociétale de l'entreprise : enjeux stratégiques et méthodologies de recherche. *Finance contrôle stratégie*, 7(1), 5–31.

Depret, M.-H. and Hamdouch, A. (2009). Quelles politiques de l'innovation et de l'environnement pour quelle dynamique d'innovation environnementale ? *Innovations*, 29, 127–147.

Desjeux, D. (2003). La consommation en société. In *Sociétés, consommation et consommateurs*, Remy, E., Garabuau-Moussaoui, I., Desjeux, D., and Filser, M. (eds). L'Harmattan, Paris.

Deslandes, G. (2012). *Le Management éthique*. Dunod, Paris.

Desreumaux, A. (2005). *Théorie des organisations*. Dunod, Paris.

Didier, M. and Prud'homme, R. (2007). *Infrastructures de transport, mobilité et croissance*. La Documentation française, Paris.

Dimaggio, P.J. and Powell, W. (1983). The iron cage revisited: Institutional isomorphism and collective rationality in organizational fields. *American Sociological Review*, 48(2), 147–160.

Djelal, H., Rigail, M., and Boyer, L. (2008). Les effluents industriels et leur traitement. *Revue Management & Avenir*, 20, 275–288.

Dubouloz, S. (2013). L'innovation organisationnelle : antécédent et complémentarité : une approche intégrative appliquée au Lean Management. Gestion et management. PhD Thesis, Université de Grenoble, Grenoble.

Dubuisson-Quellier, S. (2013). Consommation responsable. In *Dictionnaire critique de la RSE*, Postel, N. and Sobel, R. (eds). Presses Universitaires du Septentrion, Villeneuve d'Ascq, 77–82.

Dupré, M. (2014). The comparative effectiveness of persuasion, commitment and leader block strategies in motivating recycling. *Waste Management*, 34(4), 730–737.

Dupuis, J.-C. (2007). La RSE, de la gouvernance de la firme à la gouvernance de réseau. *Revue française de gestion*, 11(180), 159–175.

Dupuis, J.-C. (2008). La responsabilité sociale de l'entreprise : gouvernance partenariale de la firme ou gouvernance de réseau ? *Revue d'économie industrielle*, 22, 67–86.

Eccles, R.G. and Serafeim, G. (2014). La frontière de la performance. *Harvard Business Review*, 5, 30–39.

Edquist, C., Hommen, L., and McKelvey, M. (2001). *Innovation and Employment: Process Versus Product Innovation*. Edward Elgar, Cheltenham.

Fayolle, A. and Hernandez, E.M. (2007). Éditorial : des avancées majeures dans le champ et toujours une grande diversité des situations. *Revue gestion 2000*, 3, 15–23.

Fletcher, C. (2013). *Ryanair. Low cost mais à quel prix ?* Altipress, Levallois-Perret.

Floyd, S.W. and Wooldridge, B. (1996). *The Strategic Middle Manager. How to Create and Sustain Competitive Advantage*. Jossey-Bass, San Francisco.

Folkman, J. and Zenger, J. (2018). Vos collaborateurs veulent des feedback négatifs, même si vous détestez en faire. *Harvard Business Review*, 29, 112–115.

Fouilleux, E. and Goulet, F. (2012). Firmes et développement durable : le nouvel esprit du productivisme. *Études rurales*, 190, 131–146.

François, P.-H. and Botteman, A. (2002). Théorie sociale cognitive de Bandura et bilan de competences : applications, recherches et perspectives critiques. *Carriéologie, revue francophone internationale*, 8(3–4), 521–543.

François-Lecompte, A. (2005). La CSR : proposition et validation d'un cadre conceptuel intégrateur. PhD Thesis, Université Pierre-Mendès-France, Grenoble.

François-Lecompte, A. and Valette-Florence, P. (2006). Mieux connaître le consommateur responsable. *Décisions Marketing*, 24, 67–79.

Frechet, M. (2007). Les difficultés relationnelles dans les partenariats d'innovation, une approche par le contrat psychologique. *Finance contrôle stratégie*, 10(1), 125–148.

Freeman, R.E. (1984). *Strategic Management: A Stakeholder Approach*. Pitman, Boston.

Friedman, M. (1962). *Capitalism and Freedom*. University of Chicago Press, Chicago.

Friedman, M. (1970). The social responsibility of business is to increase its profits. *New York Times Magazine*, 13 September.

Garabedian, S. (2007). Une analyse de la consommation éthique. Le rôle de l'information et de l'accessibilité. *Revue économie rurale*, 301, 55–74.

Gardair, E. (2007). Heuristiques et biais : quand nos raisonnements ne répondent pas nécessairement aux critères de la pensée scientifique. *Revue électronique de psychologie sociale*, 1, 32–46.

Garreau, L. (2009). L'apport du concept de sens à l'étude du fonctionnement des équipes projet, études de cas de développement de centres commerciaux chez Immochan. PhD Thesis, Université Paris Dauphine, Paris.

Gasmi, N. (2014). Limites de l'appropriation des valeurs de l'entreprise comme attribut de la différenciation. *Revue Management & Avenir*, 72, 51–70.

Gasmi, N. (2017). Innovations sociales et création de valeur partagée au sein des entreprises. *Revue vie & sciences de l'entreprise (VSE)*, 204, 96–112.

Gasmi, N. (2020). Analyse des différentes formes d'innovations environnementales développées par le groupe Decathlon et de leur impact. *Revue de l'entrepreneuriat*, 4(18), 221–248.

Gasmi, N. and Grolleau, G. (2002). Économie de l'information versus économie de l'attention ? Une application aux labels agroalimentaires. *Colloque systèmes agroalimentaires localisés*. Montpellier, France.

Gasmi, N. and Grolleau, G. (2003). Spécificités des innovations environnementales – une application aux systèmes agroalimentaires. *Revue innovations – cahiers de l'économie de l'Innovation*, 18, 73–89.

Gasmi, N. and Grolleau, G. (2005). Les stratégies de Nike face à la controverse éthique relative à ses sous-traitants. *Revue française de gestion*, 31(223), 67–73.

Gautier, A., Berger-Douce, S., and Brodhag, C. (2013). La RSE, une source de création de valeur partagée en PME ? *10th International Conference of the European Society for Ecological Economics*. ESEE 2013, Lille, France.

Gibbens, D. (2018). Comment intégrer l'éthique à votre stratégie d'utilisation des drones ? *Harvard Business Review*, 28, 55–59.

Girandola, F. and Joule, R.V. (2008). La communication engageante. *Revue électronique de psychologie sociale*, 2, 41–51.

Girard, D. (2004). Les dimensions psychologiques de l'éthique : l'impact du contexte organisationnel. *Interactions*, 8(1), 81–99.

Girard, D. (2007). Culture organisationnelle, contexte d'affaires et prise de décision éthique. *Gestion*, 32, 101–111.

Girotra, K. and Netessine, S. (2015). Quatre voies pour créer un business model innovant. Le secret de la réussite, c'est savoir qui prend quelles décisions, quand et pourquoi [Online]. Available at: https://www.hbrfrance.fr/magazine/2015/01/5951-quatre-voies-pour-creer-un-business-model-innovant/.

Godet, M. (1991). Les dangers de la seule réactivité. *Revue française de gestion*, 86, 91–92.

Gonzalez, C., Korchia, M., Menuet, L., and Urbain, C. (2009). Comment les consommateurs socialement responsables se représentent-ils la consummation ? Une approche par les associations libres. *Recherche et applications en marketing*, 24(3), 25–41.

Gregersen, H. (2018). Pour un nouveau brainstorming – pour trouver les idées innovantes, concentrez-vous sur les questions, pas sur les réponses. *Harvard Business Review*, 28, 30–38.

Grimand, A. (2012). L'appropriation des outils de gestion et ses effets sur les dynamiques organisationnelles : le cas du déploiement d'un référentiel des emplois et des compétences. *Revue Management & Avenir*, 54, 237–257.

Grolleau, G., Ibanezi, L., and Mzoughi, N. (2009). Too much of a good thing? Why altruism can harm the environment. *Ecological Economics*, 68, 2145–2149.

Groysberg, B. and Slind, M. (2014). Diriger, c'est dialoguer – comment améliorer l'engagement et la mobilisation des salariés dans des entreprises aujourd'hui moins hiérarchisées et davantage organisées en réseaux ? *Harvard Business Review*, 5, 74–82.

Groysberg, B., Lee, J., Price, J., and Yo-Jud Cheng, J. (2018). Changez la culture de votre entreprise pour améliorer sa performance. *Harvard Business Review*, 27, 40–54.

Gueguen, N., Granjean, I., and Meineri, S. (2011). Adhésion de salariés à un projet d'entreprise par le biais d'actions de communication engageante. *Revue de gestion des ressources humaines*, 4(82), 19–32.

Haanaes, K., Micjael, D., Jurgens, J., and Rangan, S. (2016). Concilier développement durable et rentabilité. *Harvard Business Review*, 15, 113–118.

Hamel, G. and Prahalad, C.K. (1989). Strategic intent? *Harvard Business Review*, 67(3), 63–76.

Hart, S. (1995). A natural-resource-based view of the firm. *Academy of Management Review*, 20, 986–1014.

Hebert, N. (1987). *L'entreprise et son image*. Dunod, Paris.

Hendry, J. (2000). Strategic decision-making, discourse, and strategy as social practice. *Journal of Management Studies*, 37, 955–977.

Hill, L.A., Brandeau, G., Truelove, E., and Lineback, K. (2015). Ne se présentant plus comme des visionnaires solitaires, des dirigeants intelligents réécrivent les règles de l'innovation. *Harvard Business Review*, 9, 86–95.

Hireche, L. (2004). L'influence de l'éthique des managers sur les comportements au travail et la performance organisationnelle : esquisse d'un modèle conceptuel. *15ème Congrès de l'AGRH – la GRH mesurée*. Montreal, Canada.

Horbach, J. (2008). Determinants of environmental innovations: New evidence from German panel data sources. *Research Policy*, 37, 163–173.

d'Humières, P. and Chauveau, A. (2001). *Les pionniers de l'entreprise responsable*. Éditions d'Organisations, Paris.

Iansiti, M. and Lakhani, K. (2015). Ubiquité numérique : comment les connexions, les capteurs et les données révolutionnent le business. *Harvard Business Review*, 8, 65–74.

Ignatius, A. (2015). Les PDG les plus performants du monde. *Harvard Business Review*, 12, 85–99.

Ihrig, M. and Macmillan, I.C. (2018). Comment obtenir l'adhésion de tout l'écosystème. *Harvard Business Review*, 26, 82–87.

Jensen, M.C. (2002). Value maximisation, stakeholder theory, and the corporate objective function. *Business Ethics Quarterly*, 12(2), 235–256.

Johnson, G., Scholes, K., and Frery, F. (2002). *Stratégique*, 2nd edition. Pearson, Paris.

Johnson, G., Melin, L., and Wittington, R. (2003). Micro strategy and strategizing: Towards an activity-based-view. *Journal of Management Studies*, 40(1), 3–22.

Johnson, G., Scholes, K., and Frery, F. (2014). *Stratégique*, 11th edition. Pearson, Paris.

Joule, R.V. and Beauvois, J.L. (1998). *Les soumissions librement consenties*. PUF, Paris.

Joule, R.V. and Beauvois, J.L. (2014). *Petit traité de manipulations à l'usage des honnêtes gens*. Presses Universitaires de Grenoble, Grenoble.

Julien, P.-A. and Marchesnay, M. (1996). *L'entrepreneuriat*. Economica, Paris.

Kahle, L.R., Boush, D.M., and Phelps, M. (2000). Good morning, Vietnam: An ethical analysis of Nike activities in Southeast Asia. *Sport Marketing Quarterly*, 9(1), 43–52.

Kania, J. and Kramer, M. (2011). Collective impact. *Standford Social Innovation Review*, winter, 36–41.

Kaplan, R., Serafeim, G., and Tugendhat, E. (2018). Croissance inclusive : des stratégies rentables pour lutter contre la pauvreté et les inégalités. *Harvard Business Review*, 27, 97–104.

Kapp, K.W. (1971). Environmental disruption and social costs: A challenge to economics. *Kyklos*, 23(4), 833–848.

Kessous, E., Mellet, K., and Zouina, M. (2010). L'économie de l'attention : entre protection des ressources cognitives et extraction de la valeur. *Revue sociologie du travail*, 52, 359–373.

Keupp, M.M., Palmié, M., and Gassmann, O. (2011). The strategic management of innovation: A systematic review and paths for future research. *International Journal of Management Reviews*, 14, 367–390.

Kiesler, C.A. (1971). *The Psychology of Commitment: Experiments Linking Behavior to Belief.* Academic Press, New York.

Kline, J. and Rosenberg, N. (1986). An overview of innovation. In *The Positive Sum Strategy. Harnessing Technology for Economic Growth*, Landau, R. and Rosenberg, N. (eds). Academy Press, Washington, 275–305.

Kotler, P., Keller, K.L., Dubois, B., and Manceau, D. (2006). *Marketing Management.* Pearson, Paris.

Kramer, M.R. and Pfitzer, M.W. (2017). Écosystème de valeur partagée. *Harvard Business Review*, 23, 79–88.

de La Broise, P. (2006). Entre reddition et legitimation : le rapport annuel d'entreprise. In *Responsabilité sociale : vers une nouvelle communication des entreprises ?*, de la Broise, P. and Lamarche, T. (eds). Presses Universitaires du Septentrion, Villeneuve d'Ascq, France.

Ladwein, R. (2003). *Le comportement du consommateur et de l'acheteur*. Economica, Paris.

Lancaster, K. (1996). A new approach to consumer theory. *Journal of Political Economy, Journal des economistes et des études humaines*, 11, 156–168.

Larceneux, F. (2002). Proposition d'un modèle théorique d'analyse de l'impact des signaux de qualité sur l'évaluation des attributs du produit par le consommateur : le M.A.S.I.A. *Actes de congrès international de l'AFM.*

Laroche, H. and Nioche, J.P. (2006). L'approche cognitive de la stratégie d'entreprise. *Revue française de gestion*, 160, 81–105.

Lash, J., Wellington, F. (2007). Competitive advantage on a warming planet. *Harvard Business Review*, 85(3) 94–102.

Lassarre, D. and Roland-Lévy, C. (2011). *La psychologie sociale appliquée à l'économie.* Édition de Boeck, Paris.

Laurent, C. (2017). Le développement durable, une opportunité qui se chiffre en milliards de dollars. *Harvard Business Review*, 24, 22–23.

Lauriol, J. (2009). Développement durable et économie de la fonctionnalité : vers de nouveaux enjeux stratégiques. *Congrès international ASAC*. Niagara Falls, Canada.

de Laville, V. and Mounoud, E. (2004). Au-delà du discours : les "arts de faire" dans la fabrication de la stratégie. Proposition d'un cadre conceptuel. *13ème Conférence de l'AIMS*. Le Havre, France.

Lemire, L. and Sabat, T. (2005). Le contrat psychologique et l'engagement organisationnel : exploration empirique dans une organisation publique et une firme privée. *Actes de la XIème Conférence internationale de management stratégique*. Angers, France.

Lendrevie, J., Lévy, J., and Lindon, D. (2009). *Mercator : théorie et pratique du marketing*, 9th edition. Dunod, Paris.

Lenhardt, V. and Buratti, L. (2013). *Découvrir le coaching*. InterÉditions, Paris.

Lépineux, F., Rosé, J.-J., Bonnan, C., and Hudson, S. (2010). *La Responsabilité sociale des entreprises – théories et pratiques*. Dunod, Paris.

Lévesque, B. (2005). Innovations et transformations sociales dans le développement économique et le développement social : approches théoriques et politiques publiques. *Les Cahiers du CRISES, Collection études théoriques*.

Levitt, T.H. (1958). The dangers of social responsibility. *Harvard Business Review*, 36(5), 41–50.

Liedtka, J. (2019). Pourquoi le design thinking est efficace. *Harvard Business Review*, 31, 60–67.

Lipovetsky, G. (2006). *Le bonheur paradoxal*. Gallimard, Paris.

Lorino, P. (2002). Vers une théorie pragmatique et sémiotique des outils appliquée aux instruments de gestion. ESSEC research document, DR 02015.

Louche, C. and Lanneau, C. (2004). Effets à long terme de l'engagement dans une organisation industrielle. *Revue Psychologie de travail et des organisations*, 10, 189–203.

Louche, C., Bartolotti, C., and Papet, J. (2006). Motivation intrinsèque et présentation de soi à différentes instances dans une organisation. *Bulletin de psychologie*, 484, 351–357.

Louppe, A. and Rocaboy, A. (1994). Consumérisme vert et démarche marketing. *Revue française de gestion*, 47, 36–47.

Lowitt, E. (2015). Survivre au changement climatique tout en gardant un business prospère. *Harvard Business Review*, 8, 77–82.

Martin, R.L. (2019). Le lourd tribut de l'efficacité. *Harvard Business Review*, 33, 49–61.

Martineau, R. (2012). Une "User Based View" pour mieux définir les outils de gestion. *XXIème Conférence de l'AIMS*. Le Havre.

Martinet, A.C. and Payaud, M.A. (2007). Formes de RSE et entreprises sociales. Une hybridation des stratégies. *Revue française de gestion*, 180, 199–214.

Mathieu, A. (2008). Écostratégies et réponse industrielle aux attentes sociétales : quelles implications ? *Actes du 3ème Atelier développement durable de l'AIMS*. Lyon, France.

Maxwell, T. and Farmer, Y. (2013). La communication engageante au service des changements de comportements en matière éthique. *Communication-information médias théories pratiques*, 32(2).

McCaffery, T. and Pearson, J. (2016). Dénicher l'innovation là où l'on s'y attend le moins : comment dépasser la fixité fonctionnelle et autres obstacles à la créativité. *Harvard Business Review*, 16, 93–100.

McInnis, D., Moorman, C., and Jaworski, B. (1991). Enhancing and measuring consumers' motivation, opportunity and ability to process brand information from ads. *Journal of Marketing*, 55, 32–53.

Meinert, D. (2011). Make telecommuting pay off. *HR Magazine*, 6(6), 33–37.

Mercier, S. (1999). *L'Éthique dans les entreprises*. La Découverte et Syros, Paris.

Mercier, S. (2000). La formalisation de l'éthique : un outil stratégique pertinent pour l'entreprise ? *Finance contrôle stratégie*, 3(3), 101–123.

Mercier, S. (2001a). Institutionnaliser l'éthique dans les grandes entreprises françaises ? *Revue française de gestion*, 136, 62–69.

Mercier, S. (2001b). L'instrumentalisation des valeurs : une ressource stratégique pour l'entreprise ? La démarche du groupe Fournier. *Revue gestion*, 26, 12–18.

Mercier, S. (2003). *L'éthique dans les entreprises*. La Découverte, Paris.

Mercier, S. and Gond, J.-P. (2005). La théorie des parties prenantes. Working Papers, Université de Bourgogne, Centre de recherches en gestion des organisations.

Mialet, J.P. (1999). *L'attention*. PUF, Paris.

Mitchell, R.K., Agle, B.R., and Wood, D.J. (1997). Toward a theory of stakeholder identification and salience: Defining the principle of who and what really counts. *Academy of Management Review*, 22(4), 853–886.

Moore, J.F. (1993). Predators and prey: A new ecology of competition. *Harvard Business Review*, 71(3), 75–86.

Morrison, E. and Robinson, S.L. (1997). When employees feel be-traded: A model of how psychological contract develops. *Academy of Management Review*, 22(1), 226–256.

Mucchielli, R. (2015). *La dynamique des groupes. Processus d'influence et de changement dans la vie affective des groupes*. ESF Éditeur, Montrouge, France.

Nasr, M.I., El Akrem, A., and Vandenberghe, C. (2009). Justice organisationnelle, confiance et comportements de citoyenneté : test d'un modèle multi-sources multi-cibles de l'échange social au travail. *Revue de gestion des ressources humaines*, 74, 3–23.

Nelson, P. (1970). Information and consumer behaviour. *Journal of Political Economy*, 78, 311–329.

Nicolas, E. (2018). Vers la définition d'une gestion sociale de la chaîne logistique. Analyse lexicale de rapports d'audit fournisseurs de l'entreprise Patagonia. *RIMHE : Revue interdisciplinaire management, homme & entreprise*, 30, 46–67.

Nidumolu, R., Prahalad, C.K., and Rangaswami, M.R. (2009). Why sustainability is now the key driver of innovation. *Harvard Business Review*, 87(9), 56–64.

Nidumolu, R., Ellison, J., Whalen, J., and Billman, E. (2017). De l'impératif à collaborer – de nouveaux modèles de partenariat peuvent protéger l'environnement et créer de la valeur pour tous. *Harvard Business Review*, 24, 65–72.

Nikolaidis, S., Gu, K., Ramakrishnan, R., and Shah, J. (2015). Efficient model learning for human-robot collaborative tasks. *10th Annual ACM/IEEE International Conference on Human-Robot Interaction*, Portland, USA, 189–196.

Nye, J.S. (1990). The changing nature of world power. *Political Science Quarterly*, 105(2), 177–192.

Oltra, V. and Saint-Jean, M. (2011). Innovations environnementales et dynamique industrielle. *Industries, institutions, innovations – éléments de dynamique industrielle*, Belis-Bergouignan, M.C., Jullien, B., Lung, Y., and Yildizoglu, M. (eds). Presses Universitaires de Bordeaux, Pessac, France, 297–346.

O'Neill, G.D., Hershauer, J.C., and Golden, J.S. (2009). The cultural context of sustainability entrepreneurship. *Greener Management International*, 55, 33–46.

Osborne, S. (1994). Naming the beast: Defining and clarifying service innovations in social policy. *Human Relations*, 51(9), 1133–1154.

Pasquero, J. (2007). Commentaire : éthique des affaires, responsabilité sociale et gouvernance sociétale : démêler l'écheveau. *Gestion*, 32, 112–116.

Patris, C., Valenduc, G., and Warrant, F. (2001). L'innovation technologique au service du développement durable. Synthèse du rapport final du programme Leviers du développement durable, Fondation Travail-Université, Centre de recherche Travail & Technologies Bruxelles 1, Brussels.

Payaud, M.A. and Martinet, A.C. (2010). Stratégies RSE-BoP et soin des communautés humaines. Concepts et propositions génériques. *Revue management international*, 14(2), 31–51.

Pettigrew, A.M. (1992). The character and significance of strategy process research. *Strategic Management Journal*, 13(5), 5–16.

Petty, R.E. and Cacioppo, J.T. (1983). Central and peripheral routes to persuasion: Application to advertising. In *Advertising and Consumer Psychology*, Percy, L. and Woodside, A.G. (eds). Lexington Books, Lexington, 3–24.

Pfeffer, J. and Salancik, G.R. (1978). *The External Control of the Organization*. Harper and Row, New York.

Pfeffer, J. and Sutton, R. (2007). *Faits et foutaises dans le management*. Vuibert, Paris.

Pfitzer, M.W., Bosckstette, V., and Stamp, M. (2014). Innover pour le progrès social. *Harvard Business Review*, 2, 60–68.

Philippe, D. (2006). La communication environnementale organisationnelle comme stratégie de légitimation. *Management International*, 10(3), 49–66.

Philips, N., Lawrence, T.B., and Hardy, C. (2004). Discours and institutions. *Academy of Management Review*, 29(4), 635–652.

Pisano, G.P. (2015). Vous avez besoin d'une stratégie d'innovation – c'est la seule façon de faire les bons arbitrages et de choisir de bonnes pratiques. [Online]. Available at: https://www.hbrfrance.fr/magazine/2015/11/8819-vous-avez-besoin-dune-strategie-dinnovation/.

Pisano, G.P. (2019). Innovation : alliez créativité et discipline. *Harvard Business Review*, 33, 32–44.

Porath, C. (2018). Un salarié sur deux ne se sent pas respecté par son employeur. *Harvard Business Review*, fall, 116–117.

Porter, M.E. (1986). *L'avantage concurrentiel, comment devancer ses concurrents et maintenir son avance*. InterÉditions, Paris.

Porter, M.E. (2015). Qu'est-ce que la stratégie? [Online]. Available at: https://www.hbrfrance.fr/magazine/2015/10/8429-quest-ce-que-la-strategie/.

Porter, M.E. and Heppelmann, J.E. (2015). Comment les produits intelligents connectés changent les règles de la concurrence. *Harvard Business Review*, 8, 37–62.

Porter, M.E. and Heppelmann, J.E. (2016). Comment les objets intelligents connectés transforment les entreprises. *Harvard Business Review*, 14, 29–48.

Porter, M.E. and Kramer, M.R. (2006). Strategy & society: The link between competitive advantage and corporate social responsibility. *Harvard Business Review*, 84, December, 78–92.

Porter, M.E. and Kramer, M.R. (2010). The link between competitive advantage and corporate social responsibility. *Harvard Business Review, Hors-Série*, spring, 52–66.

Porter, M.E. and Kramer, M.R. (2011). Creating shared value. *Harvard Business Review*, 89, January–February, 62–77.

Porter, M.E. and Reinhardt, F.L. (2007). A strategic approach to climate. *Harvard Business Review*, 5(10), 22–26.

Porter, M.E. and Van Der Linde, C. (1995). Towards a new conception of the environment: Competitiveness relationship. *Journal of Economic Perspectives*, 9(4), 97–118.

Post, J., Preston, L., and Sachs, S. (2002). Managing the extended enterprise: The new stakeholder view. *California Management Review*, 45, 6–28.

Postel, N. and Rousseau, S. (2008). RSE et éthique d'entreprise : la nécessité des institutions. *M@n@gement*, 11(2), 137–160.

Prahalad, C.K. (2004). *The Fortune at the Bottom of the Pyramid*. Pearson, Paris.

Quairel, F. (2013). Concurrence. In *Dictionnaire critique de la RSE*, Postel, N. and Sobel, R. (eds). Presses Universitaires du Septentrion, Villeneuve d'Ascq, France, 70–77.

Quairel, F. and Auberger, M.N. (2005). Management responsable et PME : une relecture du concept de responsabilité sociétale de l'entreprise. *Revue des sciences de gestion, direction et gestion*, 211–212, 11–126.

Quinn, R.E. and Thakor, A.V. (2019). Donner une finalité à l'entreprise. *Harvard Business Review*, 31, 86–94.

Rabardel, P. (1995). *Les hommes et les technologies : approche cognitive des instruments contemporains*. Armand Colin, Paris.

Regnault, G. (2006). *Valeurs et comportements dans les entreprises françaises*. L'Harmattan, Paris.

Reitter, R. and Ramanantsoa, B. (2012). *Confiance et défiance dans les organisations*. Economica, Paris.

Reverdy, T. (2005). Management environnemental et dynamique d'apprentissage. *Revue française de gestion*, 158, 187–205.

Rivière, A., Bonneveux, E., Coutelle-Brillet, P., and Deville, A. (2017). Les stratégies low-cost. Synthèse et perspectives. *Revue française de gestion*, 266, 71–87.

Robins, S., Judge, T., and Gabilliet, P. (2006). *Comportements organisationnels*. Pearson, Paris.

Robinson, S.L. and Rousseau, D.M. (1994). Violating the psychological contract: Not the exception but the norm. *Journal of Organizational Behaviour*, 15, 245–259.

Roger, C. (2000). *La qualité et la sécurité sanitaire des produits alimentaires : un des enjeux du Millénium Round de l'OMC*. INRA, Paris.

Rogers, E.M. (1995). *Diffusion of Innovations*, 4th edition. Free Press of Glencoe, New York.

Rondeau, A., Lemelin, M., and Lauzon, N. (1993). Pouvoir et mobilisation : rôle stratégique du vice-président aux ressources humaines. *Revue européenne de psychologie appliquée*, 43(1), 13–17.

Rousseau, D.M. (1989). Psychological and implied contracts in organizations. *Employee Responsibilities and Rights Journal*, 2(2), 121–139.

Sanchez, C.M. and McKinley, W. (1998). Environmental regulatory influence and product innovation: The contingency effects of organizational characteristics. *Journal of Engineering and Technologies Management*, 15(4), 257–278.

Satell, G. (2018). Les quatre types d'innovations et les problèmes qu'ils résolvent. *Harvard Business Review*, 29, 60–63.

Seidman, D. (2018). De l'économie du savoir à l'économie de l'humain. *50 idées*, Special Issue, October–November, 108–109.

Soparnot, R. and Stevens, E. (2007). *Management de l'innovation*. Dunod, Paris.

Spreitzer, G. and Porath, C. (2015). Créer une performance durable. *Harvard Business Review*, 12, 48.

Straub, R. (2019). Les pouvoirs des écosystèmes. *Harvard Business Review*, 33, 21–22.

Suchman, M.C. (1995). Managing legitimacy: Strategic and institutional approaches. *Academy of Management Review*, 20(3), 571–610.

Sundaram, A.K. and Inkpen, A.C. (2004). The corporate objective revisited. *Organization Science*, 15(3), 350–363.

Thomas, D.C., Au, K., and Ravlin, E.C. (2003). Cultural variations and the psychological contract. *Journal of Organizational Behavior*, 24(5), 451–471.

Tirole, J. (2009). Motivation intrinsèque, incitations et normes sociales. *Revue Économique*, 60, 577–589.

Tremblay, M., Chenevert, D., Simard, G., Lapalme, M.E., and Doucet, O. (2005). Agir sur les leviers organisationnels pour mobiliser le personnel : le rôle de la vision, du leadership, des pratiques de GRH et de l'organisation du travail. *Gestion*, 30, 69–78.

Turetken, O., Jain, A., Quesenberry, B., and Ngwenyama, O. (2011). An empirical investigation of the impact of individual and work characteristics on telecommuting success. *IEEE Transactions of Professional Communication*, 54(1), 56–67.

Utterback, J.M. (1994). *Mastering the Dynamics of Innovation*. Harvard Business School Press, Cambridge.

Van den Berghe, L. and Louche, C. (2005). The link between corporate governance and corporate social responsibility in insurance. *The Geneva Papers on Risk and Insurance – Issues and Practice*, 30, 425–442.

de Vaujany, F.X. (2006). Pour une théorie de l'appropriation des outils de gestion : vers un dépassement de l'opposition conception-usage. *Revue Management & Avenir*, 9, 109–126.

Vézina, M., Derriennic, F., and Monfort, C. (2001). L'impact de l'organisation du travail sur l'isolement social. *Revue Martin Média, Travailler*, 5, 101–117.

Weaver, G.R. and Treviño, L.K. (1999). Compliance and values oriented ethics programs: Influence on employees' attitudes and behavior. *Business Ethics Quarterly*, 9(2), 61–90.

Weick, K.E., Sutcliffe, K.M., and Obstfeld, D. (2005). Organizing and the process of sensemaking. *Organization Science*, 16(4), 409–421.

Wellhoff, T. (2009). *Les Valeurs*. Eyrolles/Éditions d'Organisation, Paris.

Wessel, M. and Christensen, C.M. (2014). Survivre aux ruptures. *Harvard Business Review*, 1, 46–55.

Westphalen, M.H. (2000). *Communicatior – le guide de la communication d'entreprise*. Dunod, Paris.

White, K., Hardisty, D.J., and Habib, R. (2020). L'insaisissable consommateur écoresponsable. *Harvard Business Review*, 37, 76–86.

Winston, A. (2017). Être résilient dans un monde qui se réchauffe – les déréglementations climatiques et la demande des ressources exigent une stratégie complètement nouvelle. *Harvard Business Review*, 24, 42–50.

Winter, A. and Govindarajan, V. (2016). Innovation inverse : mode d'emploi. *Harvard Business Review*, 17, 108–118.

Wittington, R. (2006). Completing the practice turn in strategy research. *Organization Studies*, 27(5), 613–634.

Wolter, R.P. (2010). Les objets à forte valence affective : la notion de nexus. In *La pensée sociale*, Rouquette, M.L. (ed.). Érès, Paris.

Womack, J.P., Jones, D.T., Ballé, M., and Beauvallet, G. (2009). *Système Lean : penser l'entreprise au plus juste*. Pearson, Paris.

Yunus, M., Dalsace, F., Ménascé, D., and Faivre-Tavignot, B. (2015). Les social business qui réussissent dans les pays développés s'inscrivent paradoxalement dans une logique de fournisseurs de solution premium. *Harvard Business Review*, 7, 27–34.

Index

D, E

M, N

O, P

U, V, W

Other titles from

iSTE

in

Innovation, Entrepreneurship and Management

2020

ANDREOSSO-O'CALLAGHAN Bernadette, DZEVER Sam, JAUSSAUD Jacques, TAYLOR Robert
Sustainable Development and Energy Transition in Europe and Asia (Innovation and Technology Set – Volume 9)

BEN SLIMANE Sonia, M'HENNI Hatem
Entrepreneurship and Development: Realities and Future Prospects (Smart Innovation Set – Volume 30)

CHOUTEAU Marianne, FOREST Joëlle, NGUYEN Céline
Innovation for Society: The P.S.I. Approach (Smart Innovation Set – Volume 28)

CORON Clotilde
Quantifying Human Resources: Uses and Analysis (Technological Changes and Human Resources Set – Volume 2)

CORON Clotilde, GILBERT Patrick
Technological Change (Technological Changes and Human Resources Set – Volume 1)

CERDIN Jean-Luc, PERETTI Jean-Marie
The Success of Apprenticeships: Views of Stakeholders on Training and Learning
(Human Resources Management Set – Volume 3)

DELCHET-COCHET Karen
Circular Economy: From Waste Reduction to Value Creation
(Economic Growth Set – Volume 2)

DIDAY Edwin, GUAN Rong, SAPORTA Gilbert, WANG Huiwen
Advances in Data Science
(Big Data, Artificial Intelligence and Data Analysis Set – Volume 4)

DOS SANTOS PAULINO Victor
Innovation Trends in the Space Industry
(Smart Innovation Set – Volume 25)

GOGLIN Christian
Emotions and Values in Equity Crowdfunding Investment Choices 1: Transdisciplinary Theoretical Approach

GUILHON Bernard
Venture Capital and the Financing of Innovation
(Innovation Between Risk and Reward Set – Volume 6)

LATOUCHE Pascal
Open Innovation: Human Set-up
(Innovation and Technology Set – Volume 10)

MAKRIDES Andreas, KARAGRIGORIOU Alex, SKIADAS Christos H.
Data Analysis and Applications 3: Computational, Classification, Financial, Statistical and Stochastic Methods
(Big Data, Artificial Intelligence and Data Analysis Set – Volume 5)
Data Analysis and Applications 4: Financial Data Analysis and Methods
(Big Data, Artificial Intelligence and Data Analysis Set – Volume 6)

MASSOTTE Pierre, CORSI Patrick
Complex Decision-Making in Economy and Finance

MEUNIER François-Xavier
Dual Innovation Systems : Concepts, Tools and Methods (Smart Innovation Set – Volume 31)

MICHAUD Thomas
Science Fiction and Innovation Design (Innovation in Engineering and Technology Set – Volume 6)

MONINO Jean-Louis
Data Control: Major Challenge for the Digital Society (Smart Innovation Set – Volume 29)

MORLAT Clément
Sustainable Productive System: Eco-development versus Sustainable Development
(Smart Innovation Set – Volume 26)

SAULAIS Pierre, ERMINE Jean-Louis
Knowledge Management in Innovative Companies 2: Understanding and Deploying a KM Plan within a Learning Organization
(Smart Innovation Set – Volume 27)

2019

AMENDOLA Mario, GAFFARD Jean-Luc
Disorder and Public Concern Around Globalization

BARBAROUX Pierre
Disruptive Technology and Defence Innovation Ecosystems (Innovation in Engineering and Technology Set – Volume 5)

DOU Henri, JUILLET Alain, CLERC Philippe
Strategic Intelligence for the Future 1: A New Strategic and Operational Approach
Strategic Intelligence for the Future 2: A New Information Function Approach

FRIKHA Azza
Measurement in Marketing: Operationalization of Latent Constructs

FRIMOUSSE Soufyane
Innovation and Agility in the Digital Age
(Human Resources Management Set – Volume 2)

GAY Claudine, SZOSTAK Bérangère L.
Innovation and Creativity in SMEs: Challenges, Evolutions and Prospects
(Smart Innovation Set – Volume 21)

GORIA Stéphane, HUMBERT Pierre, ROUSSEL Benoît
Information, Knowledge and Agile Creativity
(Smart Innovation Set – Volume 22)

HELLER David
Investment Decision-making Using Optional Models
(Economic Growth Set – Volume 2)

HELLER David, DE CHADIRAC Sylvain, HALAOUI Lana, JOUVET Camille
The Emergence of Start-ups
(Economic Growth Set – Volume 1)

HÉRAUD Jean-Alain, KERR Fiona, BURGER-HELMCHEN Thierry
Creative Management of Complex Systems
(Smart Innovation Set – Volume 19)

LATOUCHE Pascal
Open Innovation: Corporate Incubator
(Innovation and Technology Set – Volume 7)

LEHMANN Paul-Jacques
The Future of the Euro Currency

LEIGNEL Jean-Louis, MÉNAGER Emmanuel, YABLONSKY Serge
Sustainable Enterprise Performance: A Comprehensive Evaluation Method

LIÈVRE Pascal, AUBRY Monique, GAREL Gilles
Management of Extreme Situations: From Polar Expeditions to Exploration-Oriented Organizations

MILLOT Michel
Embarrassment of Product Choices 2: Towards a Society of Well-being

N'GOALA Gilles, PEZ-PÉRARD Virginie, PRIM-ALLAZ Isabelle
Augmented Customer Strategy: CRM in the Digital Age

NIKOLOVA Blagovesta
The RRI Challenge: Responsibilization in a State of Tension with Market Regulation
(Innovation and Responsibility Set – Volume 3)

PELLEGRIN-BOUCHER Estelle, ROY Pierre
Innovation in the Cultural and Creative Industries
(Innovation and Technology Set – Volume 8)

PRIOLON Joël
Financial Markets for Commodities

QUINIOU Matthieu
Blockchain: The Advent of Disintermediation

RAVIX Joël-Thomas, DESCHAMPS Marc
Innovation and Industrial Policies
(Innovation between Risk and Reward Set – Volume 5)

ROGER Alain, VINOT Didier
Skills Management: New Applications, New Questions
(Human Resources Management Set – Volume 1)

SAULAIS Pierre, ERMINE Jean-Louis
Knowledge Management in Innovative Companies 1: Understanding and Deploying a KM Plan within a Learning Organization
(Smart Innovation Set – Volume 23)

SERVAJEAN-HILST Romaric
Co-innovation Dynamics: The Management of Client-Supplier Interactions for Open Innovation
(Smart Innovation Set – Volume 20)

SKIADAS Christos H., BOZEMAN James R.
Data Analysis and Applications 1: Clustering and Regression, Modeling-estimating, Forecasting and Data Mining
(Big Data, Artificial Intelligence and Data Analysis Set – Volume 2)
Data Analysis and Applications 2: Utilization of Results in Europe and Other Topics
(Big Data, Artificial Intelligence and Data Analysis Set – Volume 3)

UZUNIDIS Dimitri
Systemic Innovation: Entrepreneurial Strategies and Market Dynamics

VIGEZZI Michel
World Industrialization: Shared Inventions, Competitive Innovations and Social Dynamics
(Smart Innovation Set – Volume 24)

2018

BURKHARDT Kirsten
Private Equity Firms: Their Role in the Formation of Strategic Alliances

CALLENS Stéphane
Creative Globalization
(Smart Innovation Set – Volume 16)

CASADELLA Vanessa
Innovation Systems in Emerging Economies: MINT – Mexico, Indonesia, Nigeria, Turkey
(Smart Innovation Set – Volume 18)

CHOUTEAU Marianne, FOREST Joëlle, NGUYEN Céline
Science, Technology and Innovation Culture
(Innovation in Engineering and Technology Set – Volume 3)

CORLOSQUET-HABART Marine, JANSSEN Jacques
Big Data for Insurance Companies
(Big Data, Artificial Intelligence and Data Analysis Set – Volume 1)

CROS Françoise
Innovation and Society
(Smart Innovation Set – Volume 15)

DEBREF Romain
Environmental Innovation and Ecodesign: Certainties and Controversies
(Smart Innovation Set – Volume 17)

DOMINGUEZ Noémie
SME Internationalization Strategies: Innovation to Conquer New Markets

ERMINE Jean-Louis
Knowledge Management: The Creative Loop
(Innovation and Technology Set – Volume 5)

GILBERT Patrick, BOBADILLA Natalia, GASTALDI Lise,
LE BOULAIRE Martine, LELEBINA Olga
Innovation, Research and Development Management

IBRAHIMI Mohammed
Mergers & Acquisitions: Theory, Strategy, Finance

LEMAÎTRE Denis
Training Engineers for Innovation

LÉVY Aldo, BEN BOUHENI Faten, AMMI Chantal
Financial Management: USGAAP and IFRS Standards
(Innovation and Technology Set – Volume 6)

MILLOT Michel
Embarrassment of Product Choices 1: How to Consume Differently

PANSERA Mario, OWEN Richard
Innovation and Development: The Politics at the Bottom of the Pyramid
(Innovation and Responsibility Set – Volume 2)

RICHEZ Yves
Corporate Talent Detection and Development

SACHETTI Philippe, ZUPPINGER Thibaud
New Technologies and Branding
(Innovation and Technology Set – Volume 4)

SAMIER Henri
Intuition, Creativity, Innovation

TEMPLE Ludovic, COMPAORÉ SAWADOGO Eveline M.F.W.
Innovation Processes in Agro-Ecological Transitions in Developing Countries
(Innovation in Engineering and Technology Set – Volume 2)

UZUNIDIS Dimitri
Collective Innovation Processes: Principles and Practices
(Innovation in Engineering and Technology Set – Volume 4)

VAN HOOREBEKE Delphine
The Management of Living Beings or Emo-management

2017

AÏT-EL-HADJ Smaïl
The Ongoing Technological System
(Smart Innovation Set – Volume 11)

BAUDRY Marc, DUMONT Béatrice
Patents: Prompting or Restricting Innovation?
(Smart Innovation Set – Volume 12)

BÉRARD Céline, TEYSSIER Christine
Risk Management: Lever for SME Development and Stakeholder Value Creation

CHALENÇON Ludivine
Location Strategies and Value Creation of International Mergers and Acquisitions

CHAUVEL Danièle, BORZILLO Stefano
The Innovative Company: An Ill-defined Object
(Innovation between Risk and Reward Set – Volume 1)

CORSI Patrick
Going Past Limits To Growth

D'ANDRIA Aude, GABARRET Inés
Building 21st Century Entrepreneurship
(Innovation and Technology Set – Volume 2)

DAIDJ Nabyla
Cooperation, Coopetition and Innovation
(Innovation and Technology Set – Volume 3)

FERNEZ-WALCH Sandrine
The Multiple Facets of Innovation Project Management
(Innovation between Risk and Reward Set – Volume 4)

FOREST Joëlle
Creative Rationality and Innovation
(Smart Innovation Set – Volume 14)

GUILHON Bernard
Innovation and Production Ecosystems
(Innovation between Risk and Reward Set – Volume 2)

HAMMOUDI Abdelhakim, DAIDJ Nabyla
Game Theory Approach to Managerial Strategies and Value Creation
(Diverse and Global Perspectives on Value Creation Set – Volume 3)

LALLEMENT Rémi
Intellectual Property and Innovation Protection: New Practices and New Policy Issues
(Innovation between Risk and Reward Set – Volume 3)

LAPERCHE Blandine
Enterprise Knowledge Capital
(Smart Innovation Set – Volume 13)

LEBERT Didier, EL YOUNSI Hafida
International Specialization Dynamics
(Smart Innovation Set – Volume 9)

MAESSCHALCK Marc
Reflexive Governance for Research and Innovative Knowledge
(Responsible Research and Innovation Set – Volume 6)

MASSOTTE Pierre
Ethics in Social Networking and Business 1: Theory, Practice and Current Recommendations
Ethics in Social Networking and Business 2: The Future and Changing Paradigms

MASSOTTE Pierre, CORSI Patrick
Smart Decisions in Complex Systems

MEDINA Mercedes, HERRERO Mónica, URGELLÉS Alicia
Current and Emerging Issues in the Audiovisual Industry
(Diverse and Global Perspectives on Value Creation Set – Volume 1)

MICHAUD Thomas
Innovation, Between Science and Science Fiction
(Smart Innovation Set – Volume 10)

PELLÉ Sophie
Business, Innovation and Responsibility
(Responsible Research and Innovation Set – Volume 7)

SAVIGNAC Emmanuelle
The Gamification of Work: The Use of Games in the Workplace

SUGAHARA Satoshi, DAIDJ Nabyla, USHIO Sumitaka
Value Creation in Management Accounting and Strategic Management: An Integrated Approach
(Diverse and Global Perspectives on Value Creation Set –Volume 2)

UZUNIDIS Dimitri, SAULAIS Pierre
Innovation Engines: Entrepreneurs and Enterprises in a Turbulent World
(Innovation in Engineering and Technology Set – Volume 1)

2016

BARBAROUX Pierre, ATTOUR Amel, SCHENK Eric
Knowledge Management and Innovation
(Smart Innovation Set – Volume 6)

BEN BOUHENI Faten, AMMI Chantal, LEVY Aldo
Banking Governance, Performance And Risk-Taking: Conventional Banks Vs Islamic Banks

BOUTILLIER Sophie, CARRÉ Denis, LEVRATTO Nadine
Entrepreneurial Ecosystems (Smart Innovation Set – Volume 2)

BOUTILLIER Sophie, UZUNIDIS Dimitri
The Entrepreneur (Smart Innovation Set – Volume 8)

BOUVARD Patricia, SUZANNE Hervé
Collective Intelligence Development in Business

GALLAUD Delphine, LAPERCHE Blandine
Circular Economy, Industrial Ecology and Short Supply Chains (Smart Innovation Set – Volume 4)

GUERRIER Claudine
Security and Privacy in the Digital Era (Innovation and Technology Set – Volume 1)

MEGHOUAR Hicham
Corporate Takeover Targets

MONINO Jean-Louis, SEDKAOUI Soraya
Big Data, Open Data and Data Development (Smart Innovation Set – Volume 3)

MOREL Laure, LE ROUX Serge
Fab Labs: Innovative User (Smart Innovation Set – Volume 5)

PICARD Fabienne, TANGUY Corinne
Innovations and Techno-ecological Transition (Smart Innovation Set – Volume 7)

2015

CASADELLA Vanessa, LIU Zeting, DIMITRI Uzunidis
Innovation Capabilities and Economic Development in Open Economies (Smart Innovation Set – Volume 1)

CORSI Patrick, MORIN Dominique
Sequencing Apple's DNA

CORSI Patrick, NEAU Erwan
Innovation Capability Maturity Model

FAIVRE-TAVIGNOT Bénédicte
Social Business and Base of the Pyramid

GODÉ Cécile
Team Coordination in Extreme Environments

MAILLARD Pierre
Competitive Quality and Innovation

MASSOTTE Pierre, CORSI Patrick
Operationalizing Sustainability

MASSOTTE Pierre, CORSI Patrick
Sustainability Calling

2014

DUBÉ Jean, LEGROS Diègo
Spatial Econometrics Using Microdata

LESCA Humbert, LESCA Nicolas
Strategic Decisions and Weak Signals

2013

HABART-CORLOSQUET Marine, JANSSEN Jacques, MANCA Raimondo
VaR Methodology for Non-Gaussian Finance

2012

DAL PONT Jean-Pierre
Process Engineering and Industrial Management

MAILLARD Pierre
Competitive Quality Strategies

POMEROL Jean-Charles
Decision-Making and Action

SZYLAR Christian
UCITS Handbook

2011

LESCA Nicolas
Environmental Scanning and Sustainable Development

LESCA Nicolas, LESCA Humbert
Weak Signals for Strategic Intelligence: Anticipation Tool for Managers

MERCIER-LAURENT Eunika
Innovation Ecosystems

2010

SZYLAR Christian
Risk Management under UCITS III/IV

2009

COHEN Corine
Business Intelligence

ZANINETTI Jean-Marc
Sustainable Development in the USA

2008

CORSI Patrick, DULIEU Mike
The Marketing of Technology Intensive Products and Services

DZEVER Sam, JAUSSAUD Jacques, ANDREOSSO Bernadette
Evolving Corporate Structures and Cultures in Asia: Impact of Globalization

2007

AMMI Chantal
Global Consumer Behavior

2006

BOUGHZALA Imed, ERMINE Jean-Louis
Trends in Enterprise Knowledge Management

CORSI Patrick *et al.*
Innovation Engineering: the Power of Intangible Networks

Printed and bound by CPI Group (UK) Ltd, Croydon, CR0 4YY
15/09/2026
14962360-0001